COMPARATIVE EUROPEAN POLITICS

General Editors: Hans Daalder and Ken Newton

Editorial Board: Brian Barry, Franz Lehner,
Arend Lijphart, Seymour Martin Lipset, Mogens Pedersen,
Giovanni Sartori, Rei Shiratori, Vincent Wright

COMPARATIVE EUROPEAN POLITICS

Comparative European Politics is a series for students and teachers of political science and related disciplines, published in association with the European Consortium for Political Research. Each volume will provide an up-to-date survey of the current state of knowledge and research on an issue of major significance in European government and politics.

OTHER TITLES IN THIS SERIES

Multiparty Government: The Politics of Coalition in Europe
Michael Laver and Norman Schofield

Government and Politics in Western Europe: Britain, France, Italy, West Germany
Yves Mény

FORTHCOMING

Politics and Policy in the European Community (second edition)
Stephen George

Self-Interest and Public Interest in Western Politics
Leif Lewin

Parties and Democracy

*Coalition Formation and
Government Functioning in Twenty States*

IAN BUDGE
and
HANS KEMAN

OXFORD UNIVERSITY PRESS
1990

Oxford University Press, Walton Street, Oxford OX2 6DP

Oxford New York Toronto
Delhi Bombay Calcutta Madras Karachi
Kuala Lumpur Singapore Hong Kong Tokyo
Nairobi Dar es Salaam Cape Town
Melbourne Auckland Madrid
and associated companies in
Berlin Ibadan

Oxford is a trade mark of Oxford University Press

Published in the United States by
Oxford University Press Inc., New York

© *Ian Budge and Hans Keman 1990*

First published 1990
Published in paperback 1993

British Library Cataloguing in Publication Data
Budge, Ian, 1936–
Parties and democracy: coalition formation and government
functioning in twenty states.—(Comparative European
politics).
1. Europe. Coalition governments, history
I. Title   II. Keman, Hans   III. Series
321.8043
ISBN 0-19-827925-6

Library of Congress Cataloging in Publication Data
Budge, Ian.
Parties and democracy: coalition formation and government
functioning in twenty states/Ian Budge and Hans Keman.
(Comparative European politics)
Includes bibliographical references.
1. Coalition governments—Europe.   2. Political parties—Europe.
3. Democracy.   4. Comparative government.   I. Keman, Hans.
II. Title.   III. Series.
JN94.A979B84   1990   324.24—dc20   89-49350
ISBN 0-19-827925-6

1 3 5 7 9 10 8 6 4 2

Printed in Great Britain
on acid-free paper by
Biddles Ltd, Guildford and King's Lynn

Owing—for a long time—to Judith alone

Acknowledgements

Work on this book began as part of the project on the Future of Party Government, directed from 1981 by Rudolph Wildenmann at the European University Institute in Florence. Not only did theory and book gain intellectually from the wide-ranging seminars organized under the Party Government Programme, but they also gained necessary material support—in the shape of research assistance, photocopying, and travel costs—without which the large amount of information needed to validate the theory would not have been assembled and processed. Subsequently the European University Institute took over direct responsibility for this research and made possible the further analyses and data collection required. At an early stage the Nuffield Foundation had also contributed to these costs in its usual enlightened and timely fashion (Grant No. SOC/181/755). We warmly acknowledge this material and moral assistance in writing the book. Typing it has been the responsibility, ably undertaken through many revised drafts, of Carol Snape.

We are also grateful to all these colleagues whose indispensable help prevents them from totally disclaiming responsibility for what follows! In particular we should like to thank Rudolph Wildenmann, Klaus von Beyme, Val Herman, Norman Schofield, Dick Katz, and Michael Laver. While the book has incorporated many of their suggestions, we are solely responsible for the overall argument and the empirical analyses. We could not have carried the latter through without the collaboration of Clare Gardiner, Tibert van Dijk, Ron van Dooren, and Alfonso Nunez; we hope the book repays their efforts.

Contents

Figures

Tables

Introduction

Curiously, the behaviour of parties in elections has absorbed more attention over the past three decades than the behaviour of parties in government. Yet there can be no argument over the equal if not greater importance of the latter for our understanding of politics and in particular of modes of state intervention. No matter how free, informed, and representative elections may be, any failure to respond at government level renders them ineffective. Parties alone operate in elections as well as in governments. They are consequently in a unique position to transform broad popular preferences into specific actions, thus providing the main channel through which democratic States can be made responsive (and responsible) to their citizens. Studying the way parties do this is just as essential as the analysis of their electoral strategies for an understanding of democratic processes. It is also vital to the justification of parliamentary democracy against other types of political system. Without valid knowledge of how governments are formed and run by parties, we cannot argue with any conviction for the superiority of the parliamentary system.

Nor is it enough to review the workings of party governments in one or two well-known cases. For this, quite fairly, provokes the criticism that democratic parties may govern efficiently and sensitively under favourable conditions, but where they face the social and political traumas of the rest of the world will prove unresponsive and ineffective. To demonstrate that parliamentary democracy does live up to its claims, one must study the behaviour of parties in government for as many countries as possible, comparatively and systematically.

This book analyses party governments in twenty democracies, operating under a variety of cultural and societal conditions. Countries are chosen as having maintained a parliamentary system for most of the post-war period. Democracies which became independent more recently are excluded because their party systems and modes of government have in most cases not yet stabilized, and cannot be used as a basis for broad comparative and temporal generalizations. This permits the inclusion in the analysis of Japan, Israel, Australia, New

Zealand, and Canada, outside the core democracies of Western Europe.[1] As the object is to study countries with broadly similar government arrangements (although operating under different cultural and social circumstances), the United States are excluded. With their presidential government, where the electorally successful party takes executive powers unconditionally and with a constitutionally guaranteed term of office, they differ sharply from countries where the government's tenure of office depends upon its ability to win votes of confidence in the legislature.

The criteria of selection nevertheless allow for inclusion of most other major democracies of the world and thus for the testing of a comprehensive theory of party government in parliamentary systems. The concern to develop such a theory stems in the first place from a desire to round off previous work by the present authors on the policy instruments and policy outputs of different types of party government, and on their voting and electoral consequences.[2] In *Explaining and Predicting Elections* (1983) a systematic theory of election outcomes was developed and validated for twenty-three democracies (the ones studied here, along with the United States, India, and Sri Lanka). Explaining the behaviour of parties in government is a natural corollary to explaining how they gain the popular support necessary to sustain a governmental role. Together, the theories of elections and governments provide an overall explanation of the central political processes of parliamentary democracies.

The second impulse towards generating a systematic theory comes from a wish to develop and unify work already done in this area by others, and to put it in the context of democratic theory as a whole, rather than leave it as a narrow concern of certain specialists; while the comparative analysis of democratic governments has been neglected it has not been totally ignored. In particular, attempts have been made to create theories of the way parties enter into coalitions and distribute ministries, and to test them comparatively, within the context of an 'office-seeking' model of party behaviour. While theories vary in detail, their basic assumption has traditionally been that democratic parties aim above all at acquiring and keeping government office. More detailed implications are then derived and used to explain actual party behaviour. We discuss examples of 'office-seeking' theories and later 'policy-pursuing' developments in Chapter 1. (For an excellent review and extension of some of these ideas, see the companion volume in this series.[3])

Such models have had two enduring effects on subsequent research. One is to ensure that politicians' strategies and decisions are viewed as broadly rational and hence explicable in fairly simple terms. The theory stated in Chapter 2 stands, like the 'office-seeking' explanations, within the broad 'rational choice' tradition.

The second is apparent in the a priori, semi-deductive presentation of the book's underlying theory. After initial assumptions have been stated, their implications are drawn out before being checked against actual party behaviour to see if they hold. Such a priori theory is useful because it must fill in all the links in its chain of reasoning, and is thus more specific and detailed about all the assumptions involved than retrospective interpretations of existing data. This is not only more satisfactory in itself but provides a better basis for prediction of future behaviour. Although prediction is not the same as explanation, it is both of practical use, in directing attention to what is going to happen in such a vital institution as government, and important in selecting the best theoretical explanation. The systematic and predictive form of the theory has the advantage of dovetailing with earlier predictive theories of election outcomes.[4]

Not that inductive descriptive work has been ignored. This book is from one point of view an attempt to synthesize the findings of historical and institutional research within the framework of 'rational choice' theory. Overwhelmingly, such research has shown that party leaders' policy preferences cannot be ignored in any realistic explanation of government processes.[5] Such preferences not only limit what politicians will do and say to get elected;[6] they also make it unsatisfactory for them to govern without giving weight to ideological predispositions and policy commitments.[7] These markedly affect, for example, different governments' expenditure decisions.[8] Our discussion not only incorporates the research-attested primacy of policy as a basic motivation of parties and politicians, but uses some of the previous findings to decide between competing theories of what influence it has on government actions (Chapter 5).

The order of chapters is determined by the nature of the approach. Chapter 1 argues the need for new thinking, discusses previous theory, and reviews the criticisms and counter-evidence which lead to our specific formulation. This is presented in Chapter 2, where it is summarized in the propositions of Tables 2.1 to 2.4, with the supporting text. Together these constitute a systematic, comparative, and comprehensive theory of the major processes of democratic party government—specifically, its initial formation; distribution and reallocation of ministries; policy-making and performance; termination; and effects on future governments. Chapters 3 to 6 each start by drawing out the implications of the unified theory for their own area, and then report the fit between these implications and the actual record of post-war governments in the twenty countries. Chapter 3 is concerned with government formation; Chapter 4 with the distribution of ministries between governing parties; Chapter 5 with policies and expenditures; and Chapter 6 with the way governments end and the effects this has on component parties' electoral prospects and through this on their successors. Chapter 7 assesses the bearings on general democratic theory of all the evidence taken together.

This approach, in contrast to most others, covers all the major preoccupations of parties in government, treating formation as part of an overall life-process rather than as an isolated problem requiring specific explanation. This seems necessary if the theory is to provide a context for most of the research actually done on party government, which is of a historical and holistic nature, concerned with what governments do rather than how they originate.

Besides taking cognizance of the whole range of government activities, a satisfactory theory must also link them through a concise set of general assumptions, putting them into some kind of necessary and systematic relationship rather than leaving them contingent. If the assumptions can be shown to fit the evidence, either directly or through their implications, they can then be taken as basic principles underlying the whole operation of party government. Tables 2.1 to 2.4 attempt to present such general assumptions succinctly in the shape of verbal propositions which can be precisely discussed and whose relevance to the various implications and applications checked in later chapters can be made totally clear. The introduction and discussion of these assumptions, and of their underlying rationale, form the main concern of our first two chapters.

I

Explaining Democratic Government: Background Considerations

WHY THEORY? WHY PARTIES? WHY TWENTY COUNTRIES?

Most of us would agree that it is important to know more about democracy, if for no other reason than that we live in one—but also perhaps because it is the central political ideology to which we subscribe and naturally stands at the focus of all our political experience and reflection.

A central democratic self-justification is that the system makes the state more responsive to the wishes of the people, and gives them the opportunity to change rulers if they so desire. While in very small units various devices for achieving these goals can be envisaged (including direct democracy in which the population *is* the government), in units of greater size there has up to now been little alternative to regular elections in which citizens can choose between competing candidates for government office.[1] Within the mass societies of modern States, if some degree of responsibility and accountability is to be enforced, candidates need also to be organized in competing teams, i.e. political parties. Thus office-holders who are little known to most individual electors can at least be associated with a definite group, which is tied both to a specific record in government and to certain pronouncements about future performance.

The behaviour of parties thus dominates most modern discussions of democracy in action. There are two aspects to these: what parties ought to do and what they actually do. Recommendations about what ought to be done are contingent upon what we think is actually being done or what realistically could be done within the constraints of social and economic processes. Hence the importance of finding out more about party activities, particularly in and around government.

How exactly we find out more is another matter and open to dispute. There are of course multifarious studies of parties, of governments, and of parties in government. Almost all discuss the detailed history of a particular period, seen perhaps through the eyes of the major protagonist or protagonists, or with a particular party or government at the focus. Usually the treatment is historical and institutional, and therefore fixed in a particular time and place. It is not explicitly comparative although it involves many implicit comparisons across time or space: to take a simple example, the judgement that a certain party showed itself notably active in some policy area assumes a norm based on comparisons—thus, that the party's own activity was less before or after the period in consideration; or that other parties are less active in that area, the other parties either being similar parties abroad or competitors within the country.

Even the simplest descriptive judgement thus involves comparison. If this is made implicitly, quite arbitrary assumptions are often involved. Since the historian is not in a position to investigate activity in other parties, or in other places and times (otherwise the study itself becomes comparative) he either has to draw on other research or, since this is normally lacking, simply use his own judgement of what 'normal' activity is or was. He may or may not be right—without relevant research we do not know—but the judgement is bound to be arbitrary.

This example, which could be multiplied thousands of times, clearly makes the case for supplementing historical and institutional investigations with comparative research. There is certainly no equal, in terms of richness and detail, for studies of a single party or government. Because they depend crucially on comparative evaluations, however, they need to be supplemented by research which *explicitly* deals with the experience of more than one party or government in more than one country.

Most comparisons are constrained by the resources available, or the time within which research must be done, to limited numbers of cases. Where country comparisons are involved, two or three is generally the maximum number. Because of the trade-off between the extent and the depth of a study, such comparisons are less rich than descriptions of a single case, but certainly more detailed, as regards individual governments, than our twenty-case analysis can hope to be. The number of post-war governments we study is 380 and the number of parties involved 130. With such numbers we can obviously pick out key incidents and vivid examples, but for the most part need to summarize by counting the incidence of particular types of party behaviour within certain situations, and by statistical manipulation of such counts.

This form of presentation is very different from historical and descriptive research. In place of a directly accessible narrative of party or government actions, it seems to interpose a screen of abstractions (statistics, tables, hypotheses) between the reader and the specific behaviour he is interested in. But in fact, as we have already pointed out, the approaches are not opposed but complementary. Comparative analyses are necessary to historical/descriptive case studies because they provide them with a proper basis of evaluation. They may also suggest a general framework within which a description can be set or through which it can orientate itself. In this respect, the broader the basis of comparison and the more general the framework, the better guidance there is for specific studies which will flesh out abstract figures and statistics.

All investigations, whether of natural or of social and political phenomena, require initial ideas to guide them—if only on which aspect of behaviour would be best examined first, or which areas are to be investigated and which left out. While in a historical study initial ideas can remain vague or flexible (indeed there may be benefits in leaving them to be easily modified by subsequent research), the more dispersed the material studied, the more need there is for initial ideas to be specified clearly. Greater scope and diversity make it easier to get lost, so there is greater need for a unifying focus. Knowing clearly and in detail which ideas are upheld and which rejected also helps to clarify conclusions. This is valuable because the immense range of government and party experiences we cover could otherwise lead to confusion about what precisely *had* been discovered at the end of an elaborate investigation.

There is a premium, then, in starting with a precise but comprehensive account of what one expects to find. In our case this account needs to specify the motivations of parties and show how this affects the setting-up and running of governments. Making it comprehensive means that *all* major activities are covered and explained. For real clarity the account is best expressed in a series of hypotheses or propositions each of which can be examined and compared with what the collected information on that point actually tells us. Taken together, such propositions constitute the 'theory' or 'explanation' of why and how the parties act as they do, and if upheld should also enable us to anticipate what they are going to do in government, under given circumstances.

Again, such hypothesis-testing seems far removed from historical accounts where the writer interweaves his narrative of events with explanations of motives and analysis of successes and mistakes. The historian, however, has to operate with *some* general ideas about party behaviour. These may be taken from investigations like ours. Conversely, we base our theory upon the histories, descriptions, and more limited comparisons which have gone before. It would indeed be foolish to adopt an initial theory which did not use to the full the accumulated results of historical/descriptive research. Thus our a priori assumptions and derivations, alien in form though they may seem, are in fact a codification and extension of historical and institutional findings. From that point of view they should be of immediate use in providing a summary of the current state of knowledge in the area.[2] They will be of even more use when carefully checked against comparative party behaviour, to see whether or not they cover most of the known cases. The information we have collected for this purpose from our twenty countries is described below (Appendix B), as are our 'theory' or 'explanation' (these terms being synonymous) and our reasons for thinking it plausible in light of existing knowledge (Chapter 2). In the next section of this chapter we discuss the practical and research requirements which a general explanation ought to serve, before going on in the following two sections to review current and to our mind partial theories about party government.

THE SHAPE OF A SATISFACTORY EXPLANATION

A satisfactory explanation should focus on parties, without which the democratic State could not be responsive to the population; it should be comparative (otherwise we lack grounds for properly evaluating our findings); and it should cover all important aspects of governmental activity—which we take to be its formation, the initial allocation of posts (and subsequent changes), policy-making, termination, and effects on subsequent governments.

What do we mean by 'explanation' in this context? Probably two things. One is relating all these diverse aspects of government behaviour to each other, by postulating consistent principles and motivations which produce them. It is of course conceivable that different government activities are unrelated: that governments form without reference to the policies they are going to undertake or the way in which ministries and other offices are to be divided up. It would be damaging for the rationalistic assumptions underlying democratic theory if this were so, since these must assume *some* link between these behaviours at least through a common responsiveness to election results. A relationship probably does exist, if only because of the dominance within all these processes of the same actors —politicians and political parties. In a series of encounters, often occurring simultaneously, and involving the same protagonists, it would be difficult to isolate results in one area from the others. Policy and the allocation of office are probably at the centre of negotiations over the type of government which will form and how it will be run, and disputes over both hasten the end of governments.

Given the existence of links, it should be easier to formulate a general theory which will explain the functioning of government in a second sense; that is, simplifying diversity by specifying the precise patterns or regularities which underlie it. As previously observed, the most obvious regularity lies in the fact that the same actors with, presumably, the same motivations, participate in all aspects of government. We can start therefore by examining and codifying these motivations and making assumptions about how they affect behaviour. As we shall see, almost all existing theories do adopt this tactic, although there are differences about which motivations (or mixtures of motivations) are singled out.

An important task of explanation is to eliminate ambiguities by stating premises and the conclusions or predictions they lead to, as clearly as possible. The most effective way of achieving clarity is to put all this in mathematical form. While mathematics have been most generally and successfully applied to the natural sciences, they have been increasingly used in economics and from there have spilled over into other areas of political and social science. One consistent application has been to theories of government formation and the distribution of ministries, where applications based on game theory have become increasingly common.

To permit mathematical formulation, however, the focus of the explanation has usually to be narrowed, by imposing highly restrictive and simplified assumptions. Often an essential aspect of party behaviour has to be omitted, as it is not formally tractable. Because it *is* essential, however, it is difficult to leave it out altogether, and it is often smuggled back into the reasoning at a later point—thus subverting the clarity which was the justification of the mathematical approach in the first place.

The goals of maximal clarification through mathematics and of generality of application often therefore conflict. Various compromises and trade-offs are possible—*parts* of a theory can be mathematical, or the strengths of a mathematical presentation can as far as possible be carried over in a verbal formulation. These possibilities are examined in the next three sections. They lead us to put more of a premium than some of our predecessors have on the comprehensiveness and practical relevance of theory, and its ability to accommodate the findings of historical and descriptive research. This is not to say, however, that the theory cannot be unambiguously stated (see Tables 2.1–2.4 below).

While one may state such a theory in the abstract, it is another matter to accept it as a wholly validated explanation. One claim to be so rests on its internal consistency and plausibility, and its 'fit' with previous descriptive studies. Another depends on how well its assumptions and implications conform to the evidence we collected (*after* specifying the theory) in the twenty democracies of concern. Both 'internal' and 'external' checks are applied as rigorously as possible in Chapters 3 to 5. What emerges from the confrontation is a more comprehensive and extensively validated theory of democratic party government than has existed up to now. This provides a useful basis for the development both of more detailed empirical investigations and of better-grounded formal theories, possibilities which we take up at the end of the book.

PREVIOUS EXPLANATIONS

In discussing the best starting-point for a theory which could reduce the diversity of observed government actions to a pattern, we have suggested focusing on certain participants—the parties—and on their motivations in forming and running governments. This is on the assumption that groups of people engaging in a set of related activities within the same area will act consistently and with similar intentions, through which their activities can be related. The identification of purposes and strategies serves also to explain the activities, by showing how they fit together in a coherent overall pattern.

It is of course possible to conceive of other approaches. Party actions in government could be viewed as an immediate reaction to forces acting in the environment, on an analogy with Newtonian physics, without necessarily being unified through consistent motivations and purposes.[3] It is more natural, however—at least until its full potential has been explored—to seek an explanation through purposive action by parties; and all theories known to us do so. This idea of purposive action in pursuit of a goal is the distinguishing feature of 'rational choice' models of behaviour, which—buttressed by the success of their economic applications—now constitute the predominant approach to explanation in much of political science. The predominance of rational-choice approaches is even more marked in theorizing about governments than it is elsewhere. The particular form first assumed in this field was the office-seeking model—which has also been influential in relation to elections and voting-behaviour.[4]

The basic motivation assumed by this approach was that political parties or political factions (conceived as unitary groups acting together as collective individuals) aimed exclusively at a maximal share of the spoils of office. They must therefore, in a parliamentary democracy, organize a coalition which commands over 50 per cent of legislative seats, in order to form a government and enjoy the spoils. Otherwise their equally selfish rivals would combine against the government to get office for themselves. But the coalition must not be much over 50 per cent, or it would have to share out the spoils more widely than is strictly necessary.

The expectation that such *minimal winning coalitions* would emerge is associated with the influential work of Riker, who remarked: 'In social situations similar to n-person zero-sum games with side payments, participants create coalitions just as large as they believe will ensure winning and no larger.'[5] Through its use of the assumptions of game theory this quotation assumes a confrontation of selfish actors concerned solely with material rewards. These are fixed and limited in the sense that offices cannot be shared out indefinitely among parties. The fact that one party gains office means that another loses it: hence the situation is, in the language of game theory, both 'constant-sum' (with limited, non-expandable rewards) and 'zero-sum' (one's gain is another's loss).

Riker cites European coalitions as a possible field of application for this idea but does not himself apply it to them. Closely related principles (Leisersen's bargaining proposition; Gamson's size principle[6]) were explicitly related to coalitional experiences in government, and together with certain appealing features of Riker's formulation encouraged a direct application to government formation.

The appealing features of the constant-sum assumption, from a theoretical point of view, were its simplicity and avoidance of ambiguity. It gave, for example, an absolutely specific indication of what government formed under any distribution of legislative seats. In addition it identified crucial parties with more power than others. Potential majority coalitions must have at least one member in common, who can decide which is to form the government by opting for the one which gives it most. On this foundation various 'power indices' could be constructed in quite sophisticated mathematical terms, to identify the key actors and quantify their legislative and governmental 'weight'.[7] The greater influence of the key actors can then be seen as gaining them disproportionate rewards, in the form of office. In this way minimal-winning ideas could be extended to the allocation of government ministries and even to the determination of policy, although their main application has always been to the formation of coalition governments.

Indeed, this line of reasoning was viewed for a long time as the *only* way in which a rigorous theoretical treatment of government formation could be undertaken. This can be challenged. Why should politicians not have some concern with policy, for example, so that their strategic interactions are transformed from a constant- to a variable-sum game (in other words, from distribution of a limited number of ministries which only a few can possess, to enactment of policies from which everyone could gain without inherent restriction on the benefits to be enjoyed)? Although this extension entails more approximation, in that the range of potentially viable coalitions is broadened and identification of the likely winner becomes more judgemental, many party configurations do give rise to a probable government coalition, particularly once institutional constraints are brought in. Thus coalition-building can be formalized in other terms and alternative predictions made without over-much difficulty.[8]

If we are also willing to specify the exact nature of the policies important to politicians, we can make quite unique and powerful characterizations of what governments will form. This is the approach adopted below, which allows us to go beyond the narrow focus on the mechanics of coalition-building between roughly equal partners, to a consideration of the other modes of government formation; and beyond that to a consideration of other aspects of governments than their initial formation (see the third section of Chapter 2).

Such radical reconceptualizations are encouraged by the assumption, made even by those working within the mainstream approach to coalition formation, that policy pursuit rather than office-seeking is the major theoretical motivation.[9] However, in spite of—or perhaps because of—its drastic simplifications, it must be said that the clarity and unambiguousness of the minimal-winning formulation dominated all theoretical discussion and comparative analyses of party behaviour in government during the 1960s and 1970s. This means that a review of its strengths and weaknesses is essential to any general survey of the area; and especially that any departure from its premisses has to be convincingly justified. For that reason, most of the next section is taken up with a discussion of minimal-winning theory and its variants, along with the office-seeking assumptions which sustain them. Out of the critique we develop the idea of an alternative, policy-pursuing motivation which we discuss further, still in the context of formal spatial models, in the penultimate section.

FROM OFFICE-SEEKING TO POLICY-PURSUIT

A first point to note in relation to office-seeking is that such assumptions, based on a constant-sum approach, are not the only ones which might be postulated within the framework of 'rational choice'. Rational choice is usually conceived as adoption of the most cost-efficient course of action to achieve desired ends. Rationality as such relates only to the way given ends are pursued and cannot in itself be taken as imposing restrictions on the choice of these ends themselves.

In economics the further restrictive assumption is imposed (as money is so essential to gaining material ends) that maximizing profits and minimizing costs can be taken as a universal immediate objective for everyone in the market. By analogy, office-seeking models of party behaviour in government assume that possession of office is essential to achieving all other party goals, including 'altruistic' or ideologically motivated enactment of their policies, so that office becomes the universal immediate objective. Parties are therefore seen as trying to hold as many government ministries as they can for as long a period as possible at least cost in terms of resources expended.

While the essence of money is that, once gained, it can be freely spent on other things (or given away, if altruism is the final goal), office is usually held only on certain conditions. So the analogy with money is not perfect. What happens where the conditions of holding office preclude the achievement of preferred policy ends is not usually discussed in relation to office-holding models. One analysis indicates that under such circumstances negative utilities might emerge rather quickly.[10]

This is simply common sense. It is hard to imagine any politician in the real world agreeing to enact policies he opposes, simply to stay in office. There are prudential as well as moral reasons for this. Even in a world of selfish utility-maximizers a reputation for responsibility and reliability is worth votes.[11] Yet if politicians seek office as their immediate overriding objective, they will hang on regardless of electoral consequences, even at the next election. Office is justified as essential to the attainment of other ends, but rapidly replaces these within strict office-seeking models (partly because other 'ends' or 'goals' of action are left so vague within this framework that no serious attention is paid to them).

Historical-institutional research also indicates that office-seeking assumptions are over-simplistic since so many cases are known where politicians either refused or resigned office on grounds of principle. However, like the parent profit-maximizing assumptions in economics, they were too useful theoretically—particularly for mathematical development—to be readily discarded, even if they fitted available evidence only approximately. The power and attractiveness of the minimal-winning criterion is shown by its continued use even although the 'fit' with evidence is not good. When we look at actual governments, only 34 per cent of coalitions in twelve West European countries between 1945 and 1971 can be described as 'minimal winning'. An additional 30.2 per cent were formed by 'surplus majority' governments, i.e. by coalitions of more than enough parties to form a minimal winning group. And another 35.8 per cent were composed of coalitions with less than 50 per cent of legislative seats—an even stranger result in the contest of 'minimal winning' assumptions.[12] Other investigations of varying sets of post-war West European governments have broadly confirmed these findings.[13] The governments in question are defined as administrations formed after a general election and continuing in the absence of

(a) change of Prime Minister;
(b) change in the party composition of the Cabinet; or

(*c*) resignation in an inter-election period followed by re-formation of the government with the same Prime Minister and party composition.

This is a standard definition and it is the one adopted throughout this discussion. We normally think of such events as defining a government's period of office, and it brings our theories closer to practice when we use the common-sense definition. In a study which omits the criteria of elections and resignations, and thus bases government continuity essentially on continuity of Prime Minister and party composition, Laurence Dodd does establish a tendency for governments formed on minimal-winning principles to last longer;[14] but this has been challenged as an artefact of the 'pooling' of all cabinets in all the countries on which Dodd based his analysis, fragmentation of the underlying party system being the real cause of instability.[15] The difficulty in any case is to sort out the implications of Dodd's criteria, which would lead, for example, to the conclusion that the 1949 Menzies government in Australia lasted for seventeen years! There are good reasons why governments resign, even if they re-form later along the same party lines and with the same Prime Minister. It is likely that after such a re-formation power relationships and/or policy priorities will have changed, so it makes sense to distinguish separate administrations before and after such events.

Recent work by Schofield, using the same definition of government change as Dodd, has also found a tendency for minimal winning coalitions to last longer.[16] It further appears that minimal winning coalitions tend to form as expected where there are a reasonably small number of significant parties. As fragmentation increases, in the sense that the number of significant parties goes up, surplus coalitions alternate in increasing numbers with minority governments. This alternation can be interpreted as a reaction to the confusion and uncertainty inherent in dealing with too many independent actors, and consequent difficulties in calculating how many are needed for the coalition. In turn the strain of making concessions and compromises might provoke splits within existing parties, thus increasing fragmentation in a continuing vicious circle. These findings indicate that in certain circumstances the office-seeking, minimal-winning criteria may be relevant but they are by no means universally applicable.

Evaluations of office-seeking theory have concentrated on the emergence of government coalitions because it is here that the theory is most explicit and widely applied. Evidence on the allocation of ministries is ambiguous. Browne and Franklin related the share of ministries received by parties to their share of seats, and noted a strong proportionality between them.[17] Parties, in other words, received an allocation of ministries proportional to the share of seats they had contributed to support the government. While this might seem to fit a straightforward office-seeking interpretation,[18] maximizers of office among smaller parties crucial to the formation of government would surely exploit their powerful position by demanding a disproportionate share of ministries.[19] Since in absolute terms this would still be worth while for larger parties to concede (for relatively few offices are involved in comparison to those which can be gained), one would expect on strict office-maximizing assumptions to find strong *disproportionality* in favour of small parties. Some tendencies in this direction are noted by Browne and Franklin, but not to the extent that would be envisaged by these readings of the theory.

Considered as a whole, the results do not unequivocally support either the minimal-winning hypothesis or the related size or bargaining principles of Gamson and Leiserson.[20] The great attractiveness of such approaches to mathematically minded theorists, however, prompted attempts to retain them within a more plausible framework, through the introduction of ideology as an additional motivation but one strictly subordinated to office-seeking. Ideology was conceived and measured very crudely by locating parties on a continuum running from Left to Right. Positions on this continuum were assigned to parties on the basis of investigators' own judgements for the whole post-war period. It was in this way that spatial representations became central to theorizing about government formation and party bargaining.

On the face of it, deep ideological attachments would not seem to go well with obsessive office-seeking as a major motivation of parties. And indeed, ideology is regarded within these formulations as somewhat of an externally imposed constraint on what selfish office-seekers can do. The argument is that, given the existence of ideology, it makes sense even for those not ideologically motivated to combine with closer parties rather than those further away. The reasons stem from the tensions and disagreements which ideological disparities would introduce. These produce higher costs—time and energy spent in internal government negotiations—which in turn diminish the net profit to be made out of office-holding. Moreover, internal disagreements also render the fall of the government more likely.

For both reasons policy disagreements are viewed within office-seeking models as needing to be minimized either by ensuring that ideologically contiguous parties form the government (a minimum connected winning coalition[21]) or by reducing overall diversity—even though this may sometimes involve 'jumping' small neighbouring parties.[22] Such considerations are then assumed to enter increasingly into politicians' calculations, along with their desire to attain and keep office with the smallest group possible—a majority party of course is ideal from this point of view.

De Swaan's succinct formulation of his 'policy distance' theory most clearly summarizes the nature and limitations of this type of modification to minimal-winning ideas: 'an actor strives to bring about a winning coalition in which he is included and which he expects to adopt a policy that is as close as possible, on a scale of policies, to his own most preferred policy'.[23] Two questions arise from this: Why did these analysts think it necessary to introduce policy/ideology into the theory, and how does it fit with the office-seeking assumption?

An obvious reason for modifying a theory is lack of empirical success, and we have seen that only a third of West European governments are formed by pure minimal winning coalitions. Theorists hoped that by introducing policy they would improve the fit of theory and evidence and thus produce a more valid explanation. Unfortunately the 'policy-modified' versions of winning-coalition theory succeeded in improving the fit of the theory to actual situations only marginally (although some modified versions worked very well in particular countries—that based on minimal connected winning coalitions in Italy, for example[24]).

Improvement of the empirical fit was, however, only one inducement for introducing 'ideology' or 'policy'. Another was genuine concern about ignoring such considerations. Particularly in the European context it is difficult to overlook the ideological origins of party systems and the continuing relevance of such divisions today.[25]

This desire to render the theory more realistic even at the price of complicating it is wholly praiseworthy and an example we ourselves follow below. Unfortunately the full effects were not really thought through—basically because the modification was regarded as additive rather than combinatorial. In other words, policy/ideology was seen as supplementing the winning criterion rather than directly modifying it. But in fact the admission that parties might have concerns with policy as well as concerns with office profoundly changes the whole conception of party behaviour. Failure to realize this produced fundamental incoherences and ambiguities.

Even within the 'successor' theories which put most emphasis on ideology, such ambiguities arise. They stem from the fact that politicians who choose allies because they help them attain particular policy goals have no reason to worry about the size of the resulting coalition. If a salient policy goal can be attained either with a minority government (because parties outside the governing coalition offer sympathy and support) or with a surplus majority government (because it is best to consolidate diffuse support), why should 50 per cent of seats plus one form a crucial or even relevant figure? If policy is indeed important, any coalition that can attain major goals is normal and acceptable—even, on occasion, to non-members. The possession of a bare majority is important only in a world of selfish office-seekers, not in one where policy-based agreements and alliances occur to even a limited extent: there either minority or surplus majority coalitions may be appropriate under particular circumstances.

Besides subverting the minimal-winning criterion, this opens up the possibility that policy constitutes a motivation for party actions equal to or even more important than that of office. When ideology and policy are so important in constraining politicians' actions, why should not they, rather than desire for office, determine them? When ideology can impose insuperable costs on a coalition which ignores its constraints, why, on the positive side, would it not form a binding cement which supersedes calculations of immediate advantage? From a policy perspective the main thing about a coalition would be the strength and extent of its agreements rather than its relative size.

Such reasoning leads rapidly to the substitution of a theory based exclusively on policy-pursuing motivations for one based exclusively on office-seeking motivations. A good example of how this can be developed from the previous models is to be found in Grofman's 'dynamic model of protocoalition formation'.[26] This extends the idea of coalitions based on minimizing ideological or policy distances between government partners. However, such distances need not be confined to a single Left–Right continuum but can be measured in terms of any number of policy dimensions, as appropriate. Coalition-building is viewed as going through a number of stages, in each of which the parties which see each other as closest in terms of distance weighted by size form a proto-coalition. In the next stage each proto-coalition evaluates other proto-coalitions in the same way. The process continues until some viable government coalition is formed (which might but need not be a minimal winning or indeed a winning coalition). This formulation is eminently applicable to empirical research and a kindred approach is currently being used to relate party election programmes to government programmes in twelve post-war democracies.[27]

The proto-coalition model meets many criticisms of the earlier distance-minimizing, minimal-winning theories made above. Nevertheless it still focuses on the initial formation of governments rather than on their other and usually more interesting features. On the face of it a policy-based approach should give most leverage in explaining why governments adopt the kind of policy they do. There is potential for explaining this through proto-coalitions (government policy lies at some kind of weighted mid-point between the last two of these which join to form the government). But this line of reasoning has not been developed within the model.

Government policy is more central for another of the new generation of formal models, the theory of the core. In the next section we examine this formulation in more detail, for several reasons. In the first place, it represents one of the latest and most radical developments of formal theorizing in the tradition we are examining, so there are advantages in setting it out explicitly to see how far it has got. Doing so helps specify some of the points made in the second section of this chapter about the nature and limitations of mathematical models in this area, and highlights certain advantages, at this juncture, of proceeding less formally. A critique of some of the assumptions of core theory also provides a useful basis for comparison with those of our own model (Table 2.1), and a stimulus for the concluding discussion of the chapter, where we stress the need for realistic theorizing to rest on some 'mix' of policy-pursuing and office-seeking motivations.

A SPECIFIC EXAMPLE OF A FORMAL POLICY-BASED MODEL: CORE THEORY

From the introduction of the Left–Right continuum in the late sixties, formal theories of coalitions have, almost without exception, been spatial theories, as they all rest upon some conception of party policy as a particular location within a policy space, and of policy differences between parties as related to the distance separating these locations. The simplest example of a policy space is the Left–Right continuum, represented by a straight line with party positions falling at certain points upon it in terms of the 'Leftness' or 'Rightism' of their policies.

Core theory in its present form is not bound to such a one-dimensional representation, and indeed produces its most interesting results within a two-dimensional policy space, such as those shown in Figure 1.1. The two dimensions in Figure 1.1 represent two types of policy concerns which could be (the theory is not tied to any particular type) a 'Left–Right' divergence over socio-economic priorities, and some kind of clash between traditional and innovative societal values (such as the familiar moral questions of divorce, abortion, minority rights, etc.). Within this space party positions (as given by their programmes of preferred policies) can be represented as points.

It is on the particular configuration of these points that the reasoning and conclusions of the theory are based. The 'core' itself can be defined through a sequence of operations within the space, as follows:

1. All possible combinations of parties which control 50 per cent plus one of legislative seats (winning coalitions) are specified.

2. Lines are drawn between them to indicate the area of possible policy agreements intermediate between the members of the possible coalition. The set of points making up this area can be thought of as

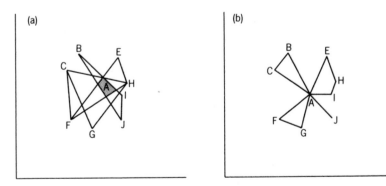

FIG. 1.1. Two-dimensional spatial representations of the theory of the core: (*a*) the core is an area; (*b*) the core is a point

Note: A–J are parties represented as points in a two-dimensional policy space. Lines define the areas of policy acceptable to all the members of the conceivable winning coalitions that could form. The shaded area in Fig. 1.1(*a*) is common to all these policy areas, as is the point occupied by party A in Fig. 1.1(*b*).

the set of policy bargains which the coalition could make to form its governmental programme on the assumption that each party wants the coalition to adopt a position as close to its own as possible.

3. The spaces delimited by the lines are then examined for a possible overlap constituting an intersection of all the potential policies of winning coalitions. Such an intersection is the *core*—which could be either an area, as in Figure 1.1(*a*), or a point designating a particular party position, as in Figure 1.1(*b*). The latter is the more common case.

The party (or parties) occupying the core position is able to move the policy of any coalition of which it is a member towards its own preferences for two reasons:

1. Since it has a greater choice of coalitions to participate in than any other party, it can bargain for concessions up to a point where policy closely approaches or even coincides with its own position.

2. Even if a coalition by some chance formed without the core party, bargaining between other parties is liable to produce a governmental compromise lying at or near the core position, given that the other parties to some extent must lie on opposite sides of it. Since this is the case, not much is lost by accepting the inevitable and going into coalition with the core party.

Much of the work undertaken on the core has been mathematical, establishing when the core is bound to exist (for instance, in the case of a one-dimensional policy space there must always be a median policy area and party (or parties)); when it could not possibly exist (when there are more than three relevant dimensions); and when it *could* exist (in two relevant dimensions), under certain conditions. Further analyses have been devoted to establishing how structurally stable the core could be in the two-dimensional situation—i.e. how far it would continue to exist despite policy movements by outlying and/or small parties (in general it will be quite stable, if formed by a single party position).[28]

Recent extensions to this reasoning have been made by McKelvey. His work has introduced the idea of an 'uncovered set' of dominant alternatives. For the special case of Euclidean preferences the 'uncovered set' is centrally located, reasonably small, and collapses to the core when the core exists: it is centred round a generalized median and gives promise of being more stable than the core itself under different institutional arrangements and shifts of party position.[29]

Whether the uncovered set can be regarded as a generalization of basic core reasoning or a new concept is probably academic. Future development of the concept has the potential for avoiding the problems of instability and non-existence which afflict the core in multi-dimensional spaces. We confine ourselves below to an exposition of core-based assumptions because:

(*a*) the complex reasoning underlying 'uncovered sets' has as yet been little explored in comparison with the core;

(*b*) in particular, the former has been applied (up to the time of writing) only to Downsian two-party competition, whereas much of our interest lies with multi-party systems and coalitions;

(*c*) the non-mathematical 'basic assumptions' which we discuss below (Table 1.1) are almost as applicable to uncovered sets as to the core, so the essential features of our discussion are applicable to both.

From the summary given above it is clear that, of the four main aspects of party behaviour in government singled out in the second section of the chapter, the theories just reviewed touch on formation, policy-making, and termination. Where a structurally stable core exists at least one member of the coalition will be known (and moreover characterized as having the most influence and initiative in coalition formation). Government policy on the most important issues can also be predicted to be that of the core party. With regard to termination, one can say that a structurally stable core will produce longer-lived governments and that formation of the succeeding government will be heavily based on the reactions of the core party to its previous partners (since it will take the initiative in forming the next coalition).

Where no structurally stable core exists theory predicts the opposite: fluctuating, short-lived coalitions with no stable membership; government policy fluctuating sharply with changes of coalition; acrimonious disputes within coalitions and a possibility of total inability to agree on any stable policy. There is a further implication from the point of view of normative democratic theory that policy solutions will be arbitrary, products of chance conjunctions of circumstances, rather than cohering round an equilibrium point produced by the electoral and legislative success of the parties. (Here, however, the existence of uncovered sets suggests some modifications, as equilibria may also exist outside the strictly defined core area.[30])

Table 1.1. Implicit assumptions of the 'core' theory of government coalitions

1. Political parties are unified actors which adopt a single programme without internal dissent (unified parties).
2. In parliamentary democracies the party or combination of parties which has at least 50 per cent plus one of legislative seats forms the government ('winning coalitions').
3. Parties seek to form that winning coalition whose governmental policy will be closest to their own policy preference (policy pursuit).
4. The important political conflicts in democracies can be represented by a one- or two-dimensional space (limited dimensionality).
5. Party and coalition policies can be represented without undue distortion by points in the one- or two-dimensional space, in such a way that points closer to the point representing their position are preferred to those further away (Euclidean space).
6. All parties have full information about the policy positions of all others on all relevant dimensions (perfect information).

Inevitably this is a broad and simplified presentation of these sets of ideas. Our intention is to examine the theories' coverage and substantive assumptions rather than the detailed mathematical reasoning which produces and qualifies conclusions. An essential point to be made, however, and one which also applies to all explanations examined in the previous section is that major assumptions of the model are generally left implicit—briefly glossed over in the verbal preamble to the mathematics or even taken totally for granted. Stating and examining such implicit assumptions brings out more clearly certain limitations and even broad inconsistencies in the reasoning. As the assumptions are verbal and institutional rather than formal and mathematical, stating them explicitly also brings out the points of contact which models in this tradition have with our own formulations (see Table 2.1 below).

These observations can be made more explicit by considering the essential presuppositions of the original core theory (Table 1.1) —presuppositions which must be made *prior* to any formal theorizing and which indeed are essential for any application of mathematics. (As noted, these apply generally to other formal theories of this type, such as the theory of uncovered sets and limited voting-cycles; and even, with modifications to the dimensionality assumption, to Grofman's proto-coalitions.)

Taking the assumptions of Table 1.1 in order, the first (that parties are totally unified to the point of being treated as single actors) is of course unique neither to formal nor indeed to coalition theory. While informal suggestions have been made that factions or other elements in parties, such as activists, might influence coalitional behaviour,[31] the possibility of internal interactions has generally been too complicated to incorporate in mathematical models. Laver and Schofield, on the basis of a detailed comparative review of factionalism in West European parties, in fact conclude that the unified-actor assumption is empirically justified for most parties at the time of coalition formation.[32]

The second assumption in Table 1.1 (on the need to have winning coalitions to form a government) is implied by the practice of using only the policy sets of such coalitions to define the core. A different method of defining viable coalitions (cf. Table 2.1 Ass. 1 below) could certainly be accommodated within core theory. However, *some* criterion for picking out those coalitions capable of forming a government is obviously necessary. Up to this point it has been 'winning' in the sense defined in Assumption 2 of Table 1.1, so it is fair to present this as it stands at the moment.

Since only policy spaces and party positions within them are considered in the theory, its implicit assumption is that parties' only motivation is to get their policies effected in government. It is thus, in the terminology introduced in the third section of the chapter, a pure policy-pursuing theory which excludes any other considerations possibly affecting party actions (such as a concern with power and office). Assumption 3 underlines the point that policy is the sole motivation. As we shall see, such an assumption does not match up very well with the emphasis on winning coalitions in Assumption 2: the theory of the core itself emphasizes that the position of the core party will be that of all coalitions, if the core is filled: there is thus no particular reason for policy-motivated parties either to join a government or to oust a minority one if the same policy will be pursued regardless.

Assumption 4 is necessary to the theory in the sense that a core will not exist in spaces of more than two dimensions. Here uncovered sets are indeed more flexible. The core is on the other hand guaranteed in one dimension and has a strong possibility of existing stably in two. As dimensions represent clusters of related policy concerns, it is necessary to assume that all important policy concerns can be grouped in one or two clusters to permit the theory to operate at all. The assumption is a strong one but is certainly not disproved by the results of empirical investigations over the last twenty years. There is of course a further implication that parties all see the space in the same way, as the logic would not apply if one party saw itself as quite differently located from the way it is seen by others (or even as existing in a different space of quite other dimensions). Given that these spaces do adequately reflect the central political questions at issue between the parties, a further assumption (5) is that party and government programmes can be represented by points within the space and that the normal conventions of (Euclidean) geometrical representation apply. The most important of these conventions is that a closer position is preferred to one further away. While this seems obvious, it is not a *necessary* attribute of party preferences: it is quite logical for strong supporters of welfare services to argue, if they cannot spend massive amounts immediately, that total neglect is preferable to marginal expenditure, since neglect will eventually create the necessary political support for total regeneration. This type of all-or-nothing reasoning, not uncommon in politics, is excluded by Assumption 5, as is a situation where one policy dimension is all-important to one party and the other of no importance at all, while the latter dimension counts for a second party with the first totally discounted. Such a situation probably occurs frequently, and would advise an additive 'city-block' type of metric rather than an Euclidean one.

We have stressed the need for general agreement among all participants on where and what the positions actually are. A prerequisite is that there are no obscurities or deliberate ambiguities about locations. This is the requirement of perfect information encapsulated in Assumption 6.

The translation of policy preferences into points in a space seems so direct and obvious that it is easy to forget that it depends on making sometimes problematical assumptions like those in Table 1.1. Any set of empirical assumptions is going to be problematical of course, but some assumptions may be more problematical than others. The ones outlined here are restrictive in that they exclude any concern with office on the side of the parties, even purely instrumental use of office to advance policies. This completely reverses earlier tendencies to attribute exclusively office-seeking concerns to parties and to exclude all interest in policy, even as a means to obtaining office!

This seeming inability to accommodate the two leading party motivations at one and the same time is perhaps a necessary feature of mathematical theorizing as it serves to render party interactions simpler and more amenable to a strictly formal treatment. This is, however, at the considerable price of leaving out of consideration central aspects of government activity—the distribution of ministries and their role in implementing policies, in the case of the theory of the core. Moreover, of the aspects it does treat, it covers only one, government policy-making, fully. The coalitions that form are only partly specified, while the exploration of duration and termination concentrates on one single cause—absence of a stable core party (or, in the extended reasoning, of an uncovered set). It seems likely that termination in particular is caused by many factors—strategic and electoral considerations and external factors among them (see Chapter 6).

None of this is to say that the theory of the core or related formal theories are inadequate for the purposes for which they are designed. They represent a great advance in their ability to accommodate subtler considerations than earlier, simpler, formal theorizing. Moreover, the ability to bring government and party behaviour within the ambit of mathematics is obviously an advantage in deriving valid logical conclusions from the assumptions.

In spite of this the core seems no more empirically successful than any of the other spatial models based on policy distances when used with party programmes to predict which parties will form a government.[33] (The theory of uncovered sets is not yet sufficiently developed in this direction to test.) Thus there is still room for a less formal treatment which can, at a non-mathematical but still systematic and rigorous level, try to integrate all the major aspects of party behaviour in government. The less restrictive assumptions of our suggested approach (Table 2.1) may not permit direct mathematical formulation but they do bear a sufficient resemblance to those of core theory (and to those of the other formulations not examined in detail here) to suggest a close affinity between the two. Because of this their development and testing is of interest for all types of theorizing within this field; specific suggestions of how to follow it up are made in Chapter 7.

POLICY PURSUIT AND OFFICE-SEEKING: COMPLEMENTARY BASES FOR EXPLAINING PARTY BEHAVIOUR IN GOVERNMENT

While the office-seeking motivation cannot provide a sufficient basis for explaining party behaviour in government, it would be foolish to discard it altogether, especially as the most up-to-date research indicates that it is through control of ministries that parties bring their main influence to bear on policy-making.[34] We have also seen that evidence does exist for minimal-winning considerations applying at least to some governments within certain countries. Moreover, if politicians are not totally selfish they are not totally altruistic either. All these considerations suggest that some mix of policy- and office-related concerns might constitute a better basis for theorizing than either taken in isolation.

If we try to consider relationships between office-seeking and policy pursuit systematically, as twin bases for theory, we come up with the following possibilities:

1. Office is valued for its own sake, as in the minimal-winning and related formulations already discussed. In this case parties are presumed only to seek office; they need to have a winning majority to gain it; there is no motivation for parties outside the government to offer support, so minority governments are ruled out; and offices will be distributed (*a*) in strict proportion to the party contribution in seats or (*b*) in proportion to the 'power' of the party in the coalition, measured in terms of its 'pivotal' position.

2. Office is sought as a means of advancing policy. This alternative takes seriously the argument that office-seeking is a way to promote policy goals—an argument used but never really investigated in previous coalition theories, and which seems to have a strong empirical basis.[35] On this assumption the value of an office and the use made of it both depend heavily on the state of policy agreements in cabinet and legislature. For example, if parties both in and out of government agree on the main policies, office has less value than when there is strong policy disagreement between parties. Minority and surplus majority governments, in the former case at least, are quite possible. The control of administration and the ability to affect policy implementation through the tenure of particular ministries constitute another aspect of political strategies opened up by this assumption. Implementation is perhaps even more important for controlling the content of policy than its initiation in cabinet. Whereas in a pure office-seeking perspective, ministries are all equivalent (provided at least they are of equal rank and power), in this policy-predominant view they are of interest also for their function. Hence, particular parties will have strong preferences for particular ministries,[36] which makes them much more than a freely interchangeable unit of power.

3. Policy is valued as a means of achieving office. This assumption

characterizes the seminal work of Downs on electoral competition,[37] which portrays electors as policy-seekers but politicians as entre-preneurs, adjusting policies to which they themselves are not neces-sarily attached so as to attract maximum numbers of voters and thus attain office. This conception does not fit neatly with minimal-winning ideas at the governmental level, as these conceive of each coalition formation as an event in its own right, outwith the historical context. So feedback effects of coalitions on elections are ignored (a party will never on minimal-winning assumptions pass by the im-mediate chance of office for longer-term electoral calculations). When, on the other hand, electoral competition and government actions are viewed as interactive, parties have to worry about effects on their electoral credibility even when considering an otherwise advantageous coalition. This may be counterbalanced by a desire to demonstrate effectiveness in government, as parties permanently out of office also suffer from lack of confidence in their ability to govern —in this case through electoral doubts that they can actually do what they say they will. A series of complicated trade-offs may then ensue between these two considerations, which can of course carry different relative weights at different times in a party's life history.

4. Policy is pursued for its own sake. This is the situation diametri-cally opposed to pure office-seeking. Here parties are seen as con-cerned only with the policies that are implemented and not at all with the holding of office—an assumption which may be quite realistic in situations of legislative supremacy over the executive. The distinction between majority and minority governments quite disappears here, since the universality of policy pay-offs renders the coalition game variable-sum—that is, policy benefits are capable of being shared by anyone without detracting from the benefits enjoyed by others. Again, we might expect the priority that parties attach to policy over office to vary with their own situation and with general political conditions —war or emergency might cause parties suddenly to elevate general policy priorities over normal concerns and form national coalitions or governments of national unity without much quibbling over who gets what.

Envisaging these different possibilities helps to make the theory of parties in government more realistic and to accommodate the results of historical and descriptive research—which would exclude neither policy nor office as a motivation at different times and different places. There can be little doubt about the desirability of developing theory along these lines. A major constraint, however, lies in making it specific enough to be really useful, without restricting it so much as to be impossibly simplified and unrealistic. One can easily say that there is a possibility of pure office-seeking giving rise to particular effects, of pure policy pursuit giving rise to radically different ones, and of the mixture of motivations producing the others sketched above; and that all these situations may crop up at different points. But without the ability to anticipate when one type of situation will arise in practice, or even to distinguish between past historical situations according to the predominance of office-seeking, policy pursuit, or a specified combination of the two, the theory would be useless for practical research, even though it clarifies certain conceptual confusions.

To illustrate this point, let us consider a central problem in the practical specification of such a theory, that is, the trade-offs between office and policy which a party is prepared to make in a particular situation. Simultaneous consideration of policy pursuit and office-seeking raises the possibility, in the bargaining to form a coalition government, that policy concessions may be compensated by portfolios, or vice versa, in a number of different ways.[38] But the way these trade-offs are made will vary between parties, countries, and time periods. In order to distinguish between the different situations outlined above we need concrete specifications of the relationship for each government. To get these we could check whether offices were distributed in strict proportion to party contributions to government strength, and whether policy concessions varied without discernible pattern. This would characterize a situation of pure office-seeking on the part of parties just as the reverse would constitute evidence for the predominance of policy pursuit.

If, however, evidence of some systematic patterning existed in regard to both, the presumption would be that office and policy were simultaneously valued. Two sets of problems arise here:

1. Do parties have different perceptions of the 'values' of different policies or policy positions? Do all parties in fact value policy positions to the same extent in comparison with office? Probably the only way to proceed is from the simplest assumption (everything valued to the same extent) to more complicated ones, checking at each stage whether the assumption produces a plausible representation.

2. In what order would bargaining proceed—would offices be allocated first and losers be compensated with policy concessions, or vice versa? Or does bargaining over both proceed simultaneously?

Again, to establish this we should have to check such matters as the time-sequence of events, and the actual results—especially if, as envisaged by this approach, different trade-off functions exist in different countries and in different time periods, or even for different parties with one country at the same time.

Estimating trade-offs is only one problem in specifying an adequate theory to cover the whole range of possibilities outlined above. It does, however, illustrate the central difficulty: as theoretical possibilities become more complicated, so we confront ever more acutely a methodological dilemma. Either we assume a priori that a particular situation (pure office-seeking, pure policy pursuit, or mixed) holds, and derive empirical estimates of the office–policy trade-off in terms of this; or we assume something about trade-off rates and use the empirical data to test theory using this independent assumption. A test of the theory's validity cannot be made on the basis of the results if we have followed the first course (because the results stem directly from the theory itself); and a test in the second case would depend heavily on the independent assumption introduced to set trade-off rates.

It follows that a theory which incorporated all the possible combinations of office-seeking and policy pursuit would be, at least in the present state of our knowledge, essentially untestable. To make it empirically relevant we have to restrict the range of theoretical possibilities considered—that is, evolve a more simplified view of the world than probably exists. Simplification to provide testable theory, with the consequent exclusion of certain real-life situations, was of course the tactic employed in the minimal-winning, pure office-seeking formulation. The problem there was that too many actual situations—two out of three—were excluded (the minority and surplus majority governments). In simplifying, therefore, one must be careful to make assumptions ʰhat do cover the commonly occurring situations.

The general strategy to be adopted is clear. This leaves two questions: What use is even a testable theory if we know in advance it cannot cover all the possibilities? And if we assume it is useful, what should the basis of the theory be?

We want a testable theory because, if validated, it tells us what are the most common relationships between office and policy—information which can then be applied in the context of more inductive investigations. Some assumptions about trade-off rates are essential to such investigations: it is better that those applied to commonly recurring situations be derived from a tested and validated explanation than made arbitrarily. The tasks of creating and checking a priori theory, on the one hand, and of inductive, theory-informed investigation, on the other, are therefore complementary—just as theoretical investigations are, or should be, complementary to historical and descriptive research.

To the second question, of what assumptions should be used as a basis for the theory, an answer has been provided, broadly, by the earlier discussion. Pure office-seeking assumptions are obviously inadequate. Pure policy-pursuing ones may be more realistic but are unlikely to cover the majority of cases. Of the two mixed situations, the one which postulates that office is used as a basis for attaining policy goals, rather than that policy is subordinated to office, is supported by the most detailed and up-to-date research[39] and is more likely to prevail in general. This is because parties in government —the principal focus of the theory—are less concerned about office than current policy-making, much of which has only a remote bearing on elections but a great deal to do with underlying ideology, the basis of party identity.

To opt for this particular mix of motivations is not however to exclude all consideration of other situations, characterized by the primacy of office-seeking or of pure policy pursuit. If our theory is to avoid the static nature of earlier formulations and envisage certain dynamic and changing historical conditions which alter the priorities and reactions of parties, it has to allow that other motivational mixes may at times prevail. This enables the formulation to cover to some extent the other three motivational conjunctions we have sketched —but they will be seen as the product of particular conditions which set aside, for limited periods, the generally prevailing use of office to attain policy goals, which assumption is the basis of our approach. In the ability to envisage an occurrence, even if limited, of the other situations, we hope that our proposed account of democratic party government avoids being simple-minded, even if it is simplified. But that can be judged directly from the presentation we now make in Chapter 2.

The General Theory of Party Government

GENERAL ASSUMPTIONS

If policy preferences are taken as the major determinant of politicians' actions, one must specify what these are and how they affect behaviour within governments. Our development of these still leaves a place for the minimal winning coalition, but as a last resort in certain special situations rather than as the general norm. As well as the shape taken by policy preferences, any theory must detail the circumstances under which a government can form, placing more emphasis on institutional and structural features such as the legislative vote of confidence, which have been ignored up till now. Parties are not necessarily united internally, although their endorsement of a large number of common interests renders it natural for many purposes to view them as single actors. This is entirely defensible for purposes of theoretical simplification, when (for example in the formation of governments) most parties have clearly defined positions on which most of their members at least temporarily agree. In the functioning of governments over a one- to four-year period, however, internal party factions emerge, even if they were not there before (but they normally are). Their existence affects the policies governments make, and perhaps even more closely the reallocations of ministries and reshuffles which occur during the lifetime of most single-party governments.

Table 2.1 spells out the general assumptions of the new theory designed to cover these and related points, and to provide an integrated basis for explaining all major aspects of party behaviour in government. As emerged in the review of existing theories in Chapter 1, strength in one direction is usually acquired at the expense of sacrifices elsewhere. Greater mathematical rigour has been secured by restricting the scope of theory, often within unrealistic limits. In our case we have bought greater comprehensiveness and realism by stating our theory in a non-mathematical, non-spatial form.

Such a reversal of priorities is justified by the impasse in which most formal theorizing now finds itself after a quarter-century of development—ever more mathematically and logically rigorous, based on ever more subtle spatial concepts, but not much more capable of 'fitting' or explaining most actual party behaviour. This state of affairs calls for a fresh approach, capable of bringing party behaviour within some comprehensible overall framework, which the tactic of devising less restrictive and more 'realistic' assumptions surely is. Nevertheless, systematic theorizing at whatever level aids development of other theories, since they always have to make closely related basic assumptions (compare Tables 1.1 and 2.1). Whatever the form such assumptions take, their elaboration and validation against comparative data provide a boost for all attempts at explanation, including mathematical and formal ones.

Informality and restrictiveness are of course highly relative concepts, and what appears informal to a mathematician may seem excessively rigorous to an historian. Our theory is stated as formally as seems compatible with the need to extend its coverage and meet the historical experience of post-war coalition governments. The presentation in Table 2.1 indeed seeks to make explicit certain assumptions which in the mathematical formulations are treated with considerable ambiguity (cf. Table 1.1).

The advantage of presenting the assumptions together is to render them more easily memorable and to emphasize their interrelationships. A tabular summary serves also to highlight the ambiguities or unforeseen complexities which we want to eliminate. In the table the assumptions form a progression from those necessary to cover the question of government formation to those dealing with other aspects of government (though most assumptions have implications for more than one area, as will appear).

Although it might be regarded as purely definitional, Assumption 1 does specify the minimal condition for a government's existence—the state of affairs which parties must create if they wish to form a government and which they must maintain if they want to stay in office. At first sight it may seem obvious (in the parliamentary regimes being discussed) that governments need to win legislative votes of confidence. The ability of the government to gain legislative support

TABLE 2.1. General assumptions of an integrated theory of democratic party government

---

1. In parliamentary democracies the party or combination of parties which can win a legislative vote of confidence forms the government.
2. Parties seek to form that government capable of surviving legislative votes of confidence which will most effectively carry through their declared policy preferences under existing conditions.
3. (*a*) The chief preference of all democratic parties is to counter threats to the democratic system.
   (*b*) Where no such threats exist, but socialist–bourgeois differences are important, the preference of all parties is to carry through policies related to these differences.
   (*c*) Where neither of the preceding conditions hold, parties pursue their own group-related preferences.
4. Within parties, and subject to overall policy agreements and disciplinary and procedural constraints, factions seek to transform their own policy preferences into government policy most effectively.

---

is, after all, specified in most constitutions (written or unwritten) as a legal requirement for its survival.

Note, however, what this very bare assumption is *not* saying—that is its real significance in our argument. It does *not* maintain, as an office-seeking approach does, that the government must have a majority of seats in order to survive votes of confidence, on the further assumption that all non-government parties impelled by the urge for immediate office will gang up on the government at every opportunity. Since office-seeking has been abandoned as the primary motivation, there is no reason why opposition parties may not offer voting-support to a government from outside, or at least abstain, if they have policy aims which may be served by these courses of action. Moreover, two non-government parties, even if they dislike the government and wish to replace it by themselves, may still like that alternative better than its replacement by the other. Hence they may rarely vote simultaneously against it. For all these reasons a government can survive quite comfortably for a considerable period with less than 50 per cent of legislative seats—sometimes, indeed, with less than 40 per cent. Thus Assumption 1 is quite compatible with the observed frequency of minority governments, which are as common as minimal winning coalitions; or for that matter with the existence of large majority governments which go substantially over the minimal-winning level. What is important in all cases is that a government is *viable* in the sense of attracting necessary support, rather than minimal winning or winning.[1]

With the question of what is at stake clarified, Assumption 2 directly states the point made generally above—that parties' main concern is with setting up governments which will carry through their preferred policies, rather than simply being in government for its own sake.

Assumption 3 states explicitly what we consider parties' preferred policies to be. In order of priority they are: to conserve democracy, if that is in any sense under threat; where such a threat is absent, to deal with distributional and planning-matters related to socialist policies (whether the parties concerned are for or against them); and where these are not salient, to pursue their own characteristic policies (which are most often designed to benefit the social groups from which the party draws its support).

In making such explicit assumptions about parties' and politicians' preferences, the new approach breaks with earlier ones. Under the desire to preserve generality wherever possible, most formal models seek to make their assumptions and implications compatible with any general aim which actors may hold (that is, by saying parties will form a government whose policy programme is as close as possible to their own preferred position—whatever the basis or metric of the policy distances involved (cf. Table 1.1 Assumptions 2–4)).

Such an assertion, however, if it is to have any practical application at all, requires that some space be specified within which distances can be measured, as appears for example in the theory of the core (Table 1.1 Assumptions 3–4). Actually setting up such a space involves singling out certain preferences as those which are most important to politicians and thus in effect making the same kind of judgement as that made by Assumption 3 (in practice Left–Right issues have been almost universally privileged). The novelty of our assumption is therefore less than it seems. It is just that it makes the theory as clear and unambiguous as possible, by attributing the specific preferences explicitly to the parties.

Preferences will of course vary with circumstances. Like anyone else, politicians tend to switch priorities in response to changed situations. The wording of Assumption 3 allows for this. Thus in a crisis of the regime it is highly unlikely that the very politicians who have been most influential in shaping its practices, and who in many ways are the chief beneficiaries of existing arrangements, will not make their main concern its support and defence. Such politicians will, by definition, be in the majority, since if they were not, the democratic regime would already have ceased to exist! Whatever their previous differences over social and economic policy, or in regard to the various group interests they represent, they will come together when the system whereby these differences is settled is itself attacked. In that, they have a common interest overlying the disputes they carry on within the democratic framework.

In a normal political situation, democracy is not seriously threatened. This gives free play for 'ordinary' disputes to emerge. Empirical research shows that the most pervasive and general of these relate to the programmes of Socialist or related 'progressive' parties.[2] Whether these are full-bloodedly Marxist or simply reformist in intent, they all threaten upsets in established relationships which tend to involve most people in the society. As a result, all parties will tend to line up on either the socialist or anti-socialist side when these issues come to the fore, sinking the differences which at other times might have separated them. Under such circumstances they will refrain from pushing points to which at other times they would have been firmly wedded, since their clients would be more decisively affected by the success or reversal of the socialist programme where there seems a real possibility of it being pushed through.

Where this is unlikely, and no threat to the democratic system exists, then parties and politicians are free to pursue the policies most characteristically associated with them. As we have noted, these are often interests or needs of associated groups. In many cases of course specific party interests and policies will not be wholly independent of the ones involved in socialist–bourgeois confrontations. Socialist parties can be expected to interest themselves in welfare, for example, at all times, and bourgeois parties in incentives and liberties. The priority given to such objectives will be less, however, than in periods of confrontation. They will be diluted by quite different goals and considerations and the style in which they are pursued will accordingly be very different.

These are strong postulates: all parties over extended periods of time are being credited with similar and quite specific motivations. It is as well at this point, therefore, to note some limitations to what is being said and to add several caveats.

(*a*) Assumption 3 is phrased so as to cover the *post-war* situation in the democracies covered here. It is certainly probable that the same specification would apply to the pre-war situation too, but its applicability to that period will not be checked and it is not necessary to the empirical success of the theory as here stated.

(*b*) This does not mean, however, that the theory and in particular the crucial Assumption 3 are simply *post hoc* rationalizations of recent events, rather than truly general explanations. The preceding point relates to evidence for testing the theory rather than the theory itself. There are clear theoretical reasons for postulating this kind of hierarchy of political preferences which give our reasoning a general rather than a purely historical significance.

At first sight the ranking we have made could be taken as counter-intuitive, given that most politico-economic discussion of what parties do in government centres round the class-partisanship model popularized by Hibbs.[3] This holds that parties, when they can, pursue policies which are in the interests of their core supporters. Thus Socialist or Labour parties promote employment, even if this also boosts inflation; and their bourgeois opponents combat inflation even at the cost of increasing unemployment.

This concern with group interests might seem to elevate the bottom-ranking set of preferences—for advancing characteristic (largely associated group) interests—to the top level. Even in the politico-economic literature, however, the second level, that of socialist–bourgeois class confrontation, is seen as overriding: one notes the central emphasis on trade-offs between inflation and unemployment, an archetypal class issue. It seems quite in line with politico-economic thinking, therefore, to postulate that other group-based issues will arise only when such trade-offs (and related distributional questions) are not at the centre of political attention (for example, in times of economic expansion, when both inflation and employment can be kept low). Class interests of course *are* group interests and will be pursued to some extent at all times, as noted above. There are, however, other groups—ethnic and regional, for a start[4]—whose situation can generate issues when they are not absolutely swamped or assimilated into the dialectic of class confrontation.

The relationship between the second and third levels of our hierarchy thus seem not only compatible with but consequential on the politico-economic literature. There remains the highest level: Can threats to democracy plausibly be postulated as overriding all other considerations, including class-based ones under certain circumstances?

One difficulty here (which we have also to tackle operationally in the second section of Chapter 3) is that politicians so often cry wolf in their own interests. This is particularly true of bourgeois parties whose appeals to national unity or the national interest are often used as tactics against working-class manifestations like strikes. But while this is true, it does appear as an operational rather than strictly theoretical problem. It is difficult to deny the existence of at least some objective threats to democracy. Coups are rare in parliamentary democracies but they have occurred (for instance in Greece and Cyprus); conspiracies and attempted coups are more common; terrorism commoner still if usually limited; external pressure and subversion are experienced by many countries. The situation envisaged in Assumption 3(a) of Table 2.1 is one of these (or a combination of more than one), where the threat is sufficient to produce feelings of common danger among both socialist and bourgeois parties. These are sufficient to override even pressing domestic conflicts, which can always be postponed to another day or even hastily patched up, whereas the response to immediate danger cannot wait. One can make a clear analogy here with Maslow's hierarchy of needs (famously popularized in political science by Inglehart[5]), where only if the need for survival is met do other needs take over. Situations of the kind we are talking about may threaten not only the survival of the democratic regime but also politicians' lives: prominent personalities of the *ancien régime* will be high on the proscription lists. Thus there is good reason for them to close ranks against anti-democratic elements and to make this their top priority.

The hierarchy of political preferences postulated in Assumption 3 thus does seem theoretically and generally, as well as historically, grounded. Certainly it ties democratic politicians to a set of fairly limited, substantive preferences. However, it is hard to see what other motives could be operating consistently and independently, across many countries and governments whether in the post-war period or at any other time. The so-called 'New Politics' and the clash between traditional morality and new views of society have both been suggested as issues which create new dimensions of conflict.[6] Both, however, have a tendency either to merge into Left–Right or group-related conflicts, or on the other hand to be shared by politicians in the different parties so that they fail to create a party-related cleavage. The only exception here would be the sharp self-differentiation of the Green parties; but these have entered into coalitional or governmental politics in only one or two countries. At the time of writing, therefore, the idea that party preferences can be summed up in terms of defence of democracy, Left–Right divisions, and group-related politics, does not seem wildly far-fetched.

(c) The explicit provision for parties having different concerns at different times marks an important theoretical innovation. The usual practice in coalition theories has been to postulate a unidimensional Left–Right continuum on which parties take up invariant positions for the whole post-war period—as if Left–Right questions were (i) always central, (ii) the only issues of political concern, and (iii) incapable of eliciting fresh or novel responses from the parties which involved some change at least in the distances separating them. If party politics were really like this they would of course be a great deal easier to explain. The failure of such one-dimensional models to fit most of the evidence suggests that things are more complicated and that such complexity needs to be recognized in theory. Recent spatial formulations (see the penultimate section of Chapter 1), concerned to picture party positions as in general multi-dimensional, go some way towards recognizing this. The practical imperatives of spatial representation (in particular, the limited numbers of cases on which it can base itself) may, however, require that even a multi-dimensional representation assume that the same cleavages dominate for the whole post-war period, or substantial slices of it, even though individual party positions may change. Our formulation allows a more flexible characterization of issue concerns as varying between different time periods and between countries (see Table 3.1 below and the related discussion in the text). As analysts have increasingly stressed the idiosyncrasies of each country's coalition politics even to the extent of suggesting that different models of coalition-making may hold true in different countries,[7] this flexibility in regard to varying issue concerns represents a necessary element of adaptability in our theory.

The last assumption (4) of Table 2.1 again innovates theoretically, by breaking with the near-universal if usually implicit postulate of previous theories that parties are, under all circumstances, totally unified actors (see Table 1.1 Assumption 1). It is of course true that Assumptions 1–3 of Table 2.1 ascribe common preferences and motivations to parties as such. This is realistic in that (i) any party which keeps together as a functioning entity must preserve a minimal set of common purposes *vis-à-vis* other parties; (ii) particular external circumstances, such as rivalry with other parties, the need to preserve a united front in negotiations (to form a government, for instance) or in elections, will all put a premium on unity, and make it realistic to treat parties in these situations as united. To the extent that a party is free from such external pressures, however, factions will try to press their own policies and get their own members into office.

Assumption 4 thus converts the fixed, invariant postulate of party unity into a variable: the degree of unity or of factionalism depends on circumstances. This is again an element of greater realism in the theory which at the same time is sufficiently simplified not to be unmanageable in a non-spatial context.

To get a better idea of the relative advantages and disadvantages of using these assumptions as the basis of a theory, we can contrast Table 2.1 with Table 1.1, which presents the comparable assumptions behind the theory of the core. A first impression is of the greater number (six to four), and greater restrictiveness, of the assumptions made by the latter—necessary of course to provide the stronger postulates required for the mathematical-spatial analysis.

Turning to specific assumptions, we have just commented on the idea (Table 1.1 Assumption 1; Table 2.1 Assumption 4) that parties are totally united internally: this is plausible in the coalition-formation situation envisaged by core theory, but less so at other points in a government's existence.[8] The presumption that only majority co-alitions can form a government (Table 1.1 Assumption 2) flies in the face of much evidence and is not actually essential to core theory, even though it has guided applications up to the present. It would be better in all developments of coalition theory from now on to shift the focus from *winning* to *viability*, in the sense of capacity to survive the legislative vote of confidence (Table 2.1 Assumption 1). Assumptions 3 of Table 1.1 and 2 of Table 2.1, on parties seeking to form the (winning/viable) government which will best serve to advance their policy preferences, are almost identical—however, ours does stress the policy-effectiveness of a resulting government as an additional consideration. This might imply, in contrast to spatial theories, that a party could choose a government somewhat less close in policy because it was expected to be more effective in implementing it, perhaps by selecting partners with governmental experience rather than ones without (cf. Table 2.2 Auxiliary Assumption 3).

As our theory is non-spatial there is nothing exactly corresponding to core theory's assumptions of the limitation of important conflicts to one or two dimensions (Table 1.1 Assumption 4) or of the relatively undistorted representation of party programmes by points in Euclidean space (Table 1.1 Assumption 5)—both of which conceal complications pointed out earlier. The equivalent assumption in non-spatial terms is 3 in Table 2.1. Postulating that certain questions predominate at certain periods might point to a lexicographic ordering, i.e. a conception of issues as clustering in three dimensions, only one of which is of concern at any one time, thus effectively postulating a varying line-up of one-dimensional preferences among the parties, which could then be analysed in spatial terms. However, we do not make any of the further assumptions about space and distance which would transform preferences into points and distances along such lexicographic dimensions. Party positions are dichotomized (for instance as socialist or bourgeois) or at most appear as categories in a purely nominal classification. This eliminates strong assumptions about Euclidean space. The attribution of a limited set of substantive preferences to parties is itself, however, a strong assumption in another sense. Differences with the seemingly contentless assumptions of core theory and related models about parties in an (undesignated) policy space are, as we have pointed out, more apparent than real. Somehow these models always end up using as one (or even the sole) dimension a Left–Right continuum—tying themselves in the end to a more specific characterization of political preferences than ours.

The assumption of perfect information in the core model (Table 1.1 Assumption 6) is necessary to a spatial theory: unless the configuration is seen in the same way by all players it will not exert the postulated effects. We have no corresponding assumption since parties will pursue their own preferences whether or not they see other parties as sharing them. The absence of precisely plotted points and distances renders exact, shared, mutual perceptions less relevant.

Freed from the need to provide a direct basis for mathematical analysis, our theory thus gets by with fewer and less restrictive assumptions than developed spatial theories; this being the case, they are, in a broad sense of the term, more likely to fit available evidence. This is not surprising. What is more interesting is the relationship of our set of assumptions to 'formal' ones. In certain cases there are close correspondences, while in others our formulation suggests modifications (for instance viable rather than winning coalitions) which should strengthen and extend them more realistically. Even in cases where there is a definite divergence, as in our attribution of different substantive preferences to parties at different times, there is a considerable pay-off for spatial theory in having this notion tested. For if upheld it will give a considerable insight into the nature of the dimensions constituting policy space.

AUXILIARY ASSUMPTIONS

For maximal clarity we also present auxiliary assumptions of our theory at this point (Table 2.2). These are discussed separately because they stand at a different level of generality from the basic postulates of Table 2.1: they range from the essential but trivial (Assumptions 1 and 2) and the essential but slightly problematic (Assumption 3) to the complementary, strictly non-essential, but substantively interesting Assumption 4.

The first two assumptions carry on from the discussion of factionalism in the preceding section. In order to build on this one has to assume, first, that party leaders will belong to factions, and that this will also apply to government ministers and to the Prime Minister. There is little problem in making such a generalization, since we recognize that 'factions' is a wide term embracing any coterie or set of associates acting with some common purpose within the party. Unless an absolute internal unity prevails, such groups will have differences of opinion from time to time and this is all we really need to derive consequences. The loyalty of ministers and Prime Minister to their faction as well as to their party will influence their behaviour, with consequences which will be most evident in the area of internal government change. A trigger for factional struggles is specified by

TABLE 2.2. Auxiliary assumptions of the integrated theory of democratic party government

---

1. Except in essentially caretaker administrations, government ministers, including the Prime Minister, are members of parties; and within them, of factions.
2. Ministers are replaced if forced to demit their post.
3. Ministries play an important policy-making and -implementing role in the area of their formal competence.
4. Normal governmental arrangements are the most effective in getting policies carried through. Subject to their declared policies being advanced, therefore, parties seek to form governments with a party composition as close to the normal as possible.

Assumption 2. This makes the trivial but none the less essential point that ministries do not normally disappear with ministers, so the quitting of office by an individual for whatever reason provides the stimulus for a change in the composition of the government. We shall follow through the consequences of this in relation to Table 2.4 below.

Assumption 3 is essential in the sense that ministries which had purely formal powers would not interest policy-orientated factions or parties. Nor, obviously, if the ministry did something different from what it was supposed to do, would the distribution of offices work in the way we expect. There have been disputes about how effective ministries are in relation to the central institutions of government on the one hand, or in actually implementing policies after they have been agreed. Few would argue, however, that ministries play only a minor role in the area of their legally defined competence. Assumption 3 asserts their importance explicitly, as essential but auxiliary to the main reasoning.

Assumption 4 also stands outside the main theory but is substantively interesting in itself. We can derive wide-ranging implications from Table 2.1 without this invocation of a principle of inertia, which privileges normal arrangements even for parties pursuing their own preferences. However, this does focus on one of the most obvious ways in which pure pursuit of policy will be tempered by practical considerations. Assumption 4 thus fleshes out the point made earlier about parties forming governments that will *effectively* carry through their policies.

The argument runs as follows. Parties are concerned with setting up governmental arrangements which will most effectively attain their policy preferences. To change the normally prevailing arrangements more drastically than is required for that purpose is self-defeating, as this might provoke all sort of alarms and resistance, thus rendering it harder to carry the preferred policy through. This is because overturning established arrangements is both a signal that further, more drastic changes are to be expected (thus giving opposition more time to rally) and anxiety-provoking in itself. In a sense, usual political guarantees are being withdrawn. Thus there is a premium—even for parties bent on radical change—on associating with some party which has often been in government.

This consideration applies mainly, of course, to parties in a coalition system, where governments tend to be made up of two or more parties. But it is not absent from two-party majority systems, where

TABLE 2.3. Hierarchical rules for government formation implied by Assumptions 1–3 of Table 2.1.

---

i Where the democratic system is immediately threatened (externally or internally) all significant pro-system parties will join the government excluding anti-system parties.

In the absence of immediate threats to democracy:

ii any party with an absolute majority of legislative votes will (*a*) form a single-party government; except where such majorities are unusual, in which case it will (*b*) form the dominant party of a government excluding anti-system parties.

Where no party has a majority of votes and socialist–bourgeois differences over current issues are salient:

iii the tendance with the majority will form a government either including or with support from all numerically significant parties in the tendance (anti-system parties can only provide support and are excluded from participating in government).

If no such socialist–bourgeois differences exist:

iv the party which is manifestly larger than any other pro-system party will either form the government alone (in countries where single-party government is normal), or will form the dominant part of a government (excluding anti-system parties).

Where socialist–bourgeois differences are not salient and no single party has sufficient votes to meet the criteria for Rules ii or iv:

v coalitions capable of winning votes of confidence form
(*a*) to group the parties most agreed on the specific issues currently salient; (*b*) failing such agreement, to minimize the numbers of parties in government to those which will win legislative votes of confidence; (*c*) in any case, to include the normal parties of government (if any) and to exclude anti-system parties.

---

one party constitutes a government on its own. Normal governments then consist of one or the other of the major parties. Where one of these parties is being replaced (as in Britain the Liberals were by Labour in the twenties) it will usually be prudent for the newer party to associate itself initially in government with one of the older parties.

Postulating a bias towards normal arrangements helps make our general reasoning more specific by further restricting some of the consequences one can draw from it. The central argument is supplemented by, rather than made dependent on, this postulate, as will be clear immediately we examine Table 2.3.

IMPLICATIONS FOR GOVERNMENT FORMATION

The implications we can draw from the theoretical assumptions cover all major aspects of party behaviour in government. We deal initially with those relating to formation. The implications here specify what the party composition of governments will be under given distributions of legislative votes between parties. They are stated in Table 2.3. Rules i, ii(*a*), iii, and iv derive directly from the first three general assumptions of Table 2.1, and Rules ii(*b*) and v from these plus the auxiliary assumption (4) we have just been considering.

The relationship between rules and assumptions is clear-cut. If (by Assumption 3(*a*)) politicians' chief concern when the democratic regime is threatened is to defend it, it must follow that all pro-system parties will seek the most effective means of doing so. This is to form a Government of National Unity, far in excess of the bare numbers needed to survive votes of confidence (Assumption 1). Only by staging an unusual show of unity and determination can threats (whether external or internal) be outfaced. Such a 'surplus majority' government is inexplicable either in terms of pure office-seeking or in terms of narrow party advantages, but it is very understandable in terms of general agreement on a burningly important question of the day—a question of survival.

The desire to safeguard the regime will also incline democratic parties to shun co-operation with parties opposed to it, under any circumstances. This is not an implication of the assumptions which appears separately in Table 2.3, but it does operate throughout as a constraint on the composition of any coalition government.

Where no threat to the regime is perceived, Rule ii in Table 2.3 states that any party with an absolute majority of legislative votes will form a government on its own, or (with an eye to the normal arrangements in a country where absolute majorities are unusual) will at least dominate the government, probably in association with a small 'party of government' (i.e. a minor party which almost always participates in the ruling coalition). Rule ii(*a*), on single-party government based on an absolute majority of legislative votes, of course covers the classic situation produced by competition between two evenly balanced major parties. Whether differences over the socialist programme are salient, or whether in their absence the party is concentrating on its own characteristic, group-related policies, a single-party government is the easiest way to achieve its preferred goals. The same applies, of course, where for prudential reasons a small party has been allowed to share in government, even though this was unnecessary in purely numeric terms.

However, taking democracies as a whole, the emergence of an absolute majority for one party is relatively rare. In its absence, a quasi-two-party system may temporarily be created by a resurgence of socialist–non-socialist divisions. As we have suggested, the repercussions of a full-blooded socialist programme strongly affect most people in society. Support or opposition to these forms a cement between parties which overrides normal conflict. The salience of the socialist programme thus creates a quasi-bipartite competition between opposing ideological tendencies, in which the opposed coalitions act like majority parties. In such situations there is no question of some of the parties on one side being detached to co-operate in government with the other. Since the socialist–non-socialist cleavage is central to party competition, such an event would be as unthinkable as some faction of a majority party joining the opposition. Even anti-system parties excluded from actual government participation are driven by ideological imperatives to offer support to their own side in this cleavage.

Socialist or non-socialist loyalties, where these become salient, are thus perfectly capable of providing a strong basis of support for government, even in a comparatively fragmented multi-party system. Their salience, like the existence of anti-democratic threats, will, of course, vary over time. In some countries the prevalance and importance of division within the socialist and non-socialist camps themselves may prevent the differences separating them from ever coming to the fore of politics. In such cases, and also at times when these differences are muted by other events or the passage of time, other arrangements emerge.

We are talking, it will be remembered, of situations where no party has a majority of legislative seats (otherwise, by Rule ii, one would automatically form and dominate a government). However, there are a wide variety of intermediate situations between the emergence of a single majority party and complete fragmentation into a range of small parties. The case considered next is a dominant-party system with one outstanding party—outstanding either because it has nearly missed a majority or because it is obviously larger and more important than any other party. Such a dominant party is likely to have been repeatedly in government in the past, so its claims to office are enhanced by the desirability of preserving normal arrangements. Its size renders it the obvious basis for building an administration—a consideration reinforced by its ability to bring down most governments excluding it. Such a party can well, with the tolerance of non-government parties, form a viable government on its own. Failing tolerance, it may be able to rely on divisions between the other parties to keep it in power as the most acceptable alternative. Of course, the position of a dominant party is strengthened if other parties will join it in a governmental coalition. Its contribution assures it a directing role in the government anyway, and the continuance of the government is more assured through the adherence of other parties.

The absence of a majority party does not, therefore, preclude the possibility of government formation on the initiative of the largest party.[9] Obviously the position of the government is weaker where it commands only a minority of seats, or is subject to the possibility of intra-party disputes. But it is not by any means untenable.

The absence of a dominant party serves to convert the situation into the classic case of multipartism, where a number of relatively equal parties exist—none being of sufficient weight numerically to take an outstanding role. In this case none of the parties forms such an obvious basis for the government as to force the other parties to negotiate with it. Coalition-building must proceed by negotiation between equals. Threats to the regime or socialist–bourgeois tensions will not provide a common focus for the negotiations since by definition they do not exist in the situation we are discussing (if they did, either a surplus majority government would form under Rule i, or a quasi-majority-tendance government under Rule iii). There is still a possibility of attitudinal cement being provided for a government through agreement, however, since in the absence of other concerns each party will have its own characteristic policies which it wishes to pursue. If potential partners' concerns do not conflict too much on the questions which are currently salient to them, a common programme can be hammered out as a basis on which to form a government. Such agreement is important since it reduces tensions and costs of internal negotiation. It renders joint progress towards desired goals more likely, thus increasing satisfaction with the existing alliance and averting the possibility of the government foundering amid mutual recriminations.

The negotiation of such a programme is one way of proceeding in a fragmented multi-party system. It is entirely possible, however, that party preferences conflict so much on salient current issues that no genuine agreements can be negotiated. Governments, on the other hand, must still be formed. Since the bargaining process cannot be based on ideology or policy, the pursuit of office becomes paramount. Here we enter the situation postulated by pure office-seeking theories —but only because prior policy-based considerations are, by definition, inoperable. In default of policy agreements, it is certainly advisable to keep the number of parties in the governing coalition as small as possible, to minimize the costs of disagreement and internal negotiations. The size will be set, however, not by the need to gain an absolute majority of all legislative seats, but by the need to group parties with enough support to win legislative votes of confidence. Policy *agreements* may be absent but enough *disagreements* can exist among the major non-governmental parties to prevent them all lining up against the governing coalition at one time. We should consequently expect parties in such a situation to form a combination of the least number necessary to win votes of confidence. (Operationally, as explained in Chapter 3, we should know what level of support is necessary for votes of confidence by considering the typical shapes which governments have assumed over the post-war period in these situations and seeing what kind of 'government formula' holds.)

Both the formation of governments by agreement and that based on legislatively winning combinations are constrained by the other factors emphasized in Rule v: they need to include normal parties of government and to exclude anti-system parties. After our earlier discussion the latter requirement requires no additional justification. The inclusion of normal government parties is of even greater importance to the fragile governments emerging under Rule v, since the repercussions of not including them might well be enough to upset the whole arrangement. Besides, such parties are often the ones motivated to begin negotiations with other parties and to smooth over differences between their partners. Their familiarity with administration also removes another potential point of friction from an already trouble-prone situation. Even where policy agreements are absent, the legislatively winning coalition may not be quite as small as in abstract it might be, owing to the need to include established government parties. We shall take this factor into account when reviewing the success of Rule v in Chapter 3.

The important point to note is the incorporation of a form of minimal-winning criterion (realistically modified) in our rules of government formation. This takes cognizance of the findings cited in the third section of Chapter 1 on the incidence and longer duration of such governments in certain situations. As the earlier critique stresses, however, the criterion becomes relevant only when ideological and policy considerations do not provide an alternative basis for the creation of a government. It is a procedure of last resort, applied in the absence of other, more satisfactory, modes of action. While our formulation offers a synthesis with earlier theory, it does so on the basis of an assumed primacy of policy considerations. This carries over to the other implications considered below.

OUTSIDE SUPPORT OF GOVERNMENT

On pure office-seeking criteria, parties which consistently or generally support a government of which they are not part are acting with total irrationality. Since they do not share in ministries or other spoils, they can have no comprehensible reason for offering support, apart from a desire to build bridges to the next government. But in pure office-seeking theories parties have a short time-perspective.

If we view the matter in the light of a concern with policy, however, there are very good reasons for some excluded parties supporting governments. This is the case whenever the existing one, however unattractive, offers a better chance of the party's policies being put into effect than any of the other likely alternatives. Even where the government's policy is only marginally better from the viewpoint of the party, the costs and trouble involved in a governmental crisis may well induce it to maintain support at crucial junctures.

This point is spelled out in Implication 1(iii) of Table 2.4 (which summarizes other derivations from the assumptions and follows overleaf. It is a difficult proposition to test since it carries the danger of circularity—immediately an outside party supports a government this might be taken as proof that it must see the alternatives as worse. However, the implication need not be circular provided there is direct evidence on how party leaders view the situation. And it does fit the commonly occurring situations in which such outside support is often given, where office-seeking hypotheses do not.

A particular case of parties offering support without participation comes with anti-system parties. These are generally excluded through

TABLE 2.4. Major implications of the general assumptions of the integrated theory of democratic party government

1. *Support of government rather than participation*
    (i) A party regarded as anti-system cannot, because of the opposition of other parties, participate in government, and can only support and not join governments which will pursue some of its preferred policies (Assumption 3(*a*)).
   (ii) Where threats to democracy are absent but socialist–bourgeois differences are salient, anti-system parties will support parties of their own tendance from outside government (Assumptions 1–3).
  (iii) A party which cannot persuade others to form a government which will put into effect any of its characteristic policies will not join the government which is formed, but will vote for/abstain in favour of that government if it considers all other practicable outcomes (including an election) would further reduce the possibility of putting its policies into effect (Assumptions 1–3).

2. *Distribution of Government Ministries between parties in a coalition* (All implications involve Table 2.2 Assumption 3 as well as assumptions specifically noted)
    (i) The largest party in a coalition will take the premiership (Assumptions 1, 2, 3(*c*)).
   (ii) Subject to rough overall proportionality, each party will seek control of ministries in their own areas of policy concern: for instance, Agrarian parties will seek the Ministries of Agriculture and Fisheries and Regional Affairs; Labour parties will seek Ministries of Social Affairs, Economic Affairs, and Labour Relations; Conservative parties will seek Ministries of Defence, the Interior, Justice, Foreign Affairs, etc. (Assumptions 2, 3(*c*)).
  (iii) Where a particular type of party does not exist, the most ideologically similar of the existing parties will seek ministries in its area of policy concern (Assumptions 2, 3(*b* and *c*)).
  (iv) These tendencies are least evident when governments are formed to counter anti-democratic threats and less evident when tendance governments are formed in a situation of socialist–bourgeois hostility (Assumptions 2, 3).
   (v) A small party in a government which could be formed by a large party on its own will not necessarily get a proportionate share of ministries (Assumptions 2, 3).

3. *Policies pursued by governments*
    (i) All parties in government agree on countering threats to the democratic order (Assumptions 1, 2, 3(*a*)).

(ii) To the extent that such threats are less evident, socialist–bourgeois differences over welfare, income distribution, and economic management will become more prominent (Assumptions 1, 2, 3(*b*)).

(iii) The direction of general policy in these areas will be decided by relative socialist or bourgeois dominance of government (Assumptions 1, 2, 3(*b*), and 3(*c*)).

(iv) Each party in the government will have some of its preferred policies put into effect: for instance, governments including an Agrarian party will pursue policies more favourable to farmers and rural interests than governments without an Agrarian party; similarly with Labour parties and the working class, Conservative/Liberal parties in regard to business, etc. (Assumptions 2, 3(*c*)).

(v) The direction of policy in specific areas will be influenced by party control of the competent ministries (Assumptions 1, 2, 3; Table 2.2 Assumption 3).

4. *Turnover of personnel*

(i) Reshuffles are more frequent and the turnover of individuals in ministries is greater where the Prime Minister has more freedom of action, and declines as the Prime Minister has less freedom of action in relation to

   (*a*) other ministries
   (*b*) party factions
   (*c*) coalition parties in government
   (Assumption 4; Table 2.2 Assumptions 1, 2).

(ii) Reshuffles will therefore be more frequent in single-party governments than in coalitions (Assumption 4; Table 2.2, Assumptions 1, 2).

5. *Durability and termination of governments*

(i) The less governments agree over policy, the more likely they are to terminate for involuntary internal reasons (Assumptions 2, 3).

(ii) Hence single-party governments are less likely to terminate for involuntary internal reasons than coalitions (Assumptions 2, 3).

(iii) Of coalitions, the more ideologically mixed are more likely than those less ideologically mixed to terminate for involuntary internal reasons. This will be particularly true for socialist–bourgeois coalitions (Assumptions 2, 3).

(iv) Governments which have been unsuccessful in implementing their policies are more likely to experience internal policy disagreements than others (and hence are more likely to terminate for involuntary internal reasons) (Assumption 2).

Table 2.4. continued

   (v) In particular, governments which have been unsuccessful in achieving their economic policy objectives are more likely to experience internal policy disagreements than others (and hence are more likely to terminate for this reason) (Assumption 2).

  (vi) When a Prime Minister can fix the date of an election, he will dissolve the government if he thinks he can improve his party's vote share or lessen vote losses (Assumption 2).

6. *Effects of activity in government on participation in future governments*

   (i) To the extent that a party fails to carry through its declared policies in government, it loses popular support (or votes, if there is a proximate election) (Assumption 2).

  (ii) Termination of a coalition government through disputes over policy between the coalition partners means that

     (*a*) they are less likely for the immediate future to associate themselves with each other in coalitions (Assumption 2).

     (*b*) where they do so associate, this will be in a minimal winning coalition without policy agreements (Assumption 2) (cf. Table 2.3 Rule v(*b*)).

---

the reactions of the other parties, inspired by their overriding urge to preserve democratic procedures (Implication 1(i)). For anti-system parties themselves, support will be most clearly called for at times when the socialist programme is salient, as it strongly affects their own clients and policies. In such a situation they will line up with the other parties on their own side of that cleavage, in order to maintain a Government of their particular tendance (Implication 1(ii)).

DISTRIBUTION OF MINISTRIES

Most theories of democratic government confine themselves to the party composition of coalitions (taking single-party governments as the extreme case of a minimal winning coalition). On office-seeking criteria, however, the distribution of ministries is equally or even more important, since control of a ministry is the main reward sought by parties for entering government in the first place. Even on policy-pursuing criteria, control of ministries is important, because it is the crucial element in the formulation and (perhaps more important) the implementation of programmes in a particular area. All this is simplified in the case of a single-party government, of course, since all ministries are then at the disposal of the one party and the problem of distribution then relates to intra-party factions—with which we deal below. Most of the discussion in this section relates to coalition governments, normally of several parties.

The few explicit treatments of the distribution of ministries, made mostly from an office-seeking perspective, have tended to stress proportionality as the major criterion for allocating offices within a coalition.[10] With this procedure each party expects, and gets, a share of ministries more or less proportionate to the share of legislative votes it contributes to government support. Empirical evidence for this has been produced from a matching of seats and ministries for European coalitions from 1945 to 1970. This produced an almost equal proportion of shares of seats to shares of ministries.[11] The original study noted that there may also be a form of 'qualitative' as well as 'quantitative' proportionality in operation, whereby the allocation of 'important' ministries may supplement mechanical proportionality. Most evidence on this comes from another investigation by Browne which produced mixed results.[12]

A policy-based perspective must put more emphasis than the office-seeking perspective on parties' concern not just with important ministries, but with ministries in the particular areas of their interest. Thus it is not just a question of getting an equivalent general return for their support, but of securing a specific ministry or ministries because of their significance for the party's policy concerns (cf. Table 2.2 Assumption 3). At the same time proportionality between seats and votes cannot be ignored. Precisely because all coalition partners wish to advance their own goals so far as possible, they will seek control of as many government ministries as they can and thus limit the numbers available to other parties. Each party has a sanction in that withdrawal will lessen the government's chances of survival. The most likely division they can agree will be one which (1) secures for each party the ministry or ministries important to it (subject to the constraint that some of these may be of equal importance to other parties in the government, so not all ministries of concern may be secured), and (2) maintains a rough equivalence between a party's support in the legislature and the number of ministries it obtains.

This provision in regard to proportionality matches Browne and Franklin's findings on European coalition governments. Whereas they interpreted this as evidence of a strict proportionality rule based on office-seeking motivations, proportionality is regarded here as the second stage in a bargaining process directed at securing policy-relevant ministries. The crucial question in deciding between these interpretations is whether there is in fact any general connection between specific types of party and the types of ministry they obtain. This point is investigated in detail in Chapter 4. Implication 2(ii) in Table 2.4 forms a summary of this argument. It should, however, also be taken in conjunction with Implication 2(iii). Not all types of party exist in all countries, although the major types of ministry do. There is no Agrarian party in Britain, France, or Germany, for example, and no Christian party in either of the first two countries. What happens in these cases to ministries which would have been allocated to the missing party? Its policy concerns are likely to be taken up by parties of a similar disposition, who seek to occupy the ministries it would otherwise have wanted to secure. For example, since the countryside is the place where traditions survive longest, one would expect religious parties to emphasize rural connections where a specifically Agrarian party is absent. This point will be expanded in Chapter 4 through a specification of the policy interests of each type of party, and listing of the ministries that are as a result most important to them.

For larger parties with a developed comprehensive ideology, most ministries are relevant. The most important in view of its centrality and dominance of the government agenda is the premiership. The largest party in the coalition can be expected to assert its claims to this, perhaps even being willing to cede otherwise important ministries and to take somewhat less than its strictly proportional share in order to get it. The rationale here is that all parties covet this central post for its policy advantages; in resulting struggles or bargaining, the party with most resources will generally get it, and this will be the largest party.

These are the major, general findings expected over all coalitions. There are the further Implications 2(iv) and 2(v), however, which state conditions under which this type of share-out will be modified. These implications follow from the assumptions that coalition governments differ considerably according to whether they form in response to an anti-democratic threat, as appendages to a majority or dominant party, as quasi-majority coalitions of a socialist or bourgeois tendance, as agreed multi-party cabinets in the absence of the preceding conditions, or as minimal winning groups unable to agree on current issues. In the case of a Government of National Unity, where the overriding imperative is preservation of the regime, it would be unreasonable to expect parties to stick out as much for ministries of their own concern. Somewhat similar considerations apply to participation in a tendance majority where the main consideration is the victory or defeat of the socialist programme rather than parties' specific policy interests. Where a small party tags along with a majority or dominant party it can similarly not expect to get more than basic demands—perhaps the one ministry of most pressing concern (provided this is not also desired by the dominant partner). The greatest scope for bargaining comes with coalitions of many relatively equal partners. The general trends mentioned in Table 2.3 should be more evident here—and even more among relatively disagreed but legislatively viable coalitions than among coalitions formed on the basis of agreements on current policy. In the latter case, parties have through the coalition agreement some guarantee that preferred policies will be pushed regardless of the particular ministries they control. Where agreement has proved impossible, however, parties have no guarantee of getting their own way otherwise than through control of particular ministries. Hence there should be an additional premium on occupying those of major concern to each partner.

POLICIES PURSUED BY GOVERNMENTS

All these points will be considered in more detail below (Chapter 4). Our summary discussion now turns to related questions of policy-making. In a policy-based approach these of course are central: not only is policy not adjusted by governments in order to gain office, but its adoption and implementation are the main reasons for parties taking office in the first place.

Since it is so central the question has been thoroughly considered already. So the way in which the implications stated in Table 2.4 follow from basic assumptions (with no auxiliaries needed) is fairly obvious. It may be less clear, however, why they have taken the particular form they have and why others which might have been derived have been omitted. In both cases the explanation lies in the limitations of the data available to check them (which again will be explained more fully in the relevant chapter below—Chapter 5).

Basically, the policy data available—on government expenditure in particular areas, legislation, and use of policy instruments—extends only from 1963 to the present. It does not therefore cover any periods of acute crisis in the democracies under consideration (cf. Table 3.1 below). The implication which follows naturally from the theoretical reasoning, that government priorities change sharply between crises and periods of normal politics, cannot therefore be directly checked in our investigation. (We have instead the related Implication 3(ii).) We can only attempt a less direct confirmation, by hypothesizing some kind of agreement on general measures against possible threats, represented in the later post-war period by the danger of external aggression and by defence expenditures (Implication 3(i)).

Nor can we anticipate abrupt discontinuities between periods of sharp socialist–bourgeois confrontation and other periods in which parties pursue their own particular goals. As pointed out above, socialists are likely to try to extend their policies in the field of welfare regardless of the centrality of the issue in the general politics of the day; and bourgeois parties will emulate them in regard to their own concerns. As such parties will be in office in most governments, we cannot expect sharp policy contrasts between periods of intense general confrontation and more diffuse pursuit of party-specific goals. All that could emerge is a general differentiation over the whole post-war period, between socialist-dominated and bourgeois-dominated governments (Implication 3(iii)). This merges into the general expectation that a party's participation in government will promote its own characteristic policies (Implication 3(iv)).

In light of what was said about party interest in office for its policy influence, Implication 3(v) makes a logical extension to party control of ministries, which it sees as exercising an independent effect on specific policies regardless of which party dominates the government. This provides the basis for a particularly interesting and direct check on reasons why parties might desire certain ministries, and on the consequences of them holding them. Checks on the effects of 'sectoral dominance' are carried through in Chapter 5 (see particularly Tables 5.2, 5.4, 5.6, and 5.8) and form an original and particularly fruitful aspect of our analysis.

TURNOVER OF PERSONNEL

Given the assumption of absolute party unity discussed above, and the consequent neglect of policy divergences which may emerge within parties and governments, previous formulations have tended to ignore internal change within the lifetime of a government. Yet this is of great significance to its functioning and behaviour and any explanation seeking to be comprehensive must cover it.

Implication 4(i) follows partly from Assumptions 1 and 2 in Table 2.2, which make the trivial but necessary point that the departure of a minister usually involves replacing him (rather than abolishing the ministry). He may be succeeded by a person from outside the current administration, but more usually by somebody from inside, who has to be replaced in turn. Thus the resignation of a single member often produces repercussions which go beyond his particular post.

The extent, however, to which such an event produces extensive transfers and turnover of personnel can be related to the power of the Prime Minister. We have already noted (Table 2.1 Assumption 4), that factions with distinct policy preferences will exist within most parties. Internally they will act in relation to each other just as externally parties do in relation to each other. That is, they will seek control of certain ministries within the overall party share, and try to advance their preferences by implementing them within ministries and seeking to influence overall party actions. Since factions will, by and large, agree more with other factions within the same party than with factions outside, overall unity will be preserved by an ability to negotiate compromises and by procedures for party unity and discipline which are explicitly designed to prevent disputes from getting out of hand. Nevertheless internal struggles, even though muted, may be expected to go on. Where there is a single-party government these will be the main source of government dissensions. In a coalition, of course, dissensions between parties overshadow internal factional jockeying and also put more of a premium on party unity.

By Assumption 1 in Table 2.2, we postulate that the Prime Minister, like other members of the party, is a member of a faction committed to forwarding its policy emphases. She will advance these in part through her agenda-setting and related powers. To exert these she has, of course, to retain office and more immediately to prevent the emergence of alternative centres of initiative within the government. The most obvious way to buttress her position and that of her faction is to move rivals fairly frequently, to prevent them consolidating a power base inside their own ministry. Quite apart from helping her own faction, the Prime Minister has also to enhance the effectiveness and unity of the overall party so far as she can. This involves fairly prompt action to replace inefficient and unpopular ministers by better nominees.

These considerations apply mainly to single-party or predominant-party governments. In coalitions the Prime Minister's power is limited by the necessity of getting other partners' agreement to the replacement of their ministerial nominees. Unilateral attempts at replacement are liable to provoke a government crisis. Because of the difficulty of replacing ministers once a coalition agreement has been hammered out, internal government change should be much less in the case of coalitions compared to single- or predominant-party governments (Implication 4(ii)). Again, of course, one has to recognize the varying situations under which coalitions come into existence. Where an overriding sense of purpose binds the coalition together, as in the case of anti-democratic threats or socialist–bourgeois confrontation, partners are probably disposed to accept changes for the sake of maintaining unity. Where the coalition is simply a convenient tactical adaptation to the circumstances of the moment, change is more likely to result in crisis.

The incidence of reshuffles and replacements can therefore be related to restrictions on Prime Ministerial power, which are least in single- and predominant-party governments and greatest in minimal winning coalitions without policy agreements. Factions within a party may, of course, be stronger or weaker, and to the extent that other factions are stronger the Prime Minister's freedom of action is less. It may also be constrained by institutional structures or constitutional conventions giving more autonomy to other ministries, although this is not likely to be the case in the parliamentary regimes with which we are concerned.

These expectations have already been upheld to some extent.[13] Further checks are carried through in Appendix A (located outside the body of the text because internal turnover does not fit squarely into the main flow of discussion, from the initial distribution of ministries to the policy consequences stemming from that distribution).

DURABILITY AND DISSOLUTION

The question of how long governments last is essentially bound up with the question of how they end. If the factors causing termination are absent, the government will go on.

In conformity with our general perspective, we regard such factors as generally linked to policy—either to success in achieving preferred objectives, which induces governments, where they can, to exploit this electorally; or to disagreements over what policy should be and to difficulties in carrying it out: these produce involuntary termination. This is the tenor of Implications 5(i)–5(v), starting with the general expectation that disagreement creates increasing internal difficulties which in the end cause the government to break up willy-nilly —especially if it is a coalition (5(ii)) and ideologically heterogeneous (5(iii)). Lack of success (5(iv)), especially of the economic success so important for other government plans (5(v)), is particularly likely to stimulate such disagreement.

Although the implications on the ways in which disagreements arise are new, the general reasoning on the effects of internal disagreement is very similar to the first models of coalition formation into which ideological considerations were introduced.[14] However, the implications for termination have not to our knowledge been systematically extended and checked before. (A partial review of a more limited set of countries than ours, and with a different definition of government, comes to the conclusion that ideological diversity has little effect.[15] This is hard to believe and our findings in Chapter 6 indicate otherwise.)

The last of the implications, 5(vi), introduces a new twist, however, as it suggests that not only failure and internal disagreement force the end of governments but also success and internal unity. In other words, when a party feels it can capitalize on its record so as to gain votes or limit losses, and when it has the premiership with the ability to call an election at will, then it will do this the better to pursue long-term policy objectives by consolidating its political position. This suggests that termination may be a more complex phenomenon than when it is seen simply as triggered by failure. When both successful and unsuccessful governments may hasten their own end, two streams of quite distinct events may lead to dissolution and the governments which last longest may be mediocre ones. This is speculation however: in the first place we need to check the implications in the table with the data available, which we do in Chapter 6.

EFFECTS OF GOVERNMENT ACTIVITY ON PARTICIPATION IN FUTURE GOVERNMENTS

The discussion of ways in which governments end has already introduced the question of what effects this may have on future governments, particularly in regard to Implication 5(vi). The parties are conceived as acting with an eye to improving their electoral position, with obvious effects on their legislative standing and bargaining-power in future governments.

It is an odd aspect of current theory that it concentrates attention on the formation of the current government, ignoring the possibility that politicians may have somewhat longer time-perspectives extending at least as far as the next government, and very probably as far as the next election and the government to be formed on the basis of its results. If parties did not take the next election into account, democratic theory would be in trouble, since it is through expectations of being punished or rewarded electorally that the accountability and responsiveness of politicians is enforced. The office-seeking theory of electoral competition (as opposed to office-seeking theories of government formation) indeed makes this a central part of its argument.[16]

The assumptions listed in Table 2.1 have implications for the effects of a government on its successors. We need not confine ourselves purely to the circumstances of termination in this regard, but can also consider the total effect of activity in government.

The most obvious, given that parties consist not only of leaders but also of committed supporters and voters, is that conspicuous failures of a party to advance its declared objectives cause it to lose electoral support (Implication 6(i)). If, in other words, a party builds its internal unity and support on promises to deliver particular government outputs, failure to achieve these naturally undermines its position. If an election occurs immediately after the termination of the government, without giving the party time to refurbish itself, the loss of support will naturally translate itself into votes—the consequence spelled out in Implication 6(i). This is not of course to imply that a government which fulfils its policy objectives will necessarily *gain* votes—this depends very much on the general effects of the policies —but it does imply that non-fulfilment is generally penalized.

At the other levels of a party, experiences in government can also carry an effect. The most immediate of these will be conclusions about the likelihood of carrying through its policies in coalition with another, or others. If a previous government has terminated because of vetoes of or disputes over characteristic party policies, it is likely not to wish to associate with its former partners in the immediate future. This may of course create an inability to find any policy agreements on which to base a coalition and hence a situation of the type envisaged in

Rule v(*b*)—that is, the creation of coalitions based on office-seeking where the party motivation is simply to obtain a share of ministries. These possibilities are codified in Implication 6(ii).

As the distribution of legislative seats is a central factor influencing what kinds of coalition can form (Table 2.3), the theory here comes full cycle, emphasizing the continual feedback effects of government on itself or on its successors. In this way it brings an element of historical continuity into coalition theory, which seems more realistic than regarding each formation of a government as an independent event, uninfluenced by anything outside the current power relationships of the negotiators.

CONCLUSIONS

The four summary tables provide a comprehensive, comparative theory of democratic government which integrates the various forms of party behaviour at that level of politics. It is comprehensive because it can be applied to all the major aspects of governments' existence —how they form and change, what they do, how they end. It is comparative because it applies to all types of government formed by elected parties—single-party, dominant-party, and coalitions of various types—and hence to all democracies.

The theory is more extensive than existing formulations. It is also more plausible than office-seeking theories. Politicans may be out for themselves some of the time (and some politicians all of the time!). But they also make stands of principle and have policies, distinct from those of other parties, to which they publicly commit themselves. If politicians merely wanted office, governments should be markedly stable once an initial division of ministries was agreed. We know, however, that this is not so: they often fall apart over policy disagreements, while even within a single-party government factions emerge which are distinguished primarily on policies.

The policy-commitment hypothesis also fits existing evidence better than earlier formulations, since it is compatible with all the types of government which actually form. The rest of this book is devoted to checking the fit further, by elaborating implications of the explanation and checking these in detail against evidence from twenty post-war democracies. Chapter 3 examines the question of government formation; Chapter 4 the allocation of ministries; Chapter 5 policy-making;

Chapter 6 termination and its effects on successor governments. Chapter 7 evaluates the results overall and discusses the modifications which they entail for our view of party behaviour at government level, and for theories of the State.

The sequence of discussion follows the actual stages in which the project was conceived, starting from an a priori theory of government formation, extending its implications to other aspects of party behaviour in government, and then collecting and analysing information to check these. As the data were collected after developing the theory, its fit with subsequent findings should validate it more convincingly than is possible with a posteriori interpretations of previously available evidence. It is to this question of how well theory matches with comparative evidence that we now turn.

3

Government Formation

This chapter begins to evaluate our ideas empirically rather than simply drawing out their theoretical implications. The specific hypotheses considered are those codifying the conditions under which various types of government emerge (see Table 2.3 for the various rules of government formation discussed in Chapter 2 above). The evidence used relates to the situations in which post-war governments formed and is mainly taken from compilations of newspaper reports like Keesing's Contemporary Archives, *The Times Index*, and the *New York Times Index*, as well as more specialized collections like those of von Beyme[1] and various Government Statistical Indexes, which are cited at the appropriate places (for a full discussion of data sources, see Appendix B). The exact form taken by the data will become evident from the specific tables below.

Our present analysis stems directly from a similar investigation carried through in 1978 for much the same democracies.[2] This was very successful: 85 per cent of governments examined conformed to our criteria as then formulated and other checks also gave very positive results. As more than ten years have elapsed since the earlier study was completed, we have to check whether the criteria can again be validated as convincingly as they were then, given new experiences of government in the 1980s and the slight modifications to the wording, particularly to Rule v(b) (where we now talk of viable governments, rather than minimal winning coalitions, forming in the absence of policy agreements).

We can also extend the investigation in certain respects. Like most analyses of government formation, our checks took each government as a separate 'case': that is, each counted as one example either for or against the hypotheses, no matter whether it lasted one month or three years. Obviously this approach is sensible from many points of view—a government is a government if it is officially constituted as one, and its exact period of office is beside the point. Hence in this new analysis, as in the earlier study, we check success by seeing what proportion of governments conform to our expectations out of all governments formed up to the end of 1984.

On the other hand, there is a sense in which a longer-lasting government constitutes more of a 'success' than one of relatively limited duration. Hence there is something to be said for using a 'government-month' as the unit of analysis, at least to supplement the counts based on governments pure and simple. Since the expectation is that governments formed in accordance with our rules will be more stable and hence last longer than those not conforming, the proportion of 'government-months' supportive of the hypothesis should be greater than the proportion of governments, as the latter must include certain 'mistakes', which we assume to terminate fairly quickly. At any rate we can compare results obtained by the two methods to see if such an expectation is confirmed.

The same logic suggests another supplementary check, this time based on the parties going into a government rather than the governments themselves. Even if governments lack one or other component party prescribed by our rules, we should still expect, to the extent that our theory is valid, that most parties which *should* go into government *do* actually go into government. The rules after all describe general tendencies towards forming a particular government, not rigidly deterministic situations which fit the criteria in all respects. The greater the number of parties expected to do so that actually enter a government, the more the rules are corroborated—even if the total constellation of parties is not exactly that assumed. Where possible, therefore, we shall use a count of the parties that are where they ought to be, as a proportion of all the parties existing in each government-formation situation. That will supplement the counts of governments as such, and of government-months, in evaluating the success of the theory in the area.

Two checks not applied in the earlier study will thus be used here. The criteria, in substantially the same form, have already survived a further and even more stringent test. This consisted of estimating the number of alternative party combinations, *not* in fact forming a government, which *would* have been predicted by our rules to do so—whether or not the latter successfully characterized the actual government. This test seems, perhaps, a little abstruse, but is really strict and demanding. The reasoning is as follows. Success in characterizing the party composition of the government which actually forms could be due to laxity, in the sense that the criteria might allow practically every conceivable combination to form a government. Such a characterization would not give us much more information than simply stipulating 'any party combination can form a government'. We would have a high success rate with such a tautology but it would not constitute a real theory nor add significantly to our information. A check on the extent to which the criteria give a unique or fairly unique characterization of the government coalition is thus a useful way of discovering how much genuine information they really give us.

As our rules in almost the same form have already been shown to give reasonably unique predictions (admittedly on the basis of a more limited data set), there is no need to expose them to it again. A straight reading of Table 2.3 shows that the criteria are far from admitting all combinations as feasible under specified circumstances: in fact the wording is rather restrictive, clear, and unambiguous. So empirical success will not be achieved through tautology. With this reassurance we pass from general considerations to specifying evidence for the checks we shall apply.

DEFINITIONS AND THEIR APPLICATIONS

Before we can proceed to an actual test, we need to say how certain key terms will be defined and applied in practice. Since concepts like 'threat to democracy' or 'Left–Right feeling' are absolutely vital to the success or failure of the rules, it is necessary to be totally clear about their meaning and application. Otherwise the ambiguities and tautologies which have, we hope, been avoided in the theoretical statement will simply creep in at this level.

The various key distinctions are applied to the democracies under consideration in Table 3.1. The first column lists the set of countries chosen for the study. The selection includes almost all those existing democracies which have autonomously maintained competitive elections over the post-war period. This excludes the majority of underdeveloped countries which became independent only in the late 1950s or 1960s; also such countries as Greece, Spain, and Portugal where democratic processes have been interrupted. The period taken is that

TABLE 3.1 Political characterizations of twenty-one post-war
parliamentary democracies

	Duration of anti-democratic threat	Duration of Left–Right feeling	Anti-system party or parties	Normal party or parties of government
Australia	—	1949–61, 1974–80	—	Liberal, Country, Labour
Austria	1945–64	1945–65	Communist,* Freedom (1945–75)	People's, Socialist
Belgium	1945–7	1961–5	Communist*	Christian Social
Canada	—	—	—	Liberal
Denmark	1945–7	1966–73	Communist,* Socialist People's, Progress	Social Deomocrat
Finland	—	—	—	Agrarian, Swedish People's
France 4	1946–7 1954–8	—	Communist,* RPF (1947–54)	Socialist, Radical, MRP
5	1958–62	1966–84	Communist (1958–69), New Right	Gaullist, Ind. Rep.

West Germany	—	1949–59	Communist	Free Democrat
Iceland	—	—	—	Independence
Ireland	—	—	Sinn Féin	Fianna Fáil
Israel	—	—	—	Labour
Italy	1945–7	—	Communist (1947–70), Monarchist, Neo-Fascist (MSI)	Christian Democrat
Japan	—	1946–84	Communist, Komeito	Liberal Democrat
Luxemburg	1945–7	—	Communist*	Christian Socialist
Netherlands	1945–7	1966–84	Communist,* Pacifist Socialist, Boeren (Farmers)	CDA, KVP
New Zealand	—	1976–84	—	Conservative, Labour
Norway	1945–7	1959–84	Socialist People's	Labour
Sweden	—	1957–84	—	Social Democrat
Switzerland	—	—	Communist	CVP, FDP, SPS, SVP
UK	—	1971–84	—	Conservative, Labour

* From April 1947.

since the war, from the first regular parliament of the regime to the end of 1984 (when data collection for our study ceased).

The next column of Table 3.1 lists the duration of anti-democratic threats (if any). Since politicians often cry wolf on this point we have tended to be conservative in defining these (for example, even though West Germany had a grand coalition between 1966 and 1969, based on the alleged threat from the Neo-Nazis, we do not consider the threat posed by their scattered provincial victories serious enough for inclusion). Emphasis is placed on the immediacy of a threat. Obviously the existence of large Communist parties in France and Italy has generated fears of a non-democratic take-over which are important in understanding the politics of these countries: nevertheless it has never seemed that they were about to complete a take-over next month, so we do not regard France and Italy as experiencing a permanent crisis throughout the post-war period.

Most European countries are regarded as having undergone a crisis immediately after the Second World War, as governments wrestled with the vast economic problems of reconstruction and unknown dangers of a Nazi Fascist reaction, which in fact would not materialize (but nobody knew this). Paradoxically, Germany and Japan did not experience such a crisis, since democratic government went through a reasonably lengthy period of emergence under the aegis of occupying troops. In spite of having to be sensitive to Russian reactions, Finland is not regarded as having at any time experienced an immediate threat, since it was obvious from the conclusion of their armistice in 1944 that the Soviet Union did not intend to take over the country—if it had, it would have done so then. Similarly, although in a sense Israel has been living dangerously since it came into existence, it has always from 1949 enjoyed an evident military dominance so no immediate threat has been experienced. Austria is obviously different, with Soviet troops actually on her soil for ten years, and their withdrawal followed by suppression of the Hungarian revolt on her border and then by the United States–Soviet confrontations of the early 1960s into which she could well have been drawn. The threats posed by the Algerian crisis, army mutinies, and terrorism in France between 1958 and 1962 are likewise immediate, in a sense in which IRA activity in the Republic of Ireland is not. While the determination of the exact periods of threat is judgemental, they are not arbitrarily imposed, and they avoid tautology by basing themselves on the 'objective' presence of a threat as reflected in contemporary discussion rather than the presence of a government of national unity, which would indeed be tautological in terms of our assumptions and hypotheses.

The same is true for the upsurge of divisive Left–Right feeling that affected most polities generally from the mid-1960s but which in some cases were triggered by specific events. Sweden is a case in point, where the Social Democrats in the mid-1950s intensified political antagonisms with all the bourgeois parties by advancing proposals for increasing State pensions and their holdings in industry, thus vastly extending government intervention in society and the economy. The continuance and strengthening of this radical programme eventually pushed the bourgeois parties into a closer alliance which maintained the Left–Right confrontation up to the end of our period.

Party politics in Norway followed this general pattern, with the emergence of the Socialist People's Party, and Labour dependence on them in the legislature, pulling Labour more decisively to the Left throughout the 1960s—a pull enhanced by the victory of the opposition to joining the European Community in the Referendum of 1973, which at first split Labour but afterwards reasserted its anti-Establishment values. A similar pattern might have emerged in Denmark, where the Socialist People's Party pulled the Social Democrats away from the more radical of the two Liberal groupings, had the extraordinary success of new populist parties in the elections of 1973 not pushed all the older established parties together again at that point.

In The Netherlands from 1966 the Labour party spontaneously raised the political temperature by deciding as a matter of principle not to join any government coalition with the Liberals. This forced the religious parties to choose decisively between a Left and a Right orientation, foreclosing any blurring of the alternatives, and thus contributed to a polarization in which the sympathy of the religious parties, if not always their immediate tactical choices, lay increasingly with the Right.

Belgium experienced an intensification of Left–Right feeling earlier. The resolution in 1958 of the schools question, with its associated clerical–anti-clerical divisions which cut across those of class, seemed to clear the way for a more focused Left–Right confrontation, sparked off by the austerity package of the Loi unique of 1961 and the violent trade-union opposition which it provoked. The elimination of religious issues also cleared the way, however, for a quite different conflict related to the relative position of Flemings and

Walloons within the country. These rapidly replaced class issues as the most important on the agenda, giving rise not only to a plethora of new parties and the division of the older ones, but to a restructuring of the Belgian State itself.

In France we have to deal with two quite different regimes and party systems—those of the parliamentary Fourth Republic and of the semi-presidential Fifth Republic. The differences make it necessary in this and subsequent discussions to treat the two as separate cases and to check hypotheses independently in each. Under the Fourth Republic the fragility of governments and of the regime itself rendered constitutional questions all-important and forced Socialists, Christian Democrats (the MRP), and Radicals into constant collaboration. The need for defence against violent subversion, and related constitutional issues, also dominated the opening years of the Fifth Republic. With the settlement in Algeria and the defeat of the Ultras by 1962 the way was opened for the events leading up to May 1968 and the continuing repercussions of that anarcho-syndicalist episode. Even if the Left subsequently became more moderate, the Gaullists and the Centre-Right then became more extreme, prolonging a Left–Right polarization to the end of our period.

In Britain the evolution of a new, anti-consensual brand of Conservatism under Heath and Thatcher, and the success of left-wing elements in dominating opposition policies (though never those of Labour governments) made the 1970s and 1980s a period of intense confrontation. The use made by the Liberal–Country coalition of the Cold War issue in Australia during the 1950s, coupled with the ideological fervour of Evatt, the Labour leader, intensified ideological opposition in that period, as did the constitutional implications of the conflict between Whitlam and Fraser in the 1970s. This was paralleled in New Zealand by the New Rightism of Muldoon during the late 1970s and early 1980s.

Austria and the Federal Republic of Germany were exceptions to the general trend for Left–Right divisions, if they occurred at all, to intensify during the 1960s and after. In both cases the rigid and rather doctrinaire positions of the Social Democrats which prevailed during the 1950s were modified by a newly pragmatic leadership for the 1960s. Japan on the other hand has always had a thoroughgoing radical Socialist party, and the attitudes of the ruling Liberal Democrats have always been more orthodox and traditional than in other countries.

For varying reasons the other democracies of our study have never experienced straightforward polarization on a Left-and-Right basis: Canadian politics, like those of the United States, are in any case less ideologically rooted than those of Europe; Finland's delicate position *vis-à-vis* the Soviet Union precludes a strong emphasis on this type of conflict; Icelandic politics are both too complex (with cross-cutting rural–urban divisions) and too personalized (in a country of very small population) to engender it; the same can be said of Luxemburg. Ireland and Israel both have dominant issues overshadowing class questions, while Italy's complex multi-party system, with splits in both Left and Right, prevents any focused division between these tendances.

Characterizations of anti-system parties are relatively straight-forward. Only in one case (Sinn Féin) is a party actually banned by law as subversive. But many parties have as their professed aim a radical change of the system, which is often interpretable as total opposition to its existing practices including those of democracy. Communist parties were commonly in this position from the take-over of the Czech regime in 1947 up to the present, with the exception of those like the Partito Comunista Italiano which strongly dissociated themselves from Stalinist tradition with their assertion of 'Euro-communism' in the 1970s. The French party, though always more Stalinist in general attitudes, began a highly pragmatic if intermittent collaboration with the Socialists in 1969. Some parties, on the other hand, have been suspect for their connections with Fascists or Nazis (the MSI in Italy, and the Freedom Party, in the early post-war era, in Austria). Others again, whether of Left or Right, have been under suspicion because of their radical populist base and expressed hostility to the system (sometimes including incitement to break existing laws). These include on the one side Komeito in Japan, Glistrup's anti-tax Progress Party in Denmark, the Poujadistes under the French Fourth Republic, and the New Right of Le Pen under the Fifth; and on the other side the various Left Socialist groupings in Western Europe.

'Normal parties of government' are of course those parties often —in some cases permanently—in government over the post-war period. So the success of the hypothesis runs the risk of being tied up tautologically with the definition. However, such parties can also be picked out on other grounds, such as their key strategic role between Left and Right, or their constant ability to complement—without dominating—a large party. Into the first category fit centre parties like the Finnish Agrarians, the Icelandic Independence Party, and the various Christian Social or Christian Democratic and other religious parties. Predominant parties are also in a sense expected to be in government, like one or other of the leading parties in a competitive two-party system. A confirmation of the presence of such parties in government is not of course world-shaking in itself. In conjunction with the other criteria of Table 2.2, however, it does serve as a useful further specification of the expected party composition.

The final definitional point is what constitutes a 'significant' party. As we confine our discussion to such parties in the rest of the book, the question again affects our results quite vitally. It arises because of the plethora of parties which exist in most countries—some being purely a name and very few gaining any electoral success. Even parties represented by a few seats in Parliament may have such limited effects either on legislation or on governments that they ought properly to be ignored in an assessment of the criteria.

The question is, where does one draw the line? Most would agree with Sartori's suggestion that relevant or significant parties in the countries we are dealing with are those which either influence the formation of governments or, if excluded from government, are too large to ignore.[3] These inclusion rules give general guidelines but need to be specified. After considering particular cases in each country, we decided that a general rule would operate quite well and accordingly defined significant parties as those with over 5 per cent of legislative seats at any stage in the post-war period. Although the actual level at which one places this boundary is always slightly arbitrary we are convinced by detailed inspection that this one does not produce gross anomalies. The proviso that we include parties who at any time cross this threshold also allows for the effects of historical record and reputation in sustaining a party (like, for example, the Italian Liberals) who for most of the post-war period fell below this level but for all that remained capable of precipitating the fall of governments.[4]

CORRESPONDENCE OF EXPECTED AND ACTUAL PARTY PARTICIPATION IN GOVERNMENT

With these decisions made, we are now in a position to distinguish each type of legislative situation highlighted by the criteria, for all twenty-one democracies (if we distinguish the Fourth and Fifth French Republics) over the post-war period, to see (1) whether the expected type of government in fact emerges, (2) whether 'predicted' governments last longer than those formed contrary to our theory, and (3) whether most parties join the governments they are expected to. It will be remembered that a government is an administration initiated in one of the following ways: (*a*) post-election formation, (*b*) change in the Prime Minister, (*c*) change in the party composition of the cabinet, (*d*) resignation in an inter-election period followed by reformation of the government with the same Prime Minister and party composition.[5] We say that a party is a *member* of a government when one or more individuals identified with that party participate in the cabinet, this participation being understood to commit individual members of that party to the support of the government whenever its continued existence is at stake.[6]

Each theoretical rule in Table 2.3 specifies a particular type of legislative situation and states what type of government will emerge under those circumstances. All the governments formed in situations of a specified type, at any time in the post-war period, are now put together and examined in aggregate. Figures for each type of situation are examined separately in a different table. This helps emphasize the fact that there is no overlap of cases: the cases included in one table appear only there and are not carried over to any of the others. All post-war governments of course appear in one or other of the tables.

Since the criteria are hierarchic in the sense that an aforementioned circumstance takes precedence over others, we start with Rule i, dealing with situations in which governments form under an immediate threat to democracy. The first column of Table 3.2 reports the total number of governments formed in periods of anti-democratic threats. Countries omitted from this table are those characterized as not having experienced such threats during the post-war era (see Table 3.1 above). The second column gives proportions of all coalitions formed during such periods which grouped the significant pro-democratic parties and which simultaneously excluded anti-system parties; in other words, the second column shows the success rate of the hypothesis, the proportions of actual cases correctly characterized.

From these a first impression emerges: that the criterion adequately characterizes actual behaviour only in certain countries, above all in Austria—which, however, represents a third of the cases owing to the

TABLE 3.2. Governments formed under an immediate threat to democracy: Inclusion of pro-system and exclusion of anti-system parties (Table 2.3. Rule i)

	Governments formed		Government-months		Parties[b]	
	Total	As predicted[a] (proportion)	Total	As predicted[a] (proportion)	Total	As predicted[a] (proportion)
Austria	11	1.00	237.6	1.00	22	1.00
Belgium	2	0.00	7.2	0.00	8	0.50
Denmark	1	0.00	24.0	0.00	6	0.33
France 4	10	0.40	60.6	0.20	61	0.83
5	3	0.00	38.4	0.00	18	0.70
Italy	2	0.00	9.6	0.00	12	0.58
Luxemburg	1	1.00	15.6	1.00	4	1.00
Netherlands	1	0.00	4.0	0.00	6	0.33
Norway	1	0.00	36.0	0.00	6	0.16
All countries	32	0.50	453.0	0.68	143	0.73

[a] The prediction of the theory is that all significant pro-system parties will join the government and all anti-system parties will be excluded.
[b] Each party is counted separately at the formation of every government.

length of time the crisis continued (nineteen years). The other notable regime, again accounting for a third of cases, is France under the Fourth Republic. The high numbers of governments here are due both to the duration of the crises (five years) and to the frequency of government change. At a proportion of only 0.40, four cases out of ten correctly characterized, compared to all cases for Austria, the success rate is comparatively much lower but still higher than for the Fifth Republic, Italy, the Low Countries, and Scandinavia. The patchy success of the criterion in different countries is reflected in an overall rate of only 0.50: exactly one-half of governments formed in crisis situations over all the countries involved were correctly characterized. Success rates in terms of government-months are no higher and sometimes lower than those for governments taken as units.

The total failure of the hypothesis to apply to Belgium, Denmark, Norway, The Netherlands, and Italy could point to one or other of several possibilities. One is that politicians in these countries simply did not feel under threat at the end of the war, in which case our operationalization (Table 3.1) would be wrong. As against this there was much talk of Nazi-sympathizers lurking behind ready to take over;[7] and Italy actually saw the formation of the MSI. The threat under the Fifth Republic from 1958–62 is hardly in doubt. It may be that parties in different countries act on the basis of diverse motivations and strategies, so that different models fit behaviour in different contexts.

Before endorsing such a conclusion on the basis of these findings, however, there are certain qualifications to be made in favour of the hypothesis we have suggested. First, the fact that the two regimes with the most prolonged experience of crisis show the most conformity to our expectations is significant in that politicians might have had more opportunity to learn from experience the best response to the situation. A more concrete qualification relates to the actual classifications made in the cases of the Fifth Republic and Italy. In both cases governments are characterized as not meeting expectations because of the non-participation of the Socialist parties, which in general are legitimist parties. In both cases, however, the Socialist party during the particular period in question (Italy just after the war, France during the first years of the Gaullist regime) could from some points of view be regarded as anti-system. In Italy the Socialists were more vociferous in criticizing the regime than the Communists and entered into an electoral alliance with the latter from 1947 to 1954. In France they were directly hostile to the Fifth Republic until well into the sixties. We have not made changes to the general operationalizations in Table 3.1 to meet these special cases, so these governments must in the end be marked down as failures of the criteria; but the extenuating circumstances deserve to be noted.

What can be said on the basis of the actual figures of Table 3.2 is that the final column, representing the proportions of parties which are where they are expected to be theoretically, shows a markedly higher success rate for the hypothesis than the government-based proportions—0.73 for all countries together, compared to 0.68 and 0.50. This is also true of certain individual countries—the Fourth Republic (a success rate of 0.83), the Fifth (0.70), and Italy (0.58). Obviously there is a tendency for significant pro-system parties to join in governments of national unity at those times, even if not all do so. The rule is tendential and statistical in nature rather than fully deterministic, therefore its success in characterizing party behaviour is perhaps more significant than its poorer performance with governments overall.

Such saving clauses could only apply, however, if the other hypotheses derived from the theory perform substantially better than this and indirectly buttress the credibility of Rule i. Turning therefore to Table 3.3, we see what actually happens when, in the absence of threats to democracy, one party or electoral alliance wins a majority of legislative seats. Not surprisingly, we find almost universal support for the hypothesis in all countries, whether success is reckoned in terms of governments as such or government-months. This success certainly acts to buttress the credibility of our formulation as a whole, though the expectation that the party with a majority of legislative seats will form a single-party government is shared with minimal-winning and many other theories of government coalition formation. It is of course natural for office-seeking as well as policy-pursuing parties to seek to take all posts for themselves.

However, the policy-pursuing model, by Rule ii(*b*) of Table 2.3, also accommodates the tendency of many majority parties to associate in government with a small party (or even more than one) which is not strictly necessary to gain a legislative majority. To gain policy ends while reassuring the uncommitted, it may be useful to share a few offices in this way provided underlying dominance is not threatened.

Two additional methodological points need to be made in regard to Table 3.3. First, one should be aware that the criteria of 'success' for

TABLE 3.3. Governments where one party or alliance has a legislative majority (no threat to democracy): Dominance of majority party, exclusion of anti-system parties (Table 2.3 Rule ii)

	Governments formed		Government-months		Parties[b]	
	Total	As predicted[a] (proportion)	Total	As predicted[a] (proportion)	Total	As predicted[a] (proportion)
Australia	23	0.95	460.0	0.95	46	0.96
Austria	5	1.00	188.4	1.00	15	1.00
Belgium	3	1.00	45.6	1.00	12	1.00
Canada	8	1.00	360.0	1.00	40	1.00
France 5	18	1.00	280.68	1.00	117	1.00
West Germany	5	1.00	153.6	1.00	15	1.00
Ireland	9	1.00	246.0	1.00	27	1.00
Italy	5	1.00	61.2	1.00	34	1.00
Japan	19	1.00	345.6	1.00	73	1.00
New Zealand	17	1.00	454.8	1.00	41	1.00
Norway	5	1.00	142.8	1.00	20	1.00
Sweden	2	1.00	37.2	1.00	10	1.00
UK	15	1.00	441.6	1.00	45	1.00
All countries[c]	127	0.99	3,304.8	0.98	442	0.98

[a] The prediction of theory is that the majority party/alliance will dominate government and anti-system parties will be excluded.

[b] Each party is counted separately at the formation of every government.

[c] India and Sri Lanka both conform to the 'prediction' of the theory in all particulars for relevant government-formation situations—11 in the case of India, 8 in the case of Sri Lanka.

Rules ii(*a*) and ii(*b*) vary somewhat with normal governmental arrangements in each country. Where single-party government is usual, no other type of arrangement has been considered a success (Australia, Canada, India, Ireland, Japan, New Zealand, Norway (for Labour governments), Sweden, United Kingdom). In the other countries, where coalitions are usual, the domination of government by the majority party, even if it has small partners has been considered a success. Secondly, electoral alliances where the partners pledged themselves in advance to form a government together should they gain a majority are regarded effectively as majority parties—the justification being that the alliance has already received a majority in the elections on the basis of their future combination in government, just like a single party. This applies particularly to the smaller Irish parties, France under the Fifth Republic, and the SPD–FDP in Germany from 1970 to 1982 (and the FDP–CDU in 1983).

In Table 3.4 we consider situations characterized by the absence of anti-democratic threats and of a majority party, where there is, however, strong Left–Right feeling on salient current issues, which induce the opposing tendances to line up against each other (Table 2.3 Rule iii). There is reasonable confirmation for this hypothesis in almost all countries, in the sense of high proportions of governments formed under strong Left–Right feeling enlisting the support of the majority tendance. Only in Belgium is the expectation totally reversed —but by only one government in a very confused political situation. Lower success in Japan is due to the disruption of normal political life and extraneous influences from the Occupation immediately after the war. In The Netherlands the success rate would have been higher had the main religious parties not been outmanœuvred into coalition with the PvdA (Labour) under den Uyl from 1973 to 1977, since when they have stuck with the increasingly right-wing Liberals. In Norway and Sweden on the other hand, even where Labour and Social Democrats were in a minority, they could always rely on crucial support from Communists or from Left Socialists, countered in turn by increasing solidarity among the bourgeois parties.

The success of Rule iii (like that of Rule v(*b*), below) is central to our whole policy-based theory of government formation as it puts so much emphasis on the binding effect of policy agreements in situations where simple rivalry for office would have forced the partners asunder. It therefore adds a strong cumulative confirmation of the theory to that of Table 3.3.

TABLE 3.4. Governments where no party or alliance has a legislative majority and Left–Right feeling is strong (no threat to democracy): Participation of all significant parties in the majority tendance, exclusion of anti-system parties (Table 2.3 Rule iii)

	Governments formed		Government-months		Parties[b]	
	Total	As predicted[a] (proportion)	Total	As predicted[a] (proportion)	Total	As predicted[a] (proportion)
Belgium	1	0.00	51.6	0.00	5	0.40
Denmark	4	1.00	85.2	0.69	20	1.00
West Germany	2	1.00	47.2	1.00	12	1.00
Japan	11	0.55	113.6	0.65	57	0.84
Netherlands	10	0.60	195.6	0.70	74	0.85
Norway	14	0.86	263.9	0.88	90	0.87
Sweden	11	0.82	311.2	0.94	55	0.90
All countries	53	0.73	1,118.3	0.80	313	0.87

[a] The prediction of the theory is that governments formed will consist of, or be supported by, all significant parties in the majority tendance, and will exclude all anti-system parties.

[b] Each party is counted separately at the formation of every government.

TABLE 3.5. Governments where no party or alliance has a legislative majority and Left–Right feeling is not strong (no threat to democracy): Dominance of the legislatively pre-eminent party, exclusion of anti-system parties (Table 2.3 Rule iv)

	Governments formed		Government-months		Parties[b]	
	Total	As predicted[a] (proportion)	Total	As predicted[a] (proportion)	Total	As predicted[a] (proportion)
Austria	3	1.00	43.2	1.00	9	1.00
Belgium	4	1.00	40.8	1.00	16	1.00
Canada	4	1.00	74.4	1.00	18	1.00
Denmark	13	0.85	322.8	0.67	94	0.81
West Germany	7	0.86	152.4	0.76	21	0.86
Iceland	1	1.00	19.2	1.00	5	1.00
Ireland	6	0.83	182.4	0.78	32	0.78
Israel	14	1.00	186.0	1.00	113	1.00
Italy	29	1.00	304.9	1.00	186	1.00
Luxemburg	3	1.00	120.7	1.00	13	1.00
Sweden	5	1.00	132.0	1.00	25	1.00
All countries[c]	92	0.95	1,578.8	0.93	532	0.93

[a] The prediction of the theory is that governments formed will be dominated by the legislatively pre-eminent party and will exclude all anti-system parties. 'Legislatively pre-eminent' is defined as: (i) having 46% of seats or more, or (ii) being ahead of the next largest party by 13% of seats or more.

[b] Each party is counted separately at the formation of every government.

[c] India (1 government) and Sri Lanka (6 governments) conform entirely to the 'prediction' of the theory for this type of situation.

Legislative situations where there is no threat to democracy, no majority party, and where the absence of strong Left–Right divisions deprives smaller parties of motives for ganging up on big ones, leave the field open for legislatively pre-eminent parties to act in a quasi-majority role, reasonably secure from concerted opposition votes against them. In such a situation these parties are expected by Rule iv of Table 2.3 either to form a single-party government or, where coalitions are more usual, to dominate a government formed in conjunction with smaller parties. Table 3.5 checks this expectation against governments formed in legislative situations with such a party, again excluding any case already considered in the preceding tables and situations where such a party did not exist. This rule successfully characterizes a high proportion of the governments formed where either one party has a near majority of legislative votes or where one of the pro-system parties is outstandingly strong. The findings are not dependent on the particular definition of 'pre-eminent' specified in the notes to the table. Various cut-off points have been experimented with and all give broadly the same results, although the numbers themselves change somewhat.

The last rule listed in Table 2.3, designed to cover the situations (and only those situations) where previous ones do not apply, groups v(*a*), v(*b*), and v(*c*). All relate to multi-party situations where, in the absence of anti-democratic threats or strong Left–Right feeling, coalitions form around agreement on specific salient issues, or, failing such agreement, through minimizing the number of coalition partners. While these rules follow logically from our Assumption 2 (on parties seeking governments which will most effectively attain their policy objectives), the point about all normal parties being included and anti-system parties excluded is fairly unrestrictive. Table 3.6, with its high success rate on all the indicators, demonstrates this. None the less the proposition it tests is not purely tautological, as demonstrated dramatically by the low proportion of successes in Canada. And its close relationship to our central argument, that parties have substantive concerns reflected in the composition of governments, renders its validation illuminating in this context.

A much severer test of our reasoning comes, however, with Table 3.7. If policy is a central concern it should provide a major basis of coalition-building in fragmented party systems, where parties cannot come together on the basis of 'national unity' or generalized Left–Right feeling. Even when these are absent, parties should still find a

TABLE 3.6. Governments where no party or alliance has a legislative majority or pre-eminence and Left–Right feeling is not strong (no threat to democracy): Inclusion of normal parties of government, exclusion of anti-system parties (Table 2.3 Rule v (c))

	Governments formed		Government-months		Parties[b]	
	Total	As predicted[a] (proportion)	Total	As predicted[a] (proportion)	Total	As predicted[a] (proportion)
Belgium	16	1.00	294.0	1.00	22	1.00
Canada	3	0.33	39.6	0.48	3	0.33
Denmark	6	0.57	110.5	0.81	26	0.90
Finland	38	0.94	466.0	0.95	38	0.92
France 4	16	0.63	76.9	0.54	80	0.91
West Germany	1	1.00	6.0	1.00	1	1.00
Iceland	13	0.69	417.6	0.78	13	0.69
Israel	17	0.58	201.6	0.61	17	0.58
Italy	12	1.00	90.5	1.00	36	1.00
Luxemburg	8	0.87	316.8	0.80	16	0.94
Netherlands	7	1.00	202.8	1.00	14	1.00
Switzerland	40	0.80	480.0	0.80	200	0.96
All countries[c]	177	0.85	2,702.3	0.79	467	0.91

[a] The prediction of the theory is that governments formed will include the normal parties of government and exclude all anti-system parties.
[b] Each party is counted separately at the formation of every government.
[c] The only Sri Lankan government formed in a situation of this type conformed to the 'prediction' of the theory.

TABLE 3.7. Governments where no party or alliance has a legislative majority or pre-eminence and Left–Right feeling is not strong (no threat to democracy): Agreement on one salient issue, exclusion of anti-system parties

	Governments[a]		Government-months	
	Total	As predicted[b] (proportion)	Total	As predicted[b] (proportion)
Belgium	11	0.63	128.4	0.50
Finland	11	0.81	124.8	0.88
France 4	6	0.16	26.5	0.50
Iceland	6	0.83	243.6	0.88
Israel	6	0.16	56.4	0.21
Italy	6	0.83	46.5	0.94
Netherlands	4	0.25	111.6	0.27
All countries	50	0.58	737.8	0.65

[a] All governments included in the figures for Table 3.6 are covered here if there was a salient issue at the time of their formation—provided that sufficient information is available on that issue; all those for which there was no salient issue or for which there is insufficient information on the salient issue are covered in Table 3.8.

[b] The 'prediction' of the theory is that governments will be formed by parties that agree on the salient issue, and will exclude all anti-system parties. Agreement on the salient issue is established as follows. The salient issue (e.g. inflation) is identified, the principal policy option (e.g. an incomes freeze) is identified; parties are considered to be in agreement on the issue if they are found to be either all 'for' or all 'against' the principal policy option. The existence of a party outside the government that shares the government preference does not infringe the criterion for government agreement as it does not affect the role of the agreement in bringing together the parties that form the government.

basis of co-operation in agreements on the most important issues of the day. These may or may not involve other long-standing party commitments, to groups or causes. They could involve areas like foreign policy where specific problems exert a pressure for their settlement. Whatever they are, their resolution provides a basis for party combination and joint action. This must be the case if our policy-pursuing assumption is correct.

The theory is clear but unfortunately the data are very scanty. Agreements of this kind are only patchily reported anywhere, even in otherwise detailed accounts of the political situation. We have been driven to record only the existence of salient issues, their character, and which parties agreed on the leading alternative. Where this information is lacking we have had by default to assume there is no agreement and relegate the governments concerned to Table 3.8, even though we suspect, in many cases, that issue agreements did exist and were important in promoting a coalition. The characterization we made even where we had some information is obviously crude and would have been improved, or even changed, had better sources existed.

Given these imperfections, the success rates of Table 3.7, even the proportion based on governments as such—which at 0.58 for all countries together might in other cases be regarded as low—are in fact very encouraging. In the majority of countries policy agreements seem to form the basis for most coalitions. Where they do not—the Fourth Republic, Israel, and The Netherlands—the extremely fragmented multi-party system may make for difficulties of perception and communication which explain the failures. However, it is notable that in the equally fragmented systems of Finland and Italy policy agreement forms an important basis for the coalitions.

It is also notable from the table that in all countries other than Belgium proportions go up for government-months compared with governments, implying that governments formed on the basis of policy agreements—at least where the opportunity for these exists—are actually more enduring and stable than those which are not so based.

Where policy agreements are lacking (though we may think that in some cases it is not the agreements themselves but accurate reports of them that are lacking), no basis for coalition formation exists other than the aim of holding office and the desire to maximize office-holding by restricting participation, as the minimal-winning criterion says. In one important respect, however, our policy-based reasoning modifies that criterion: that is, in the perception that winning legislative votes of confidence does not always require 50 per cent plus one of legislative votes, but possibly more or possibly less. Confidence may very often be a product of the proper combination of parties—perhaps with well over 50 per cent of seats—rather than numerical ability to win. Given that countries have to have governments for day-to-day administration, a minority government may often be recognized as necessary for the time being, while its very weakness and dependence may render it more tolerable. This is quite apart from hostilities among non-governmental parties which may make it impossible for them to vote together.

In estimating what was necessary to win a vote of confidence we therefore based ourselves on the post-war history of the various countries rather than an abstract figure. Where governments generally governed with just over 50 per cent of seats and never went under this, we equated winning votes of confidence with forming a party bloc holding 50 per cent plus one of legislative seats and assumed that minimal winning coalitions, in the strict sense, would form. In some cases, such as that of Belgium, the average support of governments in the post-war period was over 60 per cent; however, several governments had governed, seemingly successfully, with just over 50 per cent, so this was taken as the crucial criterion. The countries where this applied are about half of those in Table 3.8 and are asterisked.

If we go to the opposite extreme, it is clear that in Switzerland the exact percentage support of a government is irrelevant. What is important is that all four of the major parties should continue their semi-permanent coalition, and this therefore has been taken as the criterion. Similarly in the Fourth Republic governments which aimed to gain legislative confidence should have been tripartite, grouping Radicals, MRP, and Socialists. The Canadian tradition of single-party government coupled with a two-and-two-halves-party system which often prevents any party gaining a majority favours the single party with a plurality taking over control of government and getting support on this basis—even from its leading rival, since this party had also benefited from the practice in the past.

In Denmark the traditional predominance of the Social Democrats, even at 38 per cent or less of the vote, meant that government was very often carried on in the absence of alternative combinations by that party acting alone; 35 per cent could thus be a viable basis for government provided it included the proper party.

Italy resembles Switzerland in having *formule di governo*—which, however, in the case of Italy, changed over the period. After the clear Christian predominance of the fifties, the *apertura a sinistra* meant that viable governments had also to incorporate the Socialists in the sixties. The *compromesso storico* of the seventies meant that governments, however constituted, had to acknowledge the influence of the Communists. After the breakdown of this arrangement all five non-Communist parties had to form a *pentapartito* government in order to continue. Ability to win votes of confidence must be assessed therefore against the extent to which the government incorporates the appropriate *formula* for each post-war period, while including no party superfluous to that task.

In Finland the existence of a cycle of governments with large majorities alternating with minority governments has already been noted.[8] Rather than dismissing this as an aberration, it can be regarded as an essential aspect of government-making, in that the large majorities necessary to gain consensus for action tend to break down under mutual quarrels. In this situation minority administrations are the only ones possible and give a necessary pause during which negotiations for a new majority can succeed. In the case of Finland, therefore, judgements of the 'appropriateness' of governments for gaining legislative confidence were made on comparisons of the preceding government with the one under examination—one of which should have a large majority and the other a minority.

While the precise content of each formula is specified on the basis of political conditions in individual countries, the idea itself is general. Specifying the grounds on which governments may win legislative votes of confidence is necessary if we are to separate government *viability*—its ability to attract necessary support—from possession of a majority of seats.[9] The third of all governments which are minority governments can be explained only on the basis of desirable features which cause them to be supported; and as these are recurrent we arrive fairly quickly at the concept of a standing formula to which they conform and which then attracts support. Naturally the details of this vary with party system and country but the concept of formula itself is general.

On the basis, therefore, of whether a government was the minimal combination corresponding *either* to 50 per cent plus one of legislative seats *or* to another prevailing formula for viable government, the proportions of conformity to the theory shown in Table 3.8 are quite high—the notable exception being again France 4 (probably owing to a chaotic situation which prevented any formula working effectively). Proportions for government-months are generally higher than proportions for governments as such, implying greater stability for governments formed according to our norm; but the difference is less marked than in preceding tables. Possibly governments formed without policy-cement are inherently more unstable in any case.

TABLE 3.8. Governments where no party or alliance has a legislative majority or pre-eminence and Left–Right feeling is not strong (no salient issue, no threat to democracy): Composition by minimal viable combinations, exclusion of anti-system parties (Table 2.3 Rule v (6))

	Governments		Government-months	
	Total	As predicted[a] (proportion)	Total	As predicted[a] (proportion)
Belgium*	5	0.60	165.6	0.68
Canada	3	1.00	39.6	1.00
Denmark	6	0.50	110.5	0.75
Finland	27	0.44	342.0	0.38
France 4	10	0.30	50.4	0.21
West Germany*	1	1.00	6.0	1.00
Iceland*	7	0.57	174.0	0.69
Israel*	11	0.45	145.2	0.51
Italy	6	1.00	44.0	1.00
Luxemburg*	8	0.75	316.8	0.83
Netherlands*	3	0.33	91.2	0.52
Switzerland	40	0.83	480.0	0.82
All countries[b]	127	0.64	1,965.3	0.65

[a] The prediction of the theory is that each government will be formed by the minimal combination of parties that can win legislative votes of confidence, and will exclude all anti-system parties. Countries marked with an asterisk are those where the ability to win such votes coincides with the control of 50% plus one of the legislative seats.
[b] The only Sri Lankan government formed in a situation of this type failed to conform to the 'prediction' of the theory.

The proportions resulting from applying the formula for winning a vote of confidence are in any case vastly better for this group of governments than those resulting from a mechanical overall application of the minimal-winning criterion—0.15 for governments and 0.28 for government-months. While nobody could claim that our inferred norms are perfect or infallible, they do seem to correspond to political realities better than the invariant rule of 50 per cent plus one.

OVERALL ASSESSMENT OF VALIDITY OF CRITERIA

This last claim could be made with equal justice for all the criteria examined earlier, which in combination operationalize a general empirical theory of the way various types of governments emerge under different political stimuli. Of governments emerging under all types of situation in the twenty-one democracies selected for study, the proportion conforming with the combined rules of Table 2.3 is a remarkable 0.81. This is not excessively boosted by the successful characterization of single-party or dominant-party governments in a non-crisis majority situation (Rule ii)—a success shared by and large with other theories of coalition formation. For the success rate of the combined rules omitting these cases is still convincingly high (0.75). The proportion of government-months conforming to the rules is even higher (0.84), and that of individual parties higher still (0.92).

Nor is this success due to circularity in the definitions used in conjunction with the hypotheses. We have already referred to their ability to discriminate by excluding governments *not* formed, tested earlier though for a somewhat smaller data set.[10] Moreover the variation in the success rates both across countries and between criteria shows that success is far from automatic. The relatively lesser success of Rule i (that under threat all pro-system parties will join Governments of National Unity) and of Rule v(*a*) (that policy agreements from the basis for multi-party coalitions in the absence of other conditions) are tolerable within the context of overall success.

Thus, by making an allowance for the declared policy concerns of parties (Table. 2.1 Assumption 2) and establishing an order for these (Assumptions 3(*a*) and 3(*b*)), we have produced a theory of government formation that is notably more successful and informative than its predecessors. While we have relaxed the extreme mathematical formalism of some of these, the theory is still parsimonious, clear, and general.

Moreover it has the great advantage of being a theory not simply of government formation but of general party behaviour in government. Thus it relates the actual distribution of ministries in a government to the reasons for which parties joined it in the first place—that is, to the pursuit of their policies. The next chapter takes up this subject, which in turn closely relates to the making and implementation of governmental policy itself.

4

The Distribution of Ministries

This chapter continues the systematic testing of certain hypotheses already discussed in Chapter 2. Those considered here relate to the allocation of ministries among coalition partners (Table 2.4 Implications 2(i)–2(v)). As emphasized earlier, this is a particularly important aspect of our theory as the most recent research indicates that parties may influence government policy more through their tenure of specific ministries than through officially negotiated coalition accords.[1]

INITIAL ALLOCATION: HYPOTHESES AND OPERATIONALIZATION

Governments are complex phenomena to which parties must react at several levels. Not only do they have to decide whether and how to participate, but they also have to agree (usually at one and the same time) on the exact distribution of powers among partners, in the sense of ministries carrying votes and seats in the Cabinet. This may determine who is decisive in policy-planning. Even if a general government programme has been agreed, important problems of implementation and resource allocation remain. Intimately linked to these is the question of who has operational control of the relevant ministries: these give weight in planning but also confer final control over how exactly policy is effected, which can be even more important (for instance in including a certain class of beneficiaries within the legislation) than general government directives.

These dual aspects of ministries were stressed in Chapter 1. Both are crucially bound up with attainment of party goals, so the allocation of such offices is just as important for a policy-pursuing as for an office-seeking party. However, the different reasons for desiring office prompt different forms of behaviour. From the point of view of maximizing power and prestige, any office with an equal vote and roughly equivalent perquisites is equivalent to any other office. So one can be traded for another without bothering much about their specific policy remits. The only exception is the premiership because it carries more power and prestige than the others. For policy-pursuing parties on the other hand, ministries are valued because they relate closely to party objectives. Not all of them can thus be casually traded one for the other: possession of vital ministries will be a *sine qua non* of joining government, even if not all relevant ones can be obtained (possibly because of overlapping interests on the part of policy-pursuing partners).

Obviously if all parties were equally concerned with all ministries, or with the same subset, coalition formation would become impossible. However, different parties are likely to have different interests, or at least different orderings of interests, as a result of varying ideological traditions and programmatic concerns. Thus there will be room for bargaining as ministries ranking lower for one party are traded for others they rank higher, but which their partners may not value as much. Where a party is weak it can expect to get only its most valued ministry, and where it is strong it may get more ministries than it strictly requires: so the distribution will vary very much with the type of coalition that forms. The more that participation in government is linked with general objectives (such as confronting a crisis, or pushing through or opposing a full socialist programme) the less parties may insist on 'their' particular ministries. However, even in cases where a greater governmental good predominates, parties have their own particular concerns which their partners may be expected to recognize, so this should not seriously blur the overall patterns of distribution we find through the post-war period.

Trying to synthesize all these considerations is a complex task. A first step is to work out the general policy objectives of each party, in relation to ministries, and to rank the latter in order of their importance to the party—an exercise which obviously also has strong bearings on the analysis of policy-making in Chapters 5 and 6 below.

The ranking of policy priorities should indicate which ministries will be of most importance for each party and which they might be prepared to trade because they are of lesser importance. Ministries which do not come within the policy concerns of any party are available as makeweights to balance party shares of ministries with their contribution in terms of government seats, after the policy-based share-out has been made. Such a norm of overall proportionality is likely to operate after specific assignments of ministries have been made, as an obvious and uncontroversial way of assigning offices to which no party lays a special claim but which are still important in Cabinet voting.

In specifying party concern with ministries, two initial problems arise. Both derive from the comparative nature of the enterprise. The first relates to the parties. It would be difficult and unnecessarily complex to provide rankings of ministries for each individual party in every one of the twenty democracies. Instead we assign ranking for each of the five main 'families' of parties, distinguished in terms of their general ideology. It is after all in terms of their ideological traditions that we characterize their leading policy concerns and, through these, their concern with ministries. So it is appropriate to generalize across families, and to say that all individual party members of the family will share the same policy interests and hence have similar priorities in regard to ministries.

Table 4.1 accordingly distinguishes the main families and lists the individual parties which fall within these, for each country. The families we have distinguished are Conservative, Liberal, religious, Socialist, and 'single-issue' parties. The last are obviously more of a mixed bag than the others. What we mean by 'single-issue parties' is parties formed to advance one primary interest, as Agrarian parties do for country-dwellers or Nationalist parties with regard to the autonomy of a particular region or minor nationality. These are the two main types of single-issue party, although there are one or two special individual cases, such as the Danish Retsforbandet, devoted to a particular constitutional reform in the 1950s. The effect of being concerned above all with a single area of policy is to make a ministry in that area all-important to the party concerned, while others are quite secondary. This should have immediate consequences for decisions to participate in government, which will be bound closely to possession of the ministry of concern.

Members of the other families should have wider interests, as their underlying ideologies are more universal in character. Certainly religious parties (the most usual manifestation being the Christian Democrats) are concerned with the position and defence of the Church and/or religious people generally. Most religions, however, have developed social doctrines, extending to the protection of social institutions like the family and to a particular structure of traditional

TABLE 4.1. The five families of political parties

	Conservative	Liberal	Religious	Socialist	Single-issue
Australia	Liberal-Country People's	—	—	Labour	—
Austria	—	Freedom	—	Social Democratic	—
Belgium	—	Liberal	Christian Social	Socialist	Volksunie, Rassemblement wallon
Canada	Progressive Conservative, Social Credit	Liberal	—	New Democratic	Front démocratique des francophones
Denmark	Conservative, Progress	Radikale Venstre, Democratic Centre	Christian People's	Social Democratic, Left Socialist	Agrarian Liberal, Retsforbundet
Finland	KOK (National Coalition)	Liberal People's	Christian League	Social Democratic, Communist (SKDL)	Agrarian, Swedish People's, Smallholders'
France 4	Independent, Gaullist	Radical	Mouvement républicain populaire	Socialist, Communist	—
5	Gaullist	Giscardian	—	Socialist, Communist	—
West Germany	German	Free Democratic	Christian Democratic	Social Democratic	—
Iceland	National Preservation Independence	Progressive	—	Social Democratic Federation, Union of Liberals and Leftists, United Socialist	—

Country					
Ireland	Fine Gael, Fianna Fáil	—	—	Labour	—
Israel	Likud and predecessors	Independent Liberal, Progressive	Religious (various)	Labour, Alignment and predecessors, Communist	—
Italy	Movimento sociale italiano (MSI)	Liberal, Republican, Radical	Christian Democratic	Social Democratic, Socialist, Communist	—
Japan	Liberal Democratic	New Liberal Clubs	Komeito	Socialist, Communist	—
Luxemburg	—	Democratic Group	Christian Social	Social Democratic, Socialist	—
Netherlands	—	Liberal, Democraten '66, DS70	Christian Democratic Appeal and predecessors	Labour (PvdA)	—
New Zealand	National	Social Credit	—	Labour	—
Norway	Conservative, Anders Lange, Progress, New People's	Liberal	Christian People's	Labour, Left Socialist, Communist	Centre (Agrarian)
Sweden	Conservative, Moderate	People's (FP), Centre	—	Social Democratic, Communist Left, Socialist	Agrarian (Centre)
Switzerland	—	Radical Democratic	Catholic Conservative (CVP)	Social Democratic (SPS)	People's, Farmers, Traders, and Citizens (SUP)
UK	Conservative	Liberal/Alliance	—	Labour	—

morality—and also, often, extended welfare and labour philosophies not far removed from those of socialism. Socialism itself, conservatism, and liberalism all have broad but differentiated interests in wide areas of policy, which we shall describe below.

Assignment of individual parties to families is rendered easier in most cases by the fact that by both name and ideological tradition they are usually unambiguously linked to a particular political tendency. There are some difficult marginal cases, however, especially where a party has recently seemed to be revising its appeal. For example, the Italian Social Democrats have widely been regarded as a cat's-paw for American and bourgeois interests. Are they 'real' socialists therefore, to be grouped with the Socialist party itself and the Communists, or should they be put with their bourgeois allies in the Liberal camp? The trouble with the latter course is that they retain so many Leftist elements at least in their official ideology and (till the eighties anyway) among certain groups of supporters, that it is difficult to place them outside the general socialist camp. They were actually amalgamated with the Socialists in the sixties (as well as having emerged from an earlier unified socialist movement), and the Communists have always appealed to them in trying to construct alliances of the Left.

This example could be multiplied. Are the German Christian Democrats, for example, more of a Conservative than a Christian party? Many aspects of policy and ideology resemble those of the (traditional branches of the) British Conservative party. They did, however, originate with the Churches, particularly with the Catholic Church, from which they still attract disproportionate support, and that does differentiate them from secular conservatism.

On the whole, therefore, we have assigned parties to families on the basis of origins and underlying traditions, rather than more recent policy adjustments; we reason that their electoral supporters and social-group bases are more likely to derive from past traditions than from present manœuvres, and it is the interests of clients and supporters that parties will above all be concerned with in their choice of ministries.

A more general problem arises, however, with the placement of Liberal parties deriving from the existence of two rather well-attested liberal sub-traditions.[2] The first is 'Continental liberalism'—very much based on free-enterprise economics, limited State intervention, and a restrictive attitude towards welfare and labour, and emphasis on a strong defence posture. The second is 'radical liberalism'—

stressing intervention, welfare, protection of labour, and peaceful internationalism. Historically, indeed, this latter tradition was the matrix within which many Socialist and Labour parties formed. Should 'liberalism' therefore exist at all as a separate tendency, or should the sub-traditions be grouped with socialism or conservatism as the case may be?

'Liberalism' as a tendency obviously exists, as witness the existence of a Liberal International on the lines of the other major tendencies and a Liberal grouping in the European Parliament. So we feel we have no choice but to recognize it as existing in terms of *both* sub-traditions together. What they have in common, at least in the minds of activists and supporters, outweighs what separates them. And what they share is a concern with individual freedom—which has then branched out, in the one case, into a concern to remove as many external constraints as possible on individual choice and action and in the other, into a concern to give the individual a social basis for actually using his civil freedoms. The concern with freedom should give Liberal parties characteristic policies, and interests in ministries, which differ from those of Conservatives, Christians, and Socialists, none whom are averse to massive State interference and regulation of the individual to secure their particular ends.

These first approximations to party preferences provide an impetus to ordering the policy concerns of each family, as a preliminary both to the analysis of policy itself in the next two chapters, and to the consideration here of their priorities in regard to ministries.

Hypothesized party preferences are based partly on the traditional group support, ideologies, and historical origins of the parties,[3] and partly on previous analyses of their characteristic issue concerns.[4] The Conservatives first consolidated themselves in the nineteenth century as defenders of the established order and its procedures against the demands of the bourgeoisie for an extension of individual freedoms and rights of dissent. In confronting various parties pressing for some change in the status quo (whether of a Liberal or Socialist character) the Conservatives have consolidated their stance as guarantors of the existing order, its traditions, norms, laws, and constitution. Reflecting this, policy areas such as law and order and constitutional procedures appear among their first priorities. Conservative interests in preserving the existing order extend to foreign threats, through their traditional role as upholders of national interests abroad. None of the other parties are so uniquely concerned with defence issues as none of the others have grown out of the state apparatus like the Conservatives or are so closely concerned with its power and prestige.

Other areas are in a sense subsidiary to those overriding concerns. Conservatives tend to find more support among a usually more traditional rural population than in cities and large towns. But the closeness of this tie depends on the absence of a specifically Agrarian party, and of a religious party too, which would generally have a prior claim on the affections of the peasantry. In the absence of a Liberal party, Conservatives may also incorporate business elements with a strong orientation towards economic and financial affairs. Education will also interest Conservatives, as it will any party with a comprehensive ideology, as a way of inculcating its own values among the rising generation. Religious parties may well be more directly interested in this, however, as the strengthening of traditional moral orientations is more central to their *raison d'être*.

Religious parties can also expect to have more support in the countryside, at least in the absence of an Agrarian competitor. Religious doctrine, particularly Catholic doctrine, extends to the social sphere, and the overall well-being of the family (welfare, health, and work), so their interests in these areas mirror those of Socialist parties but are lower on their agenda. For the Socialist parties themselves these come first, followed by planning and regulation of the economy, which are often from their perspective seen as essential underpinnings of the Welfare State. The moral and ethical sides of socialism in turn impart a concern with education, as a distinctly lower priority, however, than it is for religious parties, who are more concerned to win young hearts and minds.

Liberalism was the first of the challenges, historically, confronting State power-holders in the nineteenth century, with its challenge to the established Church and assertion of individual freedoms—both legal and economic—against traditional constraints. Both modern branches of liberalism share this concern with freedom in the economic and political spheres. There is a particular interest in economics and finance since free trade was, historically, such a rallying-call for all varieties of liberalism. The nineteenth-century struggle against bastions of the Establishment led to anti-clericalism, mainly expressed in a desire to substitute the influence of a secular State in the schools for that of a State Church. Liberal parties tend therefore to be just as concerned with education as religious parties, though from an opposed point of view, like the Socialists.

The one area that concerns single-issue parties, as their name implies, is that of the issue: the interests of country- as opposed to city-dwellers for Agrarian parties, regional for Nationalists or autonomists. Lacking on the whole a more comprehensive ideology extending into diverse areas of life, and seeing political success as bound up particularly with their unique aim, other policy areas tend to be very much downgraded.

In the next chapter we shall extend these arguments to hypothesize particular orderings of policy priorities for each family of parties. Here we apply them to preferences for ministries, as shown in Table 4.2. The link to the policy concerns hypothesized above is obvious. If a particular type of party, like the Conservatives, for example, is most strongly concerned about law and order, it is natural for it to seek control of ministries such as the Interior, primarily, and then Justice, which are closely linked to law enforcement. Among Conservatives this concern jostles a closely related interest in the country's foreign standing and defence posture. Further down come ministries such

TABLE 4.2. Hypothesized ranking of standard ministries within the party families

Conservative	Liberal	Religious	Socialist	Single-issue
Interior	Economy/ Finance	Religious Affairs	Health/ Social Affairs/ Labour	Ministry related to issue[a]
Foreign Affairs/ Defence	Justice	Education		(Indifferent to other ministries)
Justice	Education	Agriculture	Economy	
Agriculture	Interior		Industry	
Economy	Trade/ Industry/ Commerce	Social Affairs/ Health/ Labour	Education	
Education				
Trade/ Industry/ Commerce				

[a] Agriculture/Fisheries for Agrarians, Regional for Nationalists/Regionalists.

as Agriculture, to cater for rural interests, and Economics, Trade, and Industry, which reflect lesser but still important concerns with economic management and finance, linked to business support.

As the connections with the policy interests described above are quite obvious, there is no need to labour the point with similarly detailed descriptions for other party families. Each will seek to hold ministries related to its interests, in order of priority. Of course, the interests and their ordering are hypothesized by us, so there may be some disagreement as to whether they are entirely accurate or not (since they are based on history and ideological tradition there should be *substantial* agreement). Given the link with ministries, a first check of the validity of the policy classification can be made by seeing whether party families actually choose those that we hypothesize they should. In Chapters 5 and 6 we go on to a more extensive discussion and analysis of the way in which ideology links with programmatic preferences and the functioning and termination of coalitions.

CORRESPONDENCES BETWEEN PARTY FAMILIES'
PREFERENCES AND THE ACTUAL ALLOCATION OF MINISTRIES

The parties' interest in getting ministries within their particular areas of policy concern should emerge in a general tendency for the actual allocation to give them at least the higher-ranking ministries of Table 4.2. Their policy preoccupations should also push them into trying to get the premiership if they can, because this gives them a general influence over policy. The premiership should go to the largest party: this both provides an obvious criterion for its assignment and recognizes the party's relatively greater weight in the coalition. (Even in terms of raw power, greater numbers should generally be associated with greater control over the fate of the coalition, even if smaller parties at times have substantial blackmail potential.)

We shall check distributions over all coalition governments in fifteen post-war democracies (Austria, The Netherlands, Belgium, Luxemburg, Denmark, Finland, Sweden, Norway, Iceland, West Germany, Ireland, the Fourth and Fifth French Republics, Italy, and Israel). We omit Japan because coalitions formed there only in the immediate post-war period, under the aegis of the occupation authorities, and sometimes under their vetoes and constraints. When the party system stabilized through the amalgamation of Progressives and

Liberals, it took the form of a decisive (even though faction-ridden) one-party predominance.

Switzerland is also omitted because the collegial form of its Federal Executive does not give scope for parties to claim certain ministries. The seven posts are shared out in a 2 : 2 : 2 : 1 'magic formula' between Radicals, Catholics, Socialists, and Farmers, roughly in proportion to their relative size. However each individual is voted in by the Parliament as a whole, which may at times prefer another candidate of the same party. The freedom of members of the Executive to continue for as long as they want in their particular department, if they avoid serious blunders, means that often only one position is available for a particular party nominee, so the wish of the party for control of a specific area hardly enters into the matter. Further obstacles are found in the intricate balancing of cantonal and linguistic qualifications of executive members. All this brings about the absence of conditions in which parties can assert claims to particular ministries in relatively free bargaining with potential partners. Hence it is impossible (and also unnecessary!) to test these hypotheses in Switzerland and we omit it from the analyses of this chapter.

Two further important points should be made before we get down to the examination of actual relationships. Both are related to variations in types of parties and ministries across different countries. The variation in types of ministries is not great (modern governments have broadly the same responsibilities, and, generally, assign them in comparable clusters to similarly named ministries, so we can usually also assume their area of competence is the same). However, the division does vary in minor particulars and so for the analysis we have slightly standardized descriptions across countries. This is not a major problem as the terminology we apply does not vary much from that actually in use in any country concerned. But it may explain why a specialist does not find the exact title of a particular ministry in one country appearing in the discussion.

We do base information on all cabinet ministries in each country, but specifically name only the seventeen 'general' and 'standardized' ones (Prime Ministership, Deputy Prime Ministership, Foreign Affairs, Defence, Interior, Justice, Finance, Economy, Labour, Social Affairs, Education, Health, Housing, Infrastructure, Agriculture, Industry, Religious Affairs). The remainder, a varying number for different countries and even for different governments, are counted but simply listed as 'other'.

Sometimes two of these standardized ministries are always distributed together (for instance, Health and Social Affairs). In other cases
the responsibilities may be combined into one ministry or separated
into two (for instance, Agriculture and Fisheries). Where two ministries exist in the same area we should expect them to be assigned
together where both appertain to the same party, but to be divided
between two parties if both have claims in that area (Health and
Housing, for example, between a Socialist and a Christian party which
formed part of the same coalition government).

This leads on to the second point—much more important, both
theoretically and substantively—to be made before beginning the
analysis. That is, that certain types of party are absent from some
countries (see Table 4.1) and, even more obviously, are not represented in all coalitions. In such cases the neat schematic relationship
postulated in Table 4.2 will not work (there are, for example, very few
Agrarian parties outside Scandinavia; and even in Scandinavia they do
not enter into all coalitions). What happens to Agriculture and
Fisheries when there is no Agrarian party to take them? This is of
course only one illustration of the more general problem.

Our discussion has already covered this possibility, although in a
fairly general way. Implication 2(iii) of Table 2.4 envisages that where
a particular type of party does not exist, the most similar of the
existing parties will seek the ministries in its area of policy concern.
Table 4.2 has already spelled out some of the 'inheritances' of one
party from another. Thus the Agricultural Ministry should go to the
Christians if Agrarians are absent; and if neither is represented it will
fall to the Conservatives. The latter will inherit religious concerns if a
party of that type is absent. Not all links are spelled out in Table 4.2,
however. In general we may say that religious parties are the natural
'heirs' of Agrarian parties, and Conservatives of religious parties.
Conservatives are also heirs of the Liberals in the industrial-
commercial sector. As far as Conservative concerns with order,
morality, and education go, however, we should expect them to be
inherited by the religious parties in the absence of Conservatives
themselves. Where only one bourgeois party is represented it should
take over the interests of all the others.

Socialist parties exist in all countries, so there is no question of
other parties taking over their concerns in their absence. From the
point of view of policy concerns, Communist parties are regarded
as equivalent to Labour or Social Democratic parties. In the case

of coalitions formed without Socialists, ministries will be shared out among bourgeois parties in line with their own major concerns, without any one of them becoming the unique 'heir' of the Socialists.

This general characterization of the way in which parties 'inherit' each others' concerns forms an adequate basis for the analysis of the broad connections between party family and ministry which we carry out in this section. For the more refined analysis of the next section the connections will be operationalized further in the shape of flow diagrams (Figures 4.1–4.5). We should note in passing, however, that comparative analyses of party–ministry links which ignore the possibility of one party inheriting another's interests are bound to underestimate the regularity and extent of the links. Thus the absence of a particular type of party does not imply that its target ministries go into a general pool, but rather that related parties will add them to their shopping-lists. A failure to allow for this type of substitution is a possible explanation for Browne and Feste's failure to find strong connections between party ideology and choice of particular ministries.[5] Their analysis of variance between party and ministry types, because it was aggregated across West European countries with no possibility of this form of substitution, not unnaturally undervalues the relationship. The Agricultural Ministry cannot go to the Agrarian party, for example, where the latter is absent from either the government or the system. But as we have stressed, it may go to a 'successor' party in a perfectly comprehensible manner and on the basis of recognizable policy interests.

This possibility lies at the heart of the analyses we conduct below. To save space, we organize these under successive hypotheses about relationships between parties and ministries. It will be clear from the way our discussion has proceeded that although hypotheses and data are brought into close juxtaposition, the former were clearly formulated *before* any data was even collected. Their confirmation thus gains whatever additional weight comes from validation of an a priori hypothesis.

The largest party takes the Premiership. This idea has already been introduced. Parties are anxious to have the premiership because of its general influence over discussions and implementation of policy. The clearest and most acceptable way of assigning it to a party is in terms of numerical contributions to the governmental coalition. This is of course another case where office-seeking and policy-pursuing assumptions support the same expectation. However, later hypotheses are exclusively based on policy grounds.

Over all coalitions in the fifteen countries of concern, the largest party does take the premiership in 80 per cent of the cases (214 out of 268[6]). The only country where results do not resoundingly confirm this expectation is Finland, where the largest party takes this office in only 21 out of 34 cases. This may result partly from presidential power over the nomination of ministers, and partly from several parties being fairly equal in size and the numerical criterion therefore not being as overwhelmingly obvious as elsewhere. It is striking that where coalitions are formed with predominant parties, these parties almost inevitably take the Premiership—even in Denmark (7 cases out of 7), where the predominant party is weakest of those considered.

Agrarian Parties take the Ministry of Agriculture (and related ministries such as Fisheries) in all cases of coalition governments where (i) an Agrarian party participates in the coalition and (ii) there is a Ministry of Agriculture. In contrast to the last, this hypothesis links a particular party to a ministry on the grounds of a specific policy interest. The connection is so obvious that it needs no justification (and again is a clear finding in the Browne–Feste analyses). However, the hypothesis needs to be worded cautiously to cover only the cases where the Agrarian party had an opportunity to get the ministry because it formed part of the coalition and where such a ministry existed. In fact, post-war Agrarian parties exist only in Scandinavia (with the exception of one small party in Ireland which disappeared in the fifties), and there such ministries also exist. There is overwhelming confirmation: 54 cases out of 65. Finland in this case completely conforms to expectations; it is only Ireland that produces an ambiguous result (2–2) on the point (there were two governments but four ministries involved). Clann na Talmhan was small and less able than large Agrarian parties to assert itself against its partners, but still obviously got some reward.

Perhaps more interesting is the extent to which heirs or pre-emptors of the appeal of Agrarian parties gain Agriculture. Christian parties are likely to be the nearest cognates of Agrarian parties because of their appeal to traditional values which are strongest among the rural population. For the same reason Conservative parties are likely to appeal to this group and consider their interests where there is no Agrarian *or* Christian party.

This reasoning leads to the first related hypothesis: *Christian parties take Agriculture in coalitions where (i) no Agrarian party participates, (ii) a Christian party participates in the coalition, and (iii) there is a Ministry of Agriculture.* Except in the Fourth French Republic, this link receives almost as overwhelming support as the straight Agrarian–Agriculture linkage—of the order of 83 per cent over all countries. There are no countries where the non-existence of Agrarian *and* Christian parties leaves Conservatives the heirs. In France under the Fourth Republic the MRP, in contrast to the general tendency, got Agriculture only one-third of the time—other parties such as the Radicals having strong agrarian bases. Israel with its strong religious but non-Christian parties is a special case which we consider below (Table 4.7).

Religious parties take the Ministry of Religious Affairs in all cases of coalition government where (i) a religious party participated in the coalition, and (ii) there is such a ministry. The other family within which a party particularly interested in one policy area can assert its claims to a particular ministry without encountering opposition from other parties with interests in the same area is that of the religious parties. Obviously they have a special and surely acceptable interest in Ministries of Religious Affairs. A similar formulation can be made to that for Agrarian parties. However although there are many religious parties in Western Europe the area on the whole lacks Ministries of Religious Affairs and where they do exist, religious parties have normally not participated in government. The new Danish Christian Party when it participated in two 'four-leaf clover' governments of the 1980s got the Environment Ministry rather than Religious Affairs. It is clear from the Israeli case, however, that this hypothesis is strongly upheld where religious parties normally participate in government: the relevant parties take the Ministry of Religious Affairs in 23 cases out of 29.

Either religious or Liberal or Socialist parties take the Education Ministry when one or more of them participate in the coalition. An area of conflict involving both religious and militantly secular parties is Education, where both want to have supervision of the schools area (often involving State financing or control of religious schools). In around 90 per cent of cases where one or other of these (opposing) parties participates in the governing coalition, the party in question in fact controls the Education Ministry. When one is in government without the participation of the other, it seems to establish a unique and relatively unchallenged claim to the ministry. When both are in government together, control of the Education Ministry obviously passes in a relatively unpredictable fashion between the two, depending on what trade-offs between other ministries were involved. It is interesting that for the subset of countries where the struggle over the schools question was particularly marked up to the end of the fifties (Italy, Belgium, Luxemburg, the Fourth Republic), there is a complete monopoly of the Education Ministry by the opposing sides.

Other areas where religious parties tend to confront others, and where trade-offs may affect control of the Education Ministry, are listed in the next hypothesis: *Socialist* or *Christian Parties take the Ministry of Labour/Social Affairs/Health for all coalitions where (i) Socialist or Christian parties participate in the coalition and (ii) there is such a ministry*. The wording of the hypothesis is very broad because of the postulated conflict in the coalition between two types of party which have a strong concern with social affairs. In cases where only one participates, it will have a unique claim to ministries in these areas. However, with such a number of ministries involved out of the limited set of cabinet posts available, even in these cases it would be difficult for either Christians or Socialists to defend their claim to *all* the minstries involved—especially given their other interests outside this field. Additional complications enter when both are in government together, in which case we can expect the distribution to vary with strength and local conditions in idiosyncratic ways. So the hypothesis has to be broad and assert essentially that these types of parties will always try to maintain an interest which will show up in their success in gaining at least one of the relevant ministries. Analyses of particular ministries are given below and further research will investigate links for specific parties more closely.

Probably in part because of its inclusiveness, the hypothesis receives almost 100 per cent support. It also emerges that more specific relationships hold in particular countries. In Belgium, for example, the Christian Social Party rarely takes Labour when Socialists participate in the coalition: it cedes to their more strongly held preferences in return for other ministries of interest.

The strong support received for this hypothesis is, however, slightly vitiated by its extreme inclusiveness. One of several parties is postulated to hold one of several ministries. This is probably the extreme limit to which we can go with this type of analysis without lapsing into vacuousness. We accordingly change our analytic style at this point, and in the next section investigate the same relationships through a much closer specification of the processes involved, in the shape of hypothetical flow diagrams for each party.

This broad analysis does, however, (so far as it goes) support the general thrust of the argument that parties have policy-based interests in particular ministries. Even though country- and government-specific relationships have not yet been examined, the success of the general, cross-national hypotheses indicates that ministries cannot be treated as undifferentiated coin. Having established the point with a general comparative approach, we shall proceed to consolidate it with country-specific analyses, still working, however, within the general framework of the theory presented above.

DETAILED SPECIFICATIONS OF AND CHECKS ON THE ALLOCATION OF MINISTRIES

One earlier finding which may seem to weigh against the possibility of strong party–ministry links is the very marked relationship between the proportion of seats contributed by each party to the coalition and the proportion of Cabinet Ministries which it receives.[7] We find this too: regressing the proportion of seats against the proportion of ministries given to each party over all of our coalition governments, we get a bivariate correlation coefficient of 0.91. This is of equivalent value to others obtained over varying data sets for this relationship, and is at the level of the strongest relationships ever obtained in political science. So what can we make of it within the context of a policy-based discussion?

The proportionality finding has been taken to support the following argument:

   (i) Parties are office-seekers.
  (ii) They therefore seek to maximize their share of offices in government.
 (iii) Since all are seeking to do this, the only rule that can be agreed is to relate the share of pay-offs (ministries) to contributions (seats).
 (iv) Hence we get strict proportionality between offices and seats implying, further,
  (v) that all offices (ministries) are equivalent in value for all the parties—which then goes against the idea that the latter have a substantive interest in which ministries they get.

Schofield and Laver have qualified this line of argument by pointing out that parties truly concerned to maximize office would exploit their pivotal position in the coalition to get a more than proportionate share of ministries.[8] In fragmented multi-party systems, deviations from the proportionality rule can be interpreted in this sense. However, proportionality remains as the general rule to which this is an exception.

Both proportionality and exploitation of pivotal positions can, however, also be reinterpreted in policy-based terms. Ministries are not only of interest for the implementation of specific policies but also for their relative weight in general policy formation. Maximization of the number of ministries held contributes to this weight, as it adds to the numbers of votes in Cabinet. So, desires for maximization leading to a general rule of proportionality could also derive from the attachment of parties to their policies and their desire to push them through as effectively as possible. However, we also have to take into consideration the point made earlier about their wish to obtain particular ministries because of their importance for policy implementation. Combining these two objectives (possession of designated ministries and maximization of Cabinet votes) gives to the policy-based theory distinctly different expectations about distribution from those of the office-seeking one. Instead of a simple one-stage share-out of equivalent offices, a multi-stage process can be postulated in which

(a) parties assert claims to specific ministries of interest;
(b) conflicts involved in claims to the same ministry are provisionally resolved by trading;
(c) the resulting distribution is checked against the proportionality criterion and accepted when it fits.

Negotiations may go between these different levels several times, leading to adjustments in original claims and failure because of the upper limits imposed by proportionality to gain some specific ministries of interest from the point of view of policy implementation. Distribution can be smoothed out with the aid of 'makeweight' ministries of no particular policy interest to any party, and possibly by sacrificing ministries of lower priority in the interests of keeping those of higher priority.

In this way the proportionality criterion can be incorporated into the comprehensive, policy-based interpretation of the allocation of ministries which we now attempt. This combines three elements:

(1) party attachment to particular ministries, as specified in Table 4.2, (2) the transference of concerns to cognate parties, where a particular type of party does not exist or at any rate does not participate in the coalition, and (3) proportionality. For maximum clarity we have combined these elements in flow diagrams—direct representations of every step in the process of allocation for each party type. Although the connections they make are broadly supported by the analysis of the preceding section, the diagrams are essentially hypothetical at this point. The very precise way in which processes have been specified, however, makes it possible to check them holistically against the data in our possession. By this we mean that the final set of ministries a party of a particular type would be expected to receive according to the diagram can be checked against the actual set of ministries it did receive, for all coalition governments in which that type of party participated, both in total and within each country. The analysis cannot therefore validate every stage and sequence of the postulated processes; but if the end results as postulated in the diagrams correspond to what seems to emerge in practice, there are certainly strong grounds for accepting the whole representation as a fair approximation of the actual processes of negotiation and distribution.

We start in Figure 4.1 with single-issue parties, as represented by the Agrarians, because they form the simplest case. Since the flow diagram, in specifying every step in the process of allocation, has to deal with all eventualities, it can become quite complicated. However it is in essence no more than a very precise specification of our earlier reasoning, so the various steps involved should be reasonably clear.[9]

We have said that participation is not worth while for Agrarians unless they get their own ministry of concern—Agriculture, and possibly Fisheries or Lands. Getting such ministries if they exist forms the first stage of the postulated acquisition process, as it is a necessary prerequisite to participation in government (though in itself it may not be a sufficient pay-off, depending on the size of the Agrarian contribution).

The next stage is to review possible government situations. Looking back to the circumstances under which coalitions can emerge, described in Table 2.3, we have seen that these can be very varied. Three possibilities are particularly important from the point of view of distributing ministries:

(*a*) There are situations in which one party *could* form a government on its own (because it has a majority or at least is very strongly

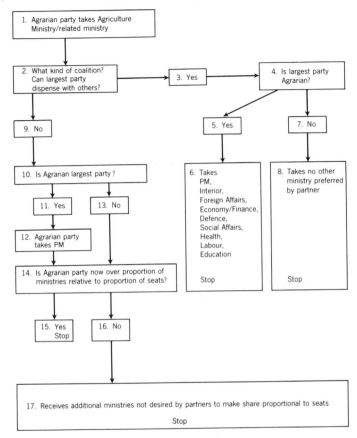

FIG. 4.1. The acquisition of ministries by an Agrarian party in a coalition government

predominant). As participation of the smaller partner(s) is purely dependent on the goodwill of the larger, the latter can take all the ministries it wants almost without regard to the former (the exception being the proviso that Agrarian parties would not participate at all without the Ministry of Agriculture and Fisheries). If the Agrarians are the largest party in this situation, they will proceed to take all the important ministries leaving to their partner or partners only one of the latter's preferred choices. If they are the smaller (and dispensable) partner, they will take (in addition to Agriculture and Fisheries) nothing which is preferred by their partner—as they are so completely dependent on its goodwill.

(*b*) A second situation is where relationships between coalition partners are more equal but where Agrarians are largest. In that case (as specified above) they will be expected to take the premiership in addition to Agriculture, which they have secured in their very first step.

(*c*) Where parties are relatively equal but Agrarians are not the largest, obviously they do not get the premiership, but they will secure Agriculture as a *sine qua non* of governmental participation.

In any case, Agrarians being satisfied on their single issue (and if largest, on the premiership) now want no more specific ministries. It is at this point that the criterion of proportionality comes in. While for other parties there might exist a possibility of having too great a proportion of ministries relative to seats, and of being docked of those of lower priority, this could not be the case with the Agrarians. To participate in the coalition at all they must have Agriculture, and if largest must have the premiership. As these are indispensable it is only if, having these, they still have less than their due proportion of ministries, that any further allocation takes place; and this can only be upwards, carrying them into box 17 and gains of enough ministries not desired by partners to make their share proportional to their contribution of seats.

It is hoped that this review of the diagram makes clear the processes which we hypothesize and their relationship with preceding theory. We turn now to Figure 4.2, which at a similar level of detail specifies the processes of allocation for Conservative parties.

Again the three possible types of coalition situation recur. In the case of coalitions with a totally dominant party, the question is again whether the Conservatives are dominant or dependent. If the former, then they will take all their preferred ministries leaving to the partner only those not preferred by them. If they themselves are dependent, on the other hand, they in turn will obtain only ministries not preferred by the partner.

In a more equal situation but where they are largest, they will take the premiership, and even if not largest they will bargain for their first priorities of Interior, Foreign Affairs, and Defence. At this point, however, they begin to compete for ministries also desired by other parties in the coalition, so whether they get Justice, Economy/

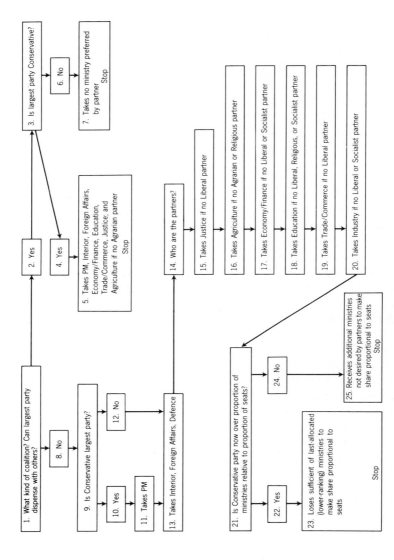

FIG. 4.2. The acquisition of ministries by a Conservative party in a coalition government

Finance, Education, Trade, etc. depends on whether interested partners are asserting claims. If there is a clash between other parties' first-priority ministries and ones which rank lower for Conservatives, the latter will obviously tend to give way.

The question of what other parties form the coalition is also of concern because the Conservatives may 'inherit' an interest in certain ministries if a partner of a certain type does not exist. This is particularly the case with regard to Agriculture if there are no Agrarian or religious partners. (Empirically, however, as we have seen above, there is no actual case in our data in which this occurs.)

With desired ministries obtained, the equalizing process based on proportionality comes into play. If Conservatives have too few ministries in relation to their seats, they will receive makeweights not especially desired by anyone else to make up their share. If too many preferred ministries have gone to them, however, they have to lose enough of their lower-ranked ones to bring them down to proportionality with seats. This final, adjusting process therefore cuts across the earlier allocation in terms of substantive preferences and can reverse some of its results. This could account for some preferred ministries not being obtained, in ways perfectly consonant with the theory, but which are not caught by broad comparisons of hypothetical preferences with actual results of the type made in the previous section.

Figure 4.3 lists the same processes for Liberal parties. As the preferences of Liberals with regard to ministries have already been specified in relation to Table 4.2, and distribution follows the same broad principles as those described for Conservatives, we do not need to discuss the figure in detail. Because Education is also a priority for religious parties—as the Interior is for Conservatives—Liberals are not assumed necessarily to get them if they have partners of these types. Again Liberals have a *sine qua non* for entry to a coalition on relatively equal terms (Economy/Finance and Justice), and again the proportionalization of ministries and seats may knock out some substantively preferred ministries from their final allocation (in the case of very small parties, entitled to only one ministry on proportional criteria, most of the preferred ministries would not in fact be obtained).

The allocation processes for religious parties (Figure 4.4) and Socialists (Figure 4.5) are again similar, once essential modifications have been made to accommodate their different preferences and

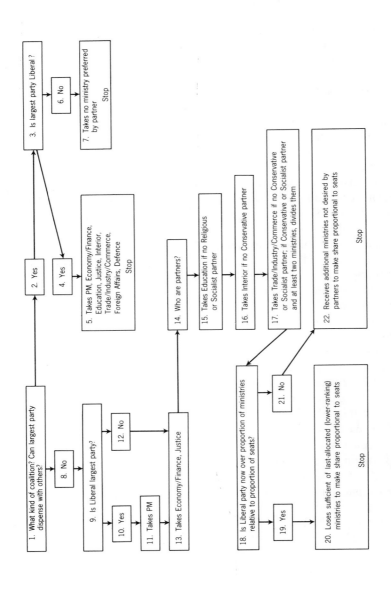

FIG. 4.3. The acquisition of ministries by a Liberal party in a coalition government

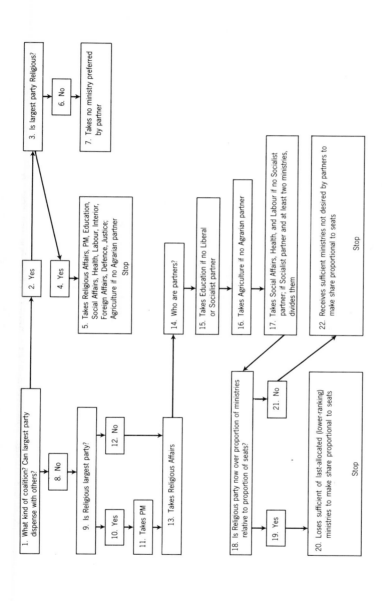

Fig. 4.4. The acquisition of ministries by a religious party in a coalition government

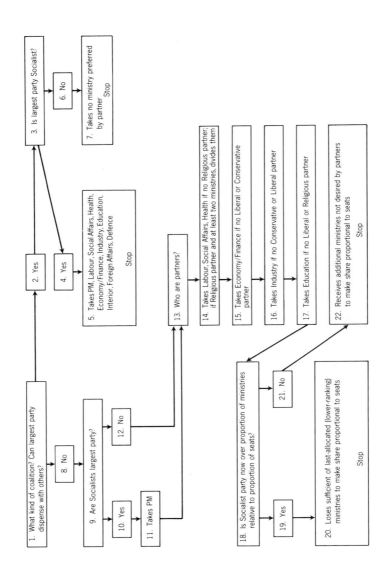

FIG. 4.5. The acquisition of ministries by a Socialist party in a coalition government

relationships with partners. Again, precisely who is a coalition partner makes a great difference to the final allocation, which is also affected by proportionalization.

These figures obviously spell out our theory in more precise detail than the general formulations made up to now. What they do for analysis is to make possible a total specification of the whole set of ministries a party should end up with in a given parliamentary situation, rather than checking the destination of particular types one by one, as in the last section. Taking the simplest case, not only do we expect the Agrarians to end up with Agriculture and Fisheries, which we know from the last analysis that they do in most cases, but where they 'earn' less than one ministry in terms of their proportion of government seats that is all they will get. Where they are largest the set will consist of Agriculture, the premiership, and additional makeweight ministries (i.e. those not specifically desired by any party) up to their level of proportionality.

We can proceed to an immediate check of this simplest case before coming to the more complicated allocation processes for the other party families. The results are shown in Table 4.3, which presents statistics on the actual allocation of ministries in the five countries (exclusive of Switzerland) where Agrarian parties took part in coalitions during the post-war period. These can be compared with the leading predictions from Figure 4.1.

As in no case was an Agrarian party large enough to dispense with partners if it so wished, the right-hand branch of the figure is irrelevant. The most important criteria for the correctness of the diagram are therefore whether in fact Agrarian parties do take the Agricultural and related ministries; whether, if largest, they take the premiership; and whether the overall relationship of their seats to their ministries is roughly proportional.

In addition we can scan the final, overall, distribution of ministries, taking account of, but not limiting ourselves to, these points, to see whether the process works generally as expected. The 'overall' evaluation is designed to complement the one-by-one, almost mechanical, checking of whether particular ministries have been assigned as they ought to be, in terms of our hypotheses. Minor deviations from such assignments (as, for instance, where a very small Agrarian party received only one agriculture-related ministry rather than two) can be discounted in the overall assessment, provided that other processes were respected. On the other hand, such achievements as gaining the

TABLE 4.3. Acquisition of ministries by Agrarian parties in five countries

	Takes Agriculture and related ministries		If largest, takes premiership		Acquires ministries in rough proportion to seats		Acquisition conforms broadly to expectations	
	Cases	Success rate of prediction	Cases	Success rate of prediction	Cases	Success rate of prediction	Cases	Success rate of prediction
Denmark	12	0.66	2	1.00	6	0.33	6	1.00
Finland	33	0.94	9	1.00	33	0.51	33	0.73
Ireland	4	0.50	—	—	2	1.00	2	1.00
Norway	10	0.70	2	0.50	5	0.60	5	0.80
Sweden	6	1.00	2	1.00	6	0.33	6	0.83
All countries	65	0.83	15	0.93	52	0.52	52	0.79

premiership while not being the largest party go against expectations, but are not specifically checked in other parts of the table; these lead to negative evaluations of overall success even though the other proportions in Table 4.3 show a relatively high rate of success.

The premiership is related less to the specific character of the party and more to its strategic situation in regard to coalition partners. In the limited number of cases in which Agrarians are the largest party it almost exclusively falls to them. In Finland, where they occupied a quasi-dominant position in the party system under the very active presidency of their former party leader, Kekkonen, they have quite often obtained the premiership when not the largest party. This counts as a failure for expectations in regard to other parties' claims to the premiership, rather than being counted in the second success-rate column of Table 4.3. However, it *is* taken into account in the overall assessment of the last column of Table 4.3, where it depresses the success of the representation in the case of Finland.

Parties' claims to particular ministries are assumed in Figure 4.1 to be made within overall limits of proportionality. It is expected, in other words, that preferences will be met only to the extent that the proportion of ministries claimed does not exceed the proportion of seats contributed to the government coalition. This assumption is upheld by the results of much other research on the relationship, and also by the high correlation for our own data. The correlation, however, only reflects a tendency for proportions of ministries received to go up or down with proportions of government seats contributed. It does not inform us about the exact limits within which the relationship holds: whether, for example, the proportions always correspond fairly precisely—40 per cent of seats being met by more or less 40 per cent of ministries in every case—or whether there are 'gaps' or 'lags' between the proportions. As a rough check here and in succeeding tables, we note the number of cases where the ministerial and seat proportions come within one ministry of each other—which normally means within about 5 per cent, as this represents one ministry in the usual case where the Cabinet numbers about twenty posts. (Where the Cabinet is seven or eight in number, as in Iceland, the equivalent percentage obviously is wider.)

The results of Table 4.3 show that some Agrarian parties (for instance in Ireland) get a very exact return for their input of government seats. Mostly, however, proportionality in this very strict sense holds in only half the relevant coalitions of each country, and this level is reflected overall. There is no clear tendency for the share of ministries to either exceed or fall short of the share of seats, either overall or within other particular countries.

The final column of Table 4.3 reports the proportion of cases in which expectations about allocations are confirmed on balance over the whole set of governments examined. In the case of an Agrarian party this would imply that it received the Agricultural Ministry, the premiership only if it was the largest party, and in addition one or two other ministries if its number of seats justified it. The overall evaluation of success does not, however, insist on close numerical proportionality, within the limit of 5 per cent. In these terms the overall representation works well—in about four-fifths of cases overall, for all cases in Denmark and Ireland, and for even more in Norway and Sweden. Owing to the success of Agrarians in obtaining the premiership even when not the largest party, the Finnish proportion is lower. Even so, this figure indicates that the representation fits nearly three-quarters of coalitions even in this rather anomalous political situation.

We started with Agrarians because, with only two types of allocation to check (Agriculture and premiership) they constitute the simplest case. Table 4.4, dealing with the family of Conservative parties, is at first sight very complicated but follows substantially the same logic. Like all the tables in this section, it checks expectations summarized in one of the earlier flow diagrams, in this case Figure 4.2. Conservatives are expected to assert claims over a much wider range than Agrarians; hence the first column indicates what proportion of all ministries expected to be taken actually are taken. For various reasons, many connected with structural inflexibilities in the allocation of small numbers of posts, this is rarely 100 per cent. For example, a Deputy Prime Ministership may be linked with the Interior or with Foreign Affairs and hence go to another party—to balance a Conservative premiership, perhaps. In such a case the associated responsibility does not go to the Conservatives either. Such situational peculiarities, however, hardly detract from the broad validity and usefulness of the representation of Figure 4.2 unless they work consistently across the board to prevent a designated ministry ever going to the Conservatives. This is not the case.

Assessments in the table generally work in a probabilistic base. Do a majority of ministries which Conservatives are presumed to put as their first priority actually go to them? (These are the Interior,

TABLE 4.4. Acquisition of ministries by Conservative parties in eleven countries

	Takes ministries expected over all criteria		If largest, takes premiership		Takes at least two of Interior, Foreign Affairs, Defence[a]		Takes other ministries as predicted[b]		Acquires ministries in rough proportion to seats		Acquisition conforms broadly to expectations	
	Cases	Success rate of prediction	Cases	Success rate of prediction	Cases	Success rate of prediction	Cases	Success rate of prediction	Cases	Success rate of prediction	Cases	Success rate of prediction
Austria	84	0.50	12	1.00	12	0.08	12	0.00	12	0.75	12	0.92
Denmark	24	0.54	3	0.66	5	0.60	5	1.00	5	0.40	5	0.80
Finland	27	0.30	1	0.00	7	0.00	7	1.00	7	0.14	7	0.00
France 4	100	0.27	8	0.00	24	0.08	24	0.67	24	0.41	24	0.08
5	75	0.56	18	0.83	18	0.27	18	0.77	18	0.55	18	0.61
West Germany	5	0.80	—	—	3	0.00	—	—	3	1.00	3	0.66
Iceland	28	0.64	8	0.75	8	0.38	8	0.37	8	0.38	8	0.75
Ireland	24	0.83	5	1.00	5	1.00	5	0.80	5	0.40	5	0.80
Israel	49	0.57	7	1.00	9	0.44	7	0.43	9	0.11	9	0.44
Norway	17	0.88	4	1.00	4	1.00	1	1.00	4	0.75	4	1.00
Sweden	7	0.43	1	0.00	2	0.50	1	0.00	2	0.50	2	0.00
All countries	440	0.50	67	0.79	97	0.29	88	0.61	97	0.44	97	0.54

[a] Successful cases include those where a small party (i.e. one entitled by proportionality to more than one ministry) takes one of these ministries.

[b] i.e. where there is no partner with competing preference and up to the limit imposed by the proportion of government seats which it contributes. The other ministries in question are Justice, Agriculture, Economy/Finance, Education, and Trade/Commerce/Industry.

Foreign Affairs, and Defence; see the third pair of columns in the table.) Do a majority of the ministries which Conservatives will take in some cases but not in others according to who they are in coalition with, actually go to them? (These are Justice, Agriculture, Economy/ Finance, Education, and Trade/Commerce/Industry; see the fourth pair of columns.) In addition we check, as with Agrarians, whether the premiership goes to the Conservatives when they are largest and whether their proportion of ministries corresponds to their proportion of government seats. Finally, we make the same assessment of overall 'fit' between the expected final allocation of ministries (as summarized in Figure 4.2) and the actual results.

The overall success rate of the Conservative representation, as estimated on this basis, is much less than that of the Agrarian equivalent, at 0.54. In six out of eleven countries the representation works reasonably well. It is pulled down particularly by its almost total failure in Finland for the National Coalition (KOK), and in the Fourth Republic of France for the Independent Conservatives. We should not wish to resort to special pleading to justify the failures, but it is worth noting that KOK has always been somewhat suspect to the Soviet Union. Given Finnish sensitivity, for obvious reasons, to Russian reactions, and the role of the President both as mediator with the USSR and as former of governments, it is not surprising that the KOK has been relegated to a less important role even on the relatively rare occasions when it has succeeded in entering government.

The Independent Conservatives under the French Fourth Republic are a different case, since it is even debatable to what extent they constituted a cohesive party. As a loose grouping of notables whose parliamentary position depended on individual local contacts, they were totally independent of any central discipline. To an even greater extent than other political groupings of the Fourth Republic they split over support of or participation within governments. Hence it is hardly surprising that they failed to assert or to agree on party priorities as far as policies and ministries were concerned. In the Fifth Republic, indeed, the Independent Conservatives emerged as a grouping much more in the liberal tradition and formed the nucleus from which the later Giscardian parties emerged. It is noticeable that when we examine the record of the Fifth Republic's Conservative party, the Gaullists, much more definite and consistent preferences for ministries emerge which are almost in line with expectations. The one case of consistent failure is in getting the Interior, Foreign Affairs, and Defence. As these are prerogatives of the President, however, it is understandable that Gaullists are less concerned about them.

The other two countries where the model fails to work well are Sweden (where Conservatives have rarely been in power and are not in a good bargaining-position) and Israel. In the latter case predictions improve as Gahal and Likud emerge as a single definite party instead of aggregating diverse, loosely associated groups.

The overall representation fits reasonably well for the well-established, influential Conservative parties of Denmark, Iceland, and Austria. The indicators of performance produce somewhat divergent results in each of these cases, however: in Denmark, for example, the Conservatives take only 54 per cent of the ministries expected, while in Iceland the Independence party is not very good in getting a majority of the Interior, Foreign Affairs, and Defence ministries (there are only eight Cabinet posts in all, however). In Austria the 'Grand Coalition' with the OSP (the other major party), and the continuing crisis from 1945 to 1964, probably enhanced the Peoples' Party's willingness to make concessions over some of its substantively preferred ministries (see the third and fourth pairs of columns). As the first pair of columns shows, it always got some preferred ministries even if not a majority. One has the feeling in examining the Austrian distributions overall that the OVP is constantly approaching the 'ideal pattern' for Conservative parties, as expected in Figure 4.2, but is being forced by the Socialists to compensate heavily for its possession of the premiership and in the presence of the crisis is obliged to make concessions. That is why the proportion of cases conforming to broad expectations, shown in the last column, is high.

The match (overall and within countries) between proportions of government seats and proportions of ministries is at much the same level as for Agrarians—that is, within about 5 per cent in about half the cases. We shall put this in context when we look at these results for all countries and parties together.

Liberal parties conform better to the corresponding model of acquisition (Figure 4.3) than Conservative parties do. This is clear from a comparison of Tables 4.4 and 4.5. The comparison is easier than with Agrarians, because both tables are presented in the same form except that Liberal parties are expected to give their highest priority to getting Economy/Finance, and Justice, with secondary preferences for Education, the Interior, and Trade/Commerce/Industry. Their success in getting one or other of the latter, however,

TABLE 4.5. Acquisition of ministries by Liberal parties in twelve countries

	Takes ministries expected over all criteria		If largest, takes premiership		Takes at least one of Economy/ Finance and Justice		Takes other ministries as predicted[a]		Acquires ministries in rough proportion to seats		Acquisition conforms broadly to expectations	
	Cases	Success rate of prediction	Cases	Success rate of prediction	Cases	Success rate of prediction	Cases	Success rate of prediction	Cases	Success rate of prediction	Cases	Success rate of prediction
Belgium	44	0.77	—	—	11	1.00	11	0.82	11	0.36	11	0.91
Denmark	34	0.53	—	—	8	0.75	6	0.33	8	0.37	8	0.63
Finland	34	0.35	—	—	22	0.32	11	0.72	22	0.64	22	0.35
France 4	81	0.73	—	—	25	0.76	18	1.00	25	0.65	25	0.72
West Germany	46	0.56	—	—	13	0.92	13	0.00	13	0.46	13	0.85
Iceland	29	0.59	2	1.00	8	0.87	8	0.37	8	0.37	8	0.37
Israel	29	0.41	—	—	19	0.53	2	0.00	19	0.77	19	0.53
Italy	52	0.69	—	—	27	0.74	—	—	27	0.48	27	0.63
Luxemburg	28	0.64	—	—	8	0.87	8	0.62	8	0.12	8	0.87
Netherlands	36	0.88	—	—	8	0.75	6	0.83	8	0.85	8	0.75
Norway	9	0.55	—	—	4	1.00	1	1.00	4	1.00	4	0.75
Sweden	12	0.58	—	—	3	1.00	3	0.33	3	1.00	3	0.66
All countries	434	0.64	2	1.00	156	0.71	87	0.59	156	0.56	156	0.64

[a] i.e. where there is no partner with competing preference and up to the limit imposed by the proportion of government seats which it contributes. The other ministries in question are Education, Interior, and Trade/Commerce/Industry.

depends crucially on who their coalition partners are, as well as when they cross the threshold of proportionality between seats and ministries.

The other points noted in Table 4.5, as in the preceding tables, are the proportion of cases in which there is rough proportionality between numbers of ministries and seats; how often, if largest, the Liberal party gets the premiership; and whether Figure 4.3 does adequately represent the overall 'flow' of acquisition. As shown by the last column, which presents the proportion of cases in which expectations are broadly confirmed by results, Figure 4.3 does emerge as an informative representation. The main exceptions are Finland (again) and Iceland—where, however, about one-third of cases do conform, vastly more than in the most deviating countries of Table 4.4.

The Radicals of the French Fourth Republic emerge in this case as a mainstream model of Liberal preferences for ministries. Even where ministries which we have posited as first priority were not taken (and thus counted as failures by our hypotheses), the ones actually taken were Education and Industry, which we had regarded as lower-ranking Liberal preferences. The same pattern holds true for the Italian Republicans and Liberals (aggregated in Table 4.5); the Republicans, however, conform in almost every respect while the PLI is much more deviant.

The vast majority of Liberal parties exhibit consistent patterns of choice in line with expectations. This contrast with Conservative parties is perhaps due, as well as to the particular circumstances discussed above, to the looser ideology and cohesion of some of the traditional Conservative groups. Nevertheless even the Conservative results do marginally confirm initial ideas, though less strikingly than Table 4.5. We now proceed to a similar test of our expectations for the fourth group, religious parties—summarized in Figure 4.4 and checked in Table 4.6.

Very consistent patterns of success appear here for the Low Countries, West Germany, and Italy. It is perhaps significant that these are the countries where Christian Democrats are strongest and practically always dominant when in government (and so, presumably, most able to see that their preferences are met). In contrast the Danish Christian People's Party is small and weak and fails to obtain any preference. Nevertheless, the corresponding Norwegian party is reasonably (and consistently) successful.

Israel is interesting in that it is the country where religious affairs

TABLE 4.6. Acquisition of ministries by religious parties in nine countries

	Takes ministries expected over all criteria		If largest, takes premiership		Takes Religious Affairs		Takes other ministries as predicted[a]		Acquires ministries in rough proportion to seats		Acquisition conforms broadly to expectations	
	Cases	Success rate of prediction	Cases	Success rate of prediction	Cases	Success rate of prediction	Cases	Success rate of prediction	Cases	Success rate of prediction	Cases	Success rate of prediction
Belgium[b]	81	0.96	19	0.84	—	—	19	1.00	19	0.64	19	0.89
Denmark	2	0.00	—	—	2	0.00	—	—	2	1.00	2	0.00
France 4[b]	76	0.51	12	0.42	—	—	25	0.36	25	0.32	25	0.16
West Germany[b]	41	0.90	9	1.00	—	—	9	0.55	9	0.60	9	1.00
Israel	94	0.52	—	—	29	0.80	29	0.00	29	0.74	29	0.55
Italy[b]	101	0.92	33	0.91	—	—	33	0.93	33	0.39	33	0.90
Luxemburg	45	0.84	12	1.00	1	1.00	11	0.73	11	0.63	11	1.00
Netherlands[b]	81	0.73	17	0.71	—	—	17	0.53	17	0.72	17	0.76
Norway	16	0.69	—	—	5	0.60	5	0.80	5	0.80	5	0.60
All countries	537	0.74	102	0.82	34	0.76	148	0.57	150	0.54	150	0.67

[a] i.e. where there is no partner with competing preference and up to the limit imposed by the proportion or government seats which it contributes. The other ministries in question are Education, Agriculture, Social Affairs, and Labour.
[b] Ministry of Religious Affairs does not exist in this country.

intrude most into everyday social and economic life. Expectations here are handsomely fulfilled as the National Religious Party almost always participates in government and takes the religious ministry in such a high proportion of cases as to make it clear that this is a normal practice. Where expectations break down in Israel is in regard to Agriculture. In light of the traditional exclusion of Jews from farming it is clear that there are none of the traditional affiliations found elsewhere between the religious party and the peasantry, so no special reason for the NRP to claim this ministry. Otherwise it does quite frequently hold Health, Social Welfare, Labour, and Education as expected, even in coalition with Socialist Labour and Liberal parties.

If Israel can be said to conform to expectations in all respects except for religious parties' possession of the Agriculture Ministry, the same cannot be said for the Mouvement républicain populaire under the French Fourth Republic. Possibly this is due to its ideology being newer and more progressive than that of other Christian Democratic parties, or perhaps to the competition of traditional established groupings like the Radicals and Independent Conservatives, which deprived it of Agriculture. Under the crisis-ridden conditions of the Fourth Republic the MRP was one of the 'natural' government parties, along with the Socialists and the Radicals, and so tended to get central ministries like the Interior and Foreign Affairs rather than the humbler, more client-orientated ones we attribute to Christian Democrats in Figure 4.4. Whatever the explanation, the MRP does not behave like most of the other parties in the table. This does not unduly depress the total results, which confirm the relative success of the representation in most countries.

The most successful representation among the 'multi-issue', more ideologically orientated parties is that for the Socialists, in Figure 4.5—results for which are given in Table 4.7. Success shows in the proportion for general fit of the representation across all countries (0.75), in the proportion of ministries going where expected (0.79), and the proportion of cases where the Welfare and Labour ministries go to Socialists (or are divided with Christian Democrats, as anticipated). Complications enter in with ministries of lower priority such as Economy, Finance, and Education, where the overall proportion of successes is only 0.56. It is of course anticipated that such lower-priority ministries are more likely to be traded, or affected by strategic and tactical considerations.

Of the individual countries, Finland and the French Fourth

TABLE 4.7. Acquisition of ministries by Socialist parties in thirteen countries

	Takes ministries expected over all criteria		If largest, takes premiership		Takes Labour, Health, Social Affairs, as predicted[a]		Takes Economy, Industry, Education, as predicted[a]		Acquires ministries in rough proportion to seats		Acquisition conforms broadly to expectations	
	Cases	Success rate of prediction	Cases	Success rate of prediction	Cases	Success rate of prediction	Cases	Success rate of prediction	Cases	Success rate of prediction	Cases	Success rate of prediction
Austria	26	0.54	1	1.00	13	1.00	13	0.08	13	0.54	13	1.00
Belgium	44	0.88	8	0.37	15	1.00	12	0.92	15	0.33	15	0.80
Denmark	26	0.92	7	1.00	7	0.71	1	0.00	7	0.14	7	0.86
Finland	96	0.62	24	0.50	25	0.80	7	0.57	25	0.54	25	0.56
France 4	44	0.79	4	0.25	18	0.66	2	1.00	18	0.33	18	0.55
West Germany	25	1.00	6	1.00	6	1.00	1	1.00	6	0.33	6	1.00
Iceland	10	0.80	1	0.00	7	1.00	2	0.50	7	0.28	7	0.71
Ireland	15	0.60	—	—	5	0.60	5	0.40	5	0.20	5	0.60
Israel	68	0.93	26	1.00	26	0.80	5	1.00	26	0.74	26	0.85
Italy	24	0.79	—	—	17	0.76	2	1.00	17	0.65	17	0.71
Luxemburg	16	0.87	1	0.00	6	0.83	4	1.00	6	0.75	6	0.83
Netherlands	25	0.80	1	1.00	9	0.88	4	0.25	9	0.55	9	0.88
Sweden	15	0.80	3	1.00	3	1.00	3	0.00	3	0.33	3	1.00
All countries	434	0.79	82	0.74	157	0.82	61	0.56	157	0.50	157	0.75

[a] i.e. where there is no partner with competing preference and up to the limit imposed by the proportion of government seats which it contributes.

Republic are less well fitted, particularly in regard to taking the premiership when largest—though in both cases Socialists take their 'core' ministries most of the time. Of course these two cases are the ones which fairly consistently deviate for other types of party too, for reasons we have gone into before. Ireland is the other exception —which is perhaps explained by the Irish Labour Party's small size and relative marginality.

The better fit of the Socialist representation compared to that for the other 'general' party families (leaving aside the single-issue Agrarian), can plausibly be accounted for by a more developed ideology and the cohesion this gives to party goals and objectives, including the possession and use of ministries. These should reveal themselves, as they seem to do, in a greater ability to obtain relevant ministries. In contrast, Conservative ideologies vary more across different countries, and at many points consist more in an adherence to pragmatism than to anything else. Hence one would expect the success of a general representation to be more mixed, as it is.

The Liberal and religious families fall between these extreme cases. Again this positioning is plausible, given the coexistence of two diverse types of liberalism on the one hand, and on the other the extreme factionalism of the Italian Christian Democrats and the relatively conservative attitudes of the Germans and Luxemburgers compared to the relatively progressive character of the Christian Democratic Appeal in the Netherlands (not to bring in Israel's National Religious or Sephardic parties!).

The actual pattern of results is thus consistent with the idea that preferences for ministries are reflections, within each party family, of a policy stance which may be more or less articulated but which is always there. Variations in the extent to which expected ministries are actually acquired, taken in conjunction with the extent to which ideology has actually been articulated, are perfectly compatible with this idea. While there are inconsistencies in the findings, on the whole they do display a remarkable degree of 'patterning' given the enormous range of situations and circumstances from which they derive —enough to make most previous researchers conclude that only limited regularities exist.[10] The relative success of the policy-based representation in explaining allocations, in this most difficult area for its presuppositions, certainly provides a good basis for the direct analysis of the policy outputs of government in the next chapter.

One aspect of Table 4.7 has not been discussed up to this point: that is the match between parties' share of seats and their share of ministries. A good correspondence is found for Israel and Luxemburg —two disparate cases in one of which the Socialists were dominant in government over most of the period, in the other of which they were strictly subordinate players on the political scene. In most other cases a small party has been able to get disproportionately high shares of ministries, which has benefited Socialists where they themselves were small (in Iceland and Ireland for example) and worked against them where they themselves were dominant (in Denmark and Germany for example). Over all the parties examined there is a match between the proportions of ministries and seats of within 5 per cent in only about half the cases examined. In this respect there is little difference between the party families.

Fifty per cent could be regarded as rather a high match or a rather low one, depending on point of view. On the one hand there is the 'lumpiness' of the distribution owing both to technical factors (per-centaging ministries which total less than ten—even where the base is twenty each step must perforce be of 5 per cent) and to considerations of tactics and bargaining, which militate against a neat final solution. The general proportionality relationship, however, has been so much emphasized and emerged so strongly from various examinations that one might have expected a closer fit in more cases.

The matter cannot in any case be resolved without a general examination of the extent to which the share of ministries goes up or down with the share of seats contributed to the government. It is only through such a general analysis that the proportionality assumptions of our theory and models, as well as the findings of previous research, can be adequately tested. Accordingly we devote the last section of this chapter to a detailed quantitative investigation of the relationship.

PROPORTIONALITY: THE GENERAL RELATIONSHIP BETWEEN SEATS AND MINISTRIES

In actual fact, once the question is stated in terms of ministries going up with seats rather than precise percentage-matching, all the evidence points in one direction—that is, towards a strong relationship. We checked this on different data sets, with slightly different assumptions built into them, on parties' shares of *ministers* in the Cabinet as opposed to their share of *ministries* (since what is at stake is a vote in Cabinet and one man casts only one vote, so the proportion of ministers might be more significant than the proportion of ministries); within the different party families across countries and within countries, and even within party families within countries! As Table 4.8 demonstrates, there is little difference whichever basis is used: the relationship remains constantly strong. (Because of limitations of space the table does not report results for party families within countries, but they show the same relationships.)

The major difference between Paloheimo's count of ministries going to each party[11] and ours (apart from inevitable errors and slightly different time periods) is in the reckoning of non-aligned ministries. In such cases we calculate the total number as being *all* Cabinet Ministries whether non-aligned or partisan, while Paloheimo bases his on the total *partisan* in the Cabinet. While the different approaches show divergences in detail, it is obvious that the broad conclusions based on them are essentially similar: shares of ministries go up and down with shares of seats. So do shares of *ministers*. This conclusion emerges so powerfully, as well as being strongly confirmed in previous research, that there is no need of measures of significance to show it is not a chance finding.

Inspection of the combined and individual figures reveals that the broad central tendency for levels of ministries and seats to correspond is always there (as it is in Tables 4.3 to 4.7), but there are many discrepancies and deviations from an exact matching. France under the Fourth Republic is the only example of a country where proportionality cannot be said to apply as a predominant tendency, however. In the case of some parties (notably small parties) the share of ministries is consistently higher than the share of seats. Large parties' shares often come below their share of seats, but this is not as general a trend.

The variations in the precise degree of correspondence between ministry shares and seat shares imply that exact proportionality is not such a dominating constraint on the final distribution of ministries as was assumed in the flow diagrams. It is obviously there as a consideration, and parties (even in pursuit of clearly cherished posts) cannot depart from it too much. Exact matching are not always possible to obtain, however, nor even desirable in some cases. Small parties benefit particularly for three reasons:

1. They must be given at least one ministry, which at 5 per cent of the Cabinet, not to say 10 per cent in some cases, may be way above their seat contribution.

TABLE 4.8. The relationship between numbers of legislative seats and of ministries gained, for various data sets, party families, and countries, 1945–1984

	Budge–Keman (Ministries)			Paloheimo (Ministries)			Budge–Keman (Ministers)		
	r	b	β	r	b	β	r	b	β
Party									
(all countries)									
All	0.89	0.75	0.89	0.91	0.78	0.91	0.91	0.77	0.91
Agrarian	0.77	0.76	0.77	0.93	0.86	0.93	0.92	0.80	0.92
Conservative	0.87	0.75	0.87	0.88	0.80	0.88	0.89	0.80	0.89
Liberal	0.85	0.97	0.85	0.79	0.83	0.79	0.84	0.94	0.84
Socialist	0.90	0.79	0.90	0.92	0.85	0.92	0.91	0.79	0.91
Religious	0.94	0.76	0.94	0.94	0.76	0.94	0.96	0.78	0.96
Country									
(all parties)									
Austria	0.81	0.83	0.81	0.78	0.88	0.78	0.81	0.86	0.81
Belgium	0.84	0.65	0.84	0.83	0.62	0.83	0.84	0.64	0.84
Denmark	0.93	0.70	0.93	0.93	0.64	0.93	0.93	0.64	0.93
Finland	0.76	0.71	0.76	0.92	0.84	0.92	0.86	0.74	0.86
France 4	0.40	0.48	0.40	0.46	0.47	0.46	0.46	0.51	0.46
5	0.83	0.66	0.83	0.85	0.72	0.85	0.87	0.68	0.87
West Germany	0.98	0.78	0.98	0.99	0.83	0.99	0.99	0.83	0.99
Iceland	0.63	0.50	0.63	0.82	0.54	0.82	0.70	0.53	0.70
Ireland	0.93	0.70	0.93	0.98	0.85	0.98	0.99	0.86	0.99
Israel	0.97	0.88	0.97	0.99	0.98	0.99	0.99	0.90	0.99
Italy	0.97	0.69	0.97	0.95	0.64	0.95	0.97	0.69	0.97
Luxemburg	0.81	0.65	0.81	0.84	0.67	0.84	0.88	0.67	0.88
Netherlands	0.90	0.84	0.90	0.96	0.83	0.96	0.94	0.82	0.94
Norway	0.94	0.80	0.94	0.97	0.85	0.97	0.97	0.86	0.97
Sweden	0.96	0.75	0.96	0.99	0.76	0.99	0.97	0.86	0.97

Note: r, the bivariate correlation coefficient, shows the extent to which the various points in a scattergram deviate from the best-fitting line for the whole set of points. b is the regression coefficient in the bivariate regression equation matching ministry-shares and seat-shares, as follows: MINSHARE = CONSTANT + b SEATSHARE. It is the slope of the best-fitting line. β is the equivalent of b when MINSHARE and SEATSHARE are expressed in the same standardized units (standard deviation units). Raw numbers were used in this statistical analysis as the 'lumpiness' of percentages based on limited numbers of cases would somewhat distort results.

2. They often have a key role in facilitating the emergence of a particular coalition, which enables them to demand more than they are strictly entitled to.

3. It costs relatively little to large parties, which in a two-partner coalition will get the lion's share anyway, to concede more to small parties.

These qualifications will be taken into account in our overall assessment in Chapter 7. They represent minor modifications, simply shifts of emphasis, in the basic argument, which has been substantially upheld by various checks in this chapter. The major point is that parties clearly do have substantive preferences for particular ministries, based on an enduring ideology and related policy concerns. So regular and strong are these that they can be specified in considerable detail, as we have done in Figures 4.1 to 4.5. It would be incredible if such concerns, besides affecting choice of ministries, did not also centrally influence government policy-making. It is to this major activity of parties in government that we dedicate the next chapter.

5

Party Influences on Government Policy

Our fundamental assumption is that parties enter governments to influence policy-making and to control policy implementation (Table 2.1 Assumption 2). The main finding of Chapter 4, that parties seek ministries related to their own interests and commitments, buttresses that view. Here we check the argument directly by seeing how far governments of different types adopt different approaches and implement different policies in line with the preferences previously attributed to party families (Table 4.2). If they do, it is a fair inference that constituent parties are actively seeking to pull policy in their own direction and that this has a great deal to do with their entry into government in the first place.

PRELIMINARY CONSIDERATIONS

Before directly checking party–policy linkages, we have as usual to clarify our procedures and to resolve certain operational difficulties. The first of these relates to the period over which we carry out the analyses—particularly of expenditures. For government formation and the distribution of ministries we have information over the whole post-war period. It is, however, almost impossible to get a reliable set of expenditure figures for even one country before the sixties in most policy fields; and totally impossible to get comparable information over a number of countries before then. The expenditures we examine are thus limited for the most part to the years between 1965 and 1983 (inclusive). Occasionally we can find more extended evidence which we bring to bear on a particular hypothesis. Most aspects of the theory have to be checked for those specific years, however, which in spite of international crisis and recession were generally more secure and prosperous than those of the first two post-war decades. This inhibits comparisons of policy-making under different circumstances (democratic crises and non-crises, socialist–bourgeois confrontations, and more relaxed political periods). However, it does not hinder us from checking the major thrust of our theoretical argument, which is squarely on the different emphases placed by party families on particular policies, in line with their long-standing preferences and commitments (Table 2.4 Implications 3(i)–3(v)).

We test these central hypotheses in three ways, each of which catches a particular aspect of party policy pursuit. In the first we look at policy differences when control is in the hands of bourgeois or socialist parties. Whether or not the questions dividing them are at the centre of political attention, with parties of the different families clustering within their own tendance, we can expect broad policy differences to emerge between the contrasting forms of party government and to be reflected in their actions and decisions. When Left–Right confrontation is not central, we do not necessarily expect governments to be purely of one tendance or another. To the extent that they are more bourgeois- or more socialist-dominated, however, we would expect their policies to veer more in the appropriate direction.

The degree to which parties are free to get their policies through depends also on whether a government is single-party or a coalition, and whether it commands a majority or minority of seats in the legislature. So we have to look at socialist–bourgeois differences in conjunction with their governmental position, in order to see how freely they have been able to put their particular preferences into effect. A Socialist party or grouping in a majority position without bourgeois partners should be freer to pass reforming measures than when it is in a minority and/or in a partly bourgeois coalition. The same holds for bourgeois parties of course with respect to their characteristic policies.

Chapter 4 especially has made the point that bourgeois parties are not an undifferentiated mass, and that Conservatives, Liberals, and Christian Democrats may differ quite sharply on priorities among themselves. The policy differences between these party families form our second level of analysis. Coalition governments will tend to associate parties of different families; to the extent that one participates in government, however, we expect to see policy differences compared to governments from which it is absent.

A third approach to the question of party influences focuses not on governments as a whole but on their constituent ministries. If parties have consistent preferences for particular types of ministry, as from our preceding analysis they appear to have, this is because control enhances their ability to influence and above all to implement policy, and thus to tilt State intervention in their own direction. In this chapter we shall see whether control over particular types of ministry is indeed reflected in their policies and outputs (Table 2.4 Implication 3(v)).

To carry through all these analyses we have developed various measures which represent the level and nature of government activity in various policy areas—social welfare, economic intervention, and external security. We examine them not only in isolation but also in regard to interactions and trade-offs between them. By looking individually at specific fields we hope to avoid the complications of comparing monetary aggregates for all the different areas lumped together, across all countries. Because of the incompatible nature of the expenditures making up the aggregate, the results of this kind of analysis often remain ambiguous. By concentrating on the individual areas of expenditure we hope not to add 'stones to rabbits'.[1]

The fact that we concentrate on specific areas also absolves us from 'controlling' for all the external disturbances which might affect the statistical results, and from employing very elaborate techniques to achieve this. As we are testing the well-defined hypothesis that political parties and their official representatives are able to direct and influence public policy in the given field, we can afford for the most part to employ very simple statistical techniques such as pairwise comparisons, which focus attention on the substantive relationships under review rather than on elaborate statistical assumptions.

It is of course true that overall characterizations of policy are sometimes necessary (to relate general policy in a field to party control of the relevant ministries, for example). In such cases we have chosen not to aggregate expenditures but to make a holistic judgement about the nature of the policy package that has been adopted (see the discussion immediately below of alternative 'types' of economic policy). While an evaluation of expenditures certainly comes in, such judgements are essentially qualitative in nature, and far from mechanical aggregation of disparate figures.

We now turn to the presentation and operationalization of the variables we shall use, which permit a precise specification of our hypotheses linking government composition to policy outputs. The empirical analysis itself will be reported in the subsequent sections.

MEASURING AND RELATING 'PARTY' AND 'POLICY'

The key factor affecting State policy we see as the ideological preferences of the party or parties in government. We classify this at our first level of analysis, that of general 'tendance', through the number of Cabinet Ministries held by bourgeois and by socialist parties, as follows:

1. If bourgeois or socialists hold 100 per cent of the Cabinet posts, we have a bourgeois or socialist *single-party government*.
2. If the percentage is between 67 and 100, we have a situation we can characterize as bourgeois or socialist *dominance*.
3. If the percentages are between 33 and 66 the tendances are taken as *balanced*.

We can locate party families in broadly the same way, taking account of whether they form a single government on their own, are in a bourgeois- or socialist-dominated coalition, or in a balanced coalition. While the nature of the coalition will affect their ability to carry through preferred policies, the assumption that they are basically in government to promote these leads to the expectation that there will be discernible policy effects from their participation.

Through these classifications we have measures both of the ideological tendances of the government and of the general ability of one or the other to impose its will within the government. There is also of course a question of how far the government is united and free to impose itself on legislature and opposition. This will vary with exact relationships between coalition partners and with the majority or minority status of the government in Parliament. The broad and approximate nature of our data does not permit us to take all these possible influences into account. We expect a party's presence in government to pull policy to some extent in the direction of its preferences (otherwise it would not be there) and therefore concentrate on the differences between bourgeois and socialist single-party government, and between dominant and balanced coalitions as we have outlined them above.

Regardless of what goes on at the Cabinet and parliamentary levels, we also expect the party which controls a particular ministry to have a disproportionate influence within the corresponding policy field. For the most part there is little problem in specifying the ministries important for each field: the external security, the Ministries of Foreign Affairs and Defence: for social welfare, those of Social Affairs, Education, and Health. The Ministry of Labour is in an ambiguous position, linked to social welfare but also extremely important in macro-economic planning, and thus more naturally grouped with Economy and Finance under 'economic affairs'.

The Prime Ministership (and Deputy Prime Ministership if there is one) will of course impinge on all fields. It will be particularly influential, however, in arranging trade-offs and deciding priorities between one area of policy and another, since Prime Ministers will naturally intervene to mediate quarrels between ministries and to co-ordinate policies generally.

Government policies within the three fields we have distinguished can all be measured most directly and easily by relevant expenditures (or, often, by the percentage change in relevant expenditures from one year to the next). As noted above, more holistic characterizations of general policy are sometimes necessary. The major area where the qualitative character of policy must be taken into account is economic affairs (and to a lesser extent, social welfare, for which see the following section).

Government policies towards the economy from 1965 to 1983 are empirically distinguishable into four main types. Each of these consists of a package of measures which, on the whole, are not logically entailed one by the other but cohere because they are pursued concurrently by governments. These packages bear a broad relationship to, and were often justified in terms of, particular economic theories, such as (in order) (i) Keynesianism, (ii) supply-side economics, (iii) Monetarism, and (iv) Neo-Liberalism. Governments, however ideologically inspired, are rarely consistent appliers of economic doctrine. So although each of the empirically distinguishable packages would find a general justification in some economic theory, it is by no means totally consistent with it. Our justification for the characterization is that this is the way governments and parties in fact put their policies together. The typology does of course meet the normal criteria of comprehensiveness and distinguishability of the categories.

The four leading types of economic policy which can be distinguished for 1965–83 are:

(i) Fiscal directiveness—a relatively strong emphasis on fiscal policy instruments, with relative indifference to the money supply. The level of public spending is manipulated to influence the level of general demand, and goes into deficit if necessary to maintain it (and as a consequence also to maintain employment levels).

(ii) Fiscal caution: the long-term aim is to reduce public spending and taxes so as to increase individual and production incentives. In the short run, however, public deficits may be tolerated so long as they are balanced by a suitable rate of economic growth.

(iii) Fiscal withdrawal, influened by a perceived need to relate the amount of money in circulation to the rate of economic growth. The normal strategy to get the money supply under control is to avoid deficit spending and indeed to reduce public expenditure in general, without taking other considerations into account.

(iv) Fiscal minimalism—dedicated to letting free markets produce their own solutions, and thus rejecting State economic activity outside its traditional narrowly defined functions.

While levels of State expenditure may be expected to go down from (i) to (iv), one needs to look at qualitative indications (government declarations, speeches, etc.) to determine precisely whether the given policy is, for instance, one of fiscal caution rather than fiscal directiveness. One obviously expects Socialist parties to be associated with the first two approaches and bourgeois parties with the latter two.

So far we have talked of the three fields of external security, social welfare, and economics separately, as if none had effects on any of the others. Such an assumption can hold only up to a certain point, however. As social welfare and defence both account for large proportions of public expenditure, it is unrealistic to regard decisions within one field as independent either of the other or of economic affairs. Indeed, the relationships are closer even than the possibility of trade-offs between warfare and welfare, as economic policy itself may aim to contribute directly to welfare by reducing unemployment. (Fiscal direction is explicitly designed to do so.) Besides ranking governments separately on their concern for 'social welfare' and 'economic welfare' (associated with the degree of interventionism) one can also rank them on a combined measure of 'overall welfare concern' incorporating both elements. We would expect Socialists and Christian Democrats to favour welfare most and Liberals and Conservatives least. As between Socialists and Christian Democrats, the former are likely to be committed equally to social and economic welfare while the latter favour social welfare more, partly because it can be channelled into direct support for the family, a main point of reference in Catholic social doctrine.

Because of the common commitment of all party families to security of the democratic order, levels of defence expenditure are likely to vary less over time than levels in the other areas. Conservatives, with their traditional support for order and security are, however, likely to adopt worst-case expectations and hold out for higher levels of expenditure even in times of *détente* and economic crisis, while Socialists and to a lesser extent Christian Democrats will tend to endorse more optimistic international scenarios and uphold welfare priorities as against military ones. Liberals with their concern for public goods provision should come between the two.

As noted above, control of the Prime Ministership may be important in deciding how money is to be allocated to areas. It is, of course, not necessarily the case that one type of expenditure must be increased at the expense of the other: both could increase or fall together, with economic growth or decline. Below we examine all four possibilities.[2]

Each of the following sections is devoted to examination of a policy field or of the relationship between them. We start with social welfare, then proceed to economics, then combined social and economic welfare, then defence, and finish with trade-offs and pay-offs between defence and social welfare. The concluding section evaluates the overall relationship between party control and government policy, and assimilates them to our previous findings on government formation and the control of ministries.

SOCIAL WELFARE

As indicated above, our judgements about the level of social welfare are based on expenditures in the areas of health, social security (pensions and direct payments to the disadvantaged), and education. State education is a social service even though, as pointed out in Chapter 4, parties' primary interest in it probably stems from a desire to spread their own beliefs and ideology rather than from concern with welfare as such. However, their general attitudes to social welfare should spill over into decisions about educational spending, so in this regard we are justified in aggregating it with other expenditures in the field.

Simply aggregating expenditures gives a reasonable but probably not optimal measure of social welfare, as additional qualitative considerations enter in. Some countries, for example, emphasize health and education at the expense of social security, and vice versa. As one may get a greater output of services for a given expenditure in one area compared to another, some countries and governments may, on a simple aggregation of expenditures across subfields, be ranked lower than the quality of their services really merits. Then again we have to take into account relative efficiency in delivery of services for a given input of money. All these considerations point to developing a rank-ordering for the strength of the Welfare State, from 1 (a highly developed welfare state) to 4 (a weakly developed one), rather than comparing expenditures directly. The relative level of expenditure is still of course an important element in the ranking.

Although rank-ordering is inevitably less sensitive than the numeric information provided by actual expenditures, which respond directly to all sorts of differences between governments, it follows from what we have said that this sensitivity may be misleading. Expenditures reflect variations which may be irrelevant to deciding whether *parties* make a difference: if differences are reflected in a considered rank-ordering, however, we can be surer that they are significant and relevant. In point of fact the need to produce enough cases to make illuminating comparisons for each cell of the table often forces us to group cases more drastically, into a dichotomy. This is not desirable but inevitable given the nature of the data. These limitations force us in Table 5.1 to dichotomize the type of government in which the parties of each family find themselves to 'single-party' (whether majority or minority) and 'coalition' (of whatever type). In later tables we have been able to classify some coalitions, for some party families (where there are enough cases), according to the type of party combination which constitutes them. This serves to give a rough idea of the ease or difficulty a party of a given type would experience in getting its policies accepted by the government as a whole.

Table 5.1 looks at the relationship between party family (within the different government situations described above) and the existence of a strong or weak Welfare State over two periods of time individually

TABLE 5.1. The relationship between party family and social welfare provision 1965–1983, across nineteen countries

Party family	Government type	Welfare State								
		1965–73			1974–84			1965–84		
		Strong (%)	Weak (%)	N	Strong (%)	Weak (%)	N	Strong (%)	Weak(%)	N
1. Conservative	Single-party	7.3	92.7	41	5.7	94.3	35	6.5	93.5	76
2. Conservative	Coalition	73.5	26.5	34	25.9	74.1	26	52.5	47.5	60
3. Liberal	Single-party	25.0	75.0	8	20.0	80.0	12	22.5	77.5	20
4. Liberal	Coalition	77.8	22.2	15	83.3	16.7	15	78.5	21.5	30
5. Religious	Single-party	33.3	66.7	6	33.3	66.7	3	33.3	66.7	9
6. Religious	Coalition	90.0	10.0	18	63.2	36.8	19	76.6	23.4	37
7. Socialist	Single-party	86.4	13.6	22	69.8	30.2	43	78.1	21.9	65
8. Socialist	Coalition	83.3	16.7	18	70.4	29.6	27	76.9	23.1	45

Note: 'Strong' indicates a ranking of 1 or 2, 'Weak' a ranking of 3 or 4; *N* stands for country-years, the units on which the table is based. Switzerland is not included in the statistics because the nature of decision-making within the permanent coalition renders inappropriate the seeking of party influences on policy.

(1965–73 and 1974–84) and together (1965–84). The reason for distinguishing between the earlier and the later period is to see whether the same relationships hold for a time of relative economic stability and prosperity and general Leftward pressures, and a time of relative instability, stagnation, and pressures towards strict economic orthodoxy.

It is evident from comparing percentages for the two periods, looking along the rows of Table 5.1, that the 'goodness' or 'badness' of the times do exert effects but that this is very much mediated by the type of parties which are in government. The cases where the 'oil shock' and the onset of economic recession made most difference are coalitions in which the Conservatives participated (row 2) and to a much lesser extent coalitions in which Christian Democrats participated (row 6). In both cases it seems likely that the arguments of the parties with more restrictive attitudes were reinforced by crisis, so that government response to economic change is far from automatic. On the contrary, it seems strongly mediated by party ideologies, as one can see from the continuing 'Welfare Statism' of governments with Socialist participation (rows 7 and 8). Obviously the world recession has *some* effects, as in the case of most types of government, but they are relatively minor in this case (though in fact coalitions with Liberal participation (row 4) not only maintain but increase welfare provision, a slight anomaly with regard to our expectations.)

Turning to direct comparisons of welfare provision between different types of government we can see immediately how important and pervasive the influence of party is. Single-party Conservative rule for example (row 1) is almost uniquely associated with less extensive welfare provision. Cases ranked at the very bottom of the ordering in terms of provision (3.5 and below) always occur under a Conservative-dominated government. The contrary is true for governments dominated by or totally composed of Socialists.

Christian Democrats presumably second the efforts of Socialists when they are in government with them (row 6). It is surprising and goes against expectations that Christian Democrats in government on their own (row 5) make relatively low provision for welfare. As against this, one can point out that (i) it is more than that made by Liberal single-party governments, as expected (Liberal expenditures are also less resistant to general economic pressures (row 3) while Christian Democratic provision remains stable between the two periods); (ii) the party families in single-party governments are ranked as expected on level of provision: Socialist, Christian Democrat, Liberal, Conservative.

The fact that the widest gap opens up between single-party Socialist governments and others points to the influence of broad tendances, rather than party family as such, being predominant in welfare decisions. And indeed the cross-national correlation coefficient between tendance on the one hand (measured in terms of the proportion of Cabinet Ministries held by each) and degree of welfare provision is 0.52 before 1973 and 0.44 after 1974. The variance associated with tendance is a not unimpressive figure given the host of other factors affecting welfare provision.

As we have constantly emphasized, however, control of implementation at ministerial level may be more important in shaping welfare than formal government decisions, certainly in a coalition. Accordingly, Table 5.2 relates party control of the relevant ministries within coalition governments to level of provision. In this table we have the full rank-order for welfare provision, from 1 (very high) to 4 (very low). Looking down the rows of the table we can see, first, the effects of Conservatives having the major share of the relevant ministries where either Liberals or Socialists have the minor share. In no case of Conservative dominance was welfare provision very high: in almost-three-quarters it was low (a little paradoxically, where Socialists held the minor share of ministries). Liberals on the other hand, even though their ministries are always shared with Conservatives, seem to ensure a very high or high degree of welfare provision.

The bulk of the cases examined, however, are ones where Christian Democrats or Socialists have most of the relevant ministries—and not by chance, if we bear in mind the hypotheses and findings of Chapter 4. For these are the ministries actively sought by the two parties on ideological grounds. (Liberals may find themselves in this field because of rather differently based interests in education.) Christian and Socialist dominance is associated overwhelmingly with very high or high provision—more so for Christians than Socialists. Christian Democratic dominance with Socialist participation seems the optimal combination for welfare, with the reverse situation also being favourable. Generally, Christian dominance, even with Liberal participation, is associated with a higher degree of welfare provision; but a Liberal presence, in other cases, even with Socialist dominance, seems to depress welfare.

TABLE 5.2. The relationship between party control of the relevant policy sector in coalition governments and social welfare provision, 1965–1983

Party family — Dominant in sector	Coalition partner	% of country-years of government — Degree of social welfare provision				% of total	Country-years of government
		1	2	3	4		
Conservative	Liberal	0.0	14.3	0.0	0.0	14.6	14
	Religious	0.0	0.0	0.0	0.0		
	Socialist	0.0	14.3	71.4	0.0		
Liberal	Conservative	50.0	50.0	0.0	0.0	10.4	10
	Religious	0.0	0.0	0.0	0.0		
	Socialist	0.0	0.0	0.0	0.0		
Religious	Conservative	0.0	4.8	0.0	0.0	43.8	42
	Liberal	14.3	14.3	2.4	0.0		
	Socialist	33.3	26.2	4.8	0.0		
Socialist	Conservative	0.0	0.0	10.0	0.0	31.3	30
	Liberal	3.3	50.0	13.3	0.0		
	Religious	20.0	3.3	0.0	0.0		

Note: The relevant ministries are Social Affairs, Health, and Education. Switzerland is not included in the statistics for the reason given in Table 5.1.

On the whole, in spite of such minor inconsistencies, our expectations are unheld by Table 5.2. The major contrast between Conservative dominance in the sector, on the one hand, and Christian and Socialist dominance on the other, comes through strongly. Coupled with the findings of Table 5.1 on the relative performance of different types of government, it clearly upholds the relevant implications of Table 2.4. By showing that parties have consistent policy records in government, it also sustains our basic assumption that the opportunity to implement policy preferences spurs party desire for office and participation in government in the first place.

ECONOMIC POLICY

We can pursue investigation of this link further by looking at economic policy. Arguably, because of its intended effect on employment and inflation and indirect effects on the financing of the Welfare State, government priorities in this area are even more important than in welfare provision. In the aftermath of the severest economic crisis in post-war history, the extent and nature of political intervention in this area has become an essential—if not *the* essential—policy concern of contemporary governments, after thirty years in which Keynesianism was an accepted (if not consistently applied) orthodoxy. As we shall see, however, party does affect the choice of policy even before 1973.

This appears graphically in Table 5.3, where one can trace a progression, albeit a slightly irregular one, from top to bottom and right to left of the table. This indicates a concentration by Conservative governments and coalitions on monetary policies linked to cuts in public expenditure, compared with the Liberal clustering on fiscal caution and the greater support of Christians and Socialists for both fiscal directiveness and caution (Socialists, paradoxically, seem more committed to directiveness in coalitions (row 8) than in single-party governments on their own account (row 7)).

Such anomalies contribute disproportionately to lowering the correlation coefficients between overall tendance and the type of economic policy adopted (attenuated in any case by relating the dichotomy socialist–bourgeois to a rank-ordering of policies, from 1 for directiveness to 4 for minimalism). Under these circumstances the

TABLE 5.3. The relationship between party family and economic policy, 1965–1983, across nineteen countries

Party family	Government type	Policy pursued (% of country-years)								Total country-years
		Fiscal directiveness		Fiscal caution		Fiscal withdrawal		Fiscal minimalism		
		65–73	74–83	65–73	74–83	65–73	74–83	65–73	74–83	
1. Conservative	Single-party	23.7	17.1	5.3	8.6	23.4	25.7	47.7	48.6	76
2. Conservative	Coalition	2.9	7.7	29.4	30.8	26.5	7.7	41.2	46.1	60
3. Liberal	Single-party	12.5	33.3	62.5	67.7	12.5	0.0	12.5	0.0	20
4. Liberal	Coalition	0.0	13.3	54.5	60.0	45.5	13.3	0.0	13.4	30
5. Religious	Single-party	50.0	66.7	33.3	33.3	16.7	0.0	0.0	0.0	9
6. Religious	Coalition	48.0	41.0	5.6	18.0	20.4	4.6	26.0	36.4	37
7. Socialist	Single-party	28.6	14.8	32.1	44.4	32.1	37.1	7.2	3.7	65
8. Socialist	Coalition	44.6	50.7	13.2	17.6	13.2	4.4	29.0	27.9	45

Switzerland is not included in the statistics for the reasons given in Table 5.1.

correlation coefficient is as low as 0.15 before 1973 and 0.25 after-wards. This result is not due entirely to outliers and methodological artefacts, however, as Table 5.3 shows clearly that the policy divide lies more between the different party families than between tend-ances: in particular it is hard to distinguish between Christians and Socialists in this area.

We can refine these conclusions by again looking at effects associ-ated with party control of the relevant ministries (Labour, Economy, Finance). The inclusion of Labour, which we have seen represents a prime objective for Socialists (and Christians, because of its effects on overall welfare), explains the high representation of these families in Table 5.4. Switzerland is again omitted from the sectoral table because the highly collective nature of the Federal Executive renders party influence in a particular ministry irrelevant.

The relationship between party family controlling ministries and type of policy is stronger and more consistent than the relationships at governmental level reported in Table 5.3. Socialists and Christians, with very few exceptions, endorse fiscal directiveness or fiscal caution. Liberals and Conservatives tend towards orthodox and restrictive policies (Conservatives more so). These findings are reinforced by twelve cases not shown in Table 5.4 because control of the sector was shared equally by three parties: in six cases between Conservatives, Liberals, and Christians, and in six cases between Socialists, Chris-tians, and Liberals. In the former fiscal withdrawal or fiscal minimal-ism were always adopted, and in the latter fiscal directiveness or fiscal caution.

In the economic field as in social welfare, parties do seem to make a difference. We should expect this to emerge even more clearly when we look at the overall 'mix' of welfare and economic policies in the next section.

SOCIAL AND ECONOMIC WELFARE

As remarked above, economic policy can have powerful effects on social welfare, both direct and indirect. Conversely, a decision to spend more on welfare has considerable economic effects, so that in policy terms they are hardly separable nowadays. It makes sense therefore to look at party influences on socio-economic policies in

TABLE 5.4. The relationship between party control of the relevant policy sector in coalition governments and economic policy, 1965–1982

Party family / Dominant in sector	Coalition partner	% of country-years of government				% of total	Country-years of government
		Fiscal directiveness	Fiscal caution	Fiscal withdrawal	Fiscal minimalism		
Conservative	Liberal	16.7	25.0	0.0	0.0	11.7	12
	Religious	0.0	0.0	0.0	0.0		
	Socialist	16.7	0.0	0.0	41.7		
Liberal	Conservative	8.7	21.8	26.1	4.3	22.3	23
	Religious	8.7	0.0	17.4	0.0		
	Socialist	13.0	0.0	0.0	0.0		
Religious	Conservative	0.0	0.0	0.0	0.0	29.1	30
	Liberal	43.3	6.7	9.1	0.0		
	Socialist	9.1	21.2	6.7	0.0		
Socialist	Conservative	13.2	0.0	0.0	0.0	36.9	38
	Liberal	15.8	23.7	0.0	10.5		
	Religious	36.8	0.0	0.0	0.0		

Note: The relevant ministries are Labour and Economy/Finance. Switzerland is not included in the statistics, for the reason given in Table 5.1.

combination, even though these are inevitably highly correlated with both sets of policies previously examined.

We can characterize overall policy mixes as follows.

1. A concern to reduce unemployment as a major economic objective, with manipulation of demand to stimulate prosperity in part to finance social welfare. In the manipulation of demand through taxation and interest policies, other social objectives such as equalization and redistribution of income can be pursued.

2. Creating economic expansion, often through extensive State intervention, to create a social spin-off for citizens. While the ultimate goal is the creation of sufficient resources to cover State expenditures, including those on welfare, the need to build up the economic base may involve directing resources from welfare in the short term. Hence this policy mix is more 'volatile' than the first, and less effective in promoting social equality.

3. The regulation of money supply in line with actual and expected economic development. While this does not preclude extra welfare expenditures under favourable conditions, they may need to be directly cut in order to reduce the amount of money in circulation.

4. Rapid reduction of any form of State intervention, including intervention in economic life. As far as possible this should be left like all other social and economic activity to private initiatives and the working of market forces.

The relationship between these policy mixes and our earlier categorizations will be obvious. However, the different party types of government do not just remain as they were, as Table 5.5 shows by contrasting the more positive policies (1 and 2 above) with the negative welfare mix of 3 and 4. Not surprisingly we have a more strongly marked differentiation between the party families, despite the general drift to less concern with welfare over time (particularly marked for Christian Democrats under the pressures of coalition partners (row 6)).

Liberals fall into a middle position, as they appear to take their creed literally: moderate State intervention with a positive eye to social welfare. However, like the Christian Democrats, they tend to change policy priorities under deteriorating economic circumstances. Socialists are more resistant to such pressures, both on their own and in coalition. Although there is some shift to a more negative position,

TABLE 5.5. The relationship between party family and socio-economic welfare, 1965–1983, across nineteen countries

Party family	Government type	Positive welfare mix			Negative welfare mix		
		% of country-years		Total country-years	% of country-years		Total country-years
		1965–73	1974–83		1965–73	1974–83	
1. Conservative	Single-party	34.2	25.7	23	65.8	74.3	53
2. Conservative	Coalition	32.3	53.9	25	67.7	46.1	35
3. Liberal	Single-party	50.0	41.7	9	50.0	58.3	11
4. Liberal	Coalition	73.3	60.0	20	26.7	40.0	10
5. Religious	Single-party	66.7	33.3	5	33.3	66.7	4
6. Religious	Coalition	83.3	57.9	26	16.7	42.1	11
7. Socialist	Single-party	86.4	69.8	48	13.6	30.2	17
8. Socialist	Coalition	72.2	66.7	31	27.8	33.3	14

Switzerland is not included for the reasons given in Table 5.1.

it is very limited. We should note finally that Conservatives in coalition seem less able to carry through their preferred policies: governments incorporating them as one element became *more* positive over time (row 2). This finding again underlines the fact that there are two factors affecting policy—party family as such and the extent of control a particular family has over policy.

Before the economic crisis the rank-order correlation coefficient between Socialist/Bourgeois tendance and welfare policy mix was 0.43, and after it 0.38, a fairly respectable level considering the dichotomy and rank-ordering on which it is based.

Checking connections between socio-economic welfare and party control over both sets of relevant ministries, Table 5.6 reveals an expected pattern of behaviour as far as the Conservatives are concerned, with a strongly negative mix in half the cases where they are dominant (though paradoxically all of these occur where Socialists also hold some ministries. As the relevant offices are not high among Conservative priorities, they dominate in less than 10 per cent of cases, however. The other party families each dominate about one-third of the time; they all pursue a positive welfare mix; and, contrary to expectations, there is little difference between them. (Indeed, Socialist dominance produces a less positive mix than in the cases of religious parties and Liberals.)

It might be argued that over this broad mix of policy, involving not just central aspects but the greater part of the government programme, overall control is more important than sectoral dominance. However this may be, it would be hard, in light of evidence examined in this and the preceding sections, to deny the influence of party in either of the areas of welfare and economics. We now move on to the rather different area of military expenditure, where the situation is less clear.

EXTERNAL SECURITY

As noted earlier, the assumption that parties have as their leading preference the defence of democracy (Table 2.1 Assumption 3(*a*)) implies that there should be less variation between governments in the area of external security than in the areas just examined. Nevertheless, parties can differ in terms of their assessment of risk when there is no

TABLE 5.6. The relationship between party control of the relevant policy sector in coalition governments and the socio-economic welfare mix, 1965–1983

Party family / Dominant in sector	Coalition partner	% of country-years of government — Socio-economic welfare mix				% of total	Country-years of government
		Strongly positive	Moderately positive	Moderately negative	Strongly negative		
Conservative	Liberal	10.0	40.0	0.0	0.0		
	Religious	0.0	0.0	0.0	0.0	8.6	10
	Socialist	0.0	0.0	0.0	50.0		
Liberal	Conservative	21.2	12.1	3.0	0.0		
	Religious	42.4	9.1	0.0	0.0	28.2	33
	Socialist	0.0	9.1	3.0	0.0		
Religious	Conservative	0.0	9.3	12.5	0.0		
	Liberal	40.6	12.5	3.1	0.0	27.4	32
	Socialist	12.5	9.3	0.0	0.0		
Socialist	Conservative	4.8	11.9	4.8	0.0		
	Liberal	4.8	23.8	9.6	2.4	35.8	42
	Religious	35.7	2.4	0.0	0.0		

Note: The relevant ministries are Social Affairs, Health, Education, Labour, and Economy/Finance. Switzerland is not included in the statistics, for the reason given in Table 5.1.

imminent crisis, as is the case during the period we examine. More-over, the extent to which they have priorities in other areas will also affect their judgement: thus all other parties should be less keen on military expenditure than the Conservatives, and Socialists most evidently so.

Table 5.7 goes quite strongly against this assumption: of single-party governments, it is the Socialists who have the highest levels of military expenditure, with the Conservatives next up to 1973, but surpassed by the Liberals from 1974. And it is Christian Democrats in sole control who spend least on security. The effect of coalitions seems to be to push up expenditures moderately, but there are differences between the two time periods. The major findings remain therefore, the unexpected ones of low Christian Democrat expenditure and the higher level for Socialists than for Conservatives. These anomalies are underlined by the low rank-order correlation coefficients between tendance and our categorization of expenditures: $r = 0.18$ before 1974 and -0.26 after 1974. The second (negative) value demonstrates the reversal of expected relationships between Conservatives and Social-ists. As we remarked previously, external security can be regarded as a perpetual defence of democracy and hence some dilution of party divisions might be expected. This might account for the absence of the Socialist–Conservative contrast but not for the one which opens up with the Christians.

Tenure of individual ministries is probably less important in determining military expenditures than overall government policy. However, this should be checked, in view of the connection between policy and party control in other areas. Table 5.8 reveals no clear pattern, other than a tendency for all governments (and indeed countries) to cluster in the 'high' and 'medium' categories of expenditure. This reinforces the inference from Table 5.7, that coalitions show less clear-cut differences than single-party governments.

TRADE-OFFS AND PAY-OFFS BETWEEN WELFARE AND SECURITY

Looking at areas in isolation or even at the overarching socio-economic mix does not inform us fully about party influences on policy. For this we have also to look at the priority given to one area as against another. Given that their combined share accounts for the

TABLE 5.7. The relationship between party family and military expenditure, 1965–1983, across nineteen countries

Party family	Government type	Level of military expenditure								
		High			Medium			Low		
		% of country-years		Total country-years	% of country-years		Total country-years	% of country-years		Total country-years
		1965–73	1974–83		1965–73	1974–83		1965–73	1974–83	
1. Conservative	Single-party	51.2	25.7	30	19.5	54.2	27	29.3	20.0	29
2. Conservative	Coalition	44.1	50.0	28	14.7	—	5	41.2	50.0	27
3. Liberal	Single-party	37.5	41.7	8	50.0	58.3	11	12.5	—	1
4. Liberal	Coalition	46.7	20.0	10	40.0	60.0	15	13.3	20.0	5
5. Religious	Single-party	—	—	—	33.3	100.0	5	66.7	—	4
6. Religious	Coalition	44.4	63.2	20	38.9	36.8	10	16.7	—	7
7. Socialist	Single-party	59.1	34.9	28	22.7	37.2	21	18.2	27.9	17
8. Socialist	Coalition	33.3	44.4	18	38.9	29.7	15	27.8	25.9	12

Note: 'High' = above average; 'Medium' = below average, but within one standard deviation of the mean; 'Low' = more than one standard deviation below the mean. Switzerland is not included.

TABLE 5.8. The relationship between party control of the relevant policy sector in coalition governments and military expenditure, 1965–1983

Party family Dominant in sector	Coalition partner	% of country-years of government Level of military expenditure				% of total	Country-years of government
		Very high	High	Moderate	Low		
Conservative	Liberal	10.0	20.0	0.0	10.9		
	Religious	0.0	15.0	10.0	0.0	16.7	20
	Socialist	0.0	25.3	0.0	10.0		
Liberal	Conservative	10.3	17.2	24.1	6.9		
	Religious	0.0	34.5	0.0	0.0	24.2	29
	Socialist	0.0	0.0	6.9	0.0		
Religious	Conservative	0.0	22.6	0.0	0.0		
	Liberal	0.0	25.7	12.9	0.0	25.8	31
	Socialist	0.0	25.7	9.7	3.2		
Socialist	Conservative	0.0	0.0	25.0	15.0		
	Liberal	0.0	27.5	0.0	0.0	33.3	40
	Religious	0.0	20.0	10.0	2.5		

Note: Sector dominance implies control of the Defence Ministry plus at least one out of the Prime Ministership and the Foreign Affairs Ministry. As for the levels of expenditure, 'Very high' = more than one standard deviation above the mean; 'High' = within one standard deviation above the mean; 'Moderate' = within one standard deviation below the mean; 'Low' = below this. Switzerland is not included.

largest part of the Budget, social welfare and external security are the natural ones to examine. While economic policy may have a general impact in the sense of increasing or decreasing resources available to both, the actual trade-offs or pay-offs between them are not determined by economic policy but result from relative policy priorities. In light of our assumptions about party preferences, we expect Socialists (in spite of their reversal on security expenditure as such) and Christian Democrats to be biased in favour of social welfare, and Liberals and especially Conservatives to put external security first. Contrasting the two areas should sharpen up party contrasts. We can examine these possibilities directly by seeing what kind of relationships hold for single-party governments and coalitions of the different families already examined.

The expenditure data on which Table 5.9 is based differ from those used before, however, since instead of examining the total amounts spent each year, we look at the change in expenditure from one year to the next: in particular, whether an increase in welfare spending is accompanied by an increase or decrease in security-related expenditure and vice versa. We concentrate on these annual, incremental changes for two reasons:

(*a*) The aggregate levels of expenditure in these areas are so massive that in relation to the overall total spent there is hardly any variation from one year to the next. In particular, expenditure on security is extremely stable. Only five countries (Canada, France, The Netherlands, Sweden, and the United Kingdom) change security expenditure by more than 0.1 per cent of the total in any one year. This confirms our theoretical expectations about the commitment of all parties to this area, but renders it advisable to concentrate on change as such rather than the massive and relatively stable aggregates underlying it.

(*b*) Concentrating on change in any case has the advantage, for this analysis, of focusing directly on the priorities a particular party has decided on for a specific year. Most expenditures are not within the control of the parties, being devoted to core programmes which cannot be cut, or committed for years ahead to long-term developments. It is the incremental, marginal decisions that privilege one type of policy in regard to another, and that stem much more from the parties' underlying preferences and values. This is what Table 5.9 reveals.

To allow for the effects of the general squeeze on expenditures after

TABLE 5.9. The relationship between party family and expenditure
on social welfare in relation to expenditure on external security, 1965–1983, across nineteen countries

Party family	Government type	% of country-years						Total country-years
		Welfare increases, security decreases		Welfare and security increase/decrease together		Welfare decreases, security increases		
		1965–73	1974–83	1965–73	1974–83	1965–73	1974–83	
1. Conservative	Single-party	46.3	31.4	29.3	48.6	24.4	20.0	76
2. Conservative	Coalition	70.6	34.6	23.5	26.2	5.9	39.2	60
3. Liberal	Single-party	75.0	25.0	25.0	50.0	–	25.0	20
4. Liberal	Coalition	66.7	26.7	26.7	53.3	6.7	20.0	30
5. Religious	Single-party	33.3	33.3	50.0	33.3	16.7	33.3	9
6. Religious	Coalition	27.8	31.6	50.0	47.4	22.2	21.1	37
7. Socialist	Single-party	68.2	39.5	31.8	48.8	–	11.6	65
8. Socialist	Coalition	55.6	37.1	33.3	48.2	11.1	14.8	45

Note: Policy-mixes are based on H. E. Keman, 'Welfare and Warfare: Critical Opinions and Conscious Choice in Public Policy', in F. Castles, F. Lehner, and M. G. Schmidt (eds.), *Managing Mixed Economies* (Berlin: De Gruyter, 1988), 104–8. The data are taken from OECD and SIPRI (see Appendix B). Switzerland is not included.

1973 we have again distinguished between an earlier period (1965–73) and a later period (1974–83). For each year of the two periods we examine the percentage of times welfare expenditure has increased while security expenditure has decreased (first two columns of the table), and the reverse (last two columns). In the middle two columns we examine the cases in which welfare and security increase or decrease together.

As expected, the Socialists, whether on their own or in coalition, generally favour welfare, with Christian Democrats more inclined to compromises which increase or decrease the areas together. There are inconsistencies in the percentages for increase of welfare in the 'good years' of 1965–73: Conservatives in coalition and Liberal single-party governments are actually the ones which favour welfare in the highest proportion of years. When the going gets tougher between 1974 and 1983, Socialists and Christian Democrats stand up for welfare more than Conservatives (though the latter in coalitions (row 2) are comparable with both Christians and Socialists in coalition). Socialists, whether in their own government or in coalition, stick out against welfare cuts more than any of the other parties, as their very low figures in the last two columns of the table show.

The evidence of the table is supported by the correlation coefficient between overall tendance (Socialists versus the rest) and expenditure changes favouring welfare: $r = 0.44$. Clearly in this case it is not over-simplifying to see the main division as before between Socialists and all bourgeois parties. Assigning priorities as between 'welfare and warfare' is a severer test of commitments, seemingly, than simple decisions about how much to spend on security (cf. Table 5.7).

CONCLUSIONS: PARTIES DO AFFECT POLICIES

There is little to add at this point to the detailed findings as they have emerged from the analysis of each policy area and of the trade-offs and pay-offs between them, other than to note the importance of the sectoral analyses in confirming parties' policy-based attachments to particular ministries (Chapter 4). Despite some detailed inconsistencies there are clear overall divergencies between the different party families. There is not always a sharp socialist–bourgeois difference: sometimes the main divide is socialist versus bourgeois, but equally often it is Conservative versus the rest, while Christian parties often adopt a quite distinctive profile.

Rather than upsetting initial expectations this helps to refine them. We should expect sharply contrasting socialist–bourgeois divisions if all countries had experienced intense Left–Right conflicts between 1965 and 1983. But as a glance at Table 3.1 reveals, these occurred in less than half the countries; in five out of the nine countries with two-party competition; and in only one case (The Netherlands) where there exists a Christian Democratic Party. The fact that the Christians often emerge close to the Socialists in the comparative analysis is perfectly understandable in terms of the type of goals and ideological preferences we attribute to them (see Table 4.2 and related discussion); indeed, the presence of such a party, sharing many social objectives of the Left but clearly non-socialist, is probably an important reason why straight socialist–bourgeois confrontations do not emerge in most cases.

These findings clearly strengthen the case for regarding parties as (*a*) being concerned with policy, since they exert a consistent and important influence over it, (*b*) being important decision-makers and actors in politics, since they move policies in the direction of their own preferences and values. One could only negate these findings by arguing that the areas examined are unimportant—which they clearly are not, being central to any government programme and consuming a major share of resources—or claiming that other factors account for the seeming relationship between party participation and particular policy lines.

But if so, what are they? We have explicitly allowed for the effects of world economic crises. By noting whether parties wholly control the government or only participate in a coalition the research design also incorporates a measure of the party's ability to effect its policies. Whereas the onus at the beginning of the study was to show that parties really do 'make a difference' (even though this had been shown before[3]), after this demonstration it surely rests with the sceptics to show what unknown factor can be accounting for the relationships which so clearly emerge.

We prefer the obvious interpretation that parties exert a strong, and even determining, influence on government decision-making. This raises another and (in more senses than one) a final question for our analysis: What are the effects on parties themselves, their electoral prospects, and their future participation in government of the policies they initiate? This is the question we address in Chapter 6.

6

Government Termination: Causes and Effects

INTRODUCTION

Coalition literature approaches the question of government break-down in a curiously indirect way, dominated by its characteristic concern with how governments formed in the first place. This is because lack of success in specifying the form coalitions take (e.g. the existence of as many surplus majority and minority coalitions as minimal winning ones) can be excused by the lesser stability and shorter duration of governments not conforming to the prescribed criteria.[1] There is no clear evidence upholding such a saving outcome in the case of minimal winning theories.[2] As we have seen in Chapter 1, the same reasoning is employed with core theory: it is indeed a natural extension to any argument which prescribes how rationally constructed coalitions should form.[3]

This leads to breakdown and termination being ignored as phenomena requiring explanation in their own right. Certainly, they might be rendered more probable by the basic composition of the government. We ourselves have noted (Table 2.4 Implications 5(ii) and 5(iii)) that policy disagreements and consequent involuntary collapse are more likely in coalitions, particularly Left–Right ones, than in single-party governments. We examine the direct effects of government composition in the third section of this chapter. But one cannot rule out, either, the effects of ongoing disagreements (Implication 5 (i)), of policy failure (Implications 5 (iv) and 5 (v)), or of tactical electoral considerations (Implication 5 (vi)). These effects will also be investigated, in the fourth and fifth sections.

Breaking from the constraints of traditional coalition theory also means that termination qualifies as cause as well as consequence. The breakdown of a coalition rendered ineffectual by continued policy

TABLE 6.1. Duration and mode of termination of governments, 1950–1983

Country	No. of governments		Average duration		Reason for termination						
					Election		Resignation of PM		Political		Constitutional intervention
	1950–83	1965–83	1950–83	1965–83	Fixed	Anticipated	Voluntary	Health	Governmental dissension	Parliamentary dissension	
Australia	19	13	1.8	1.4	8	3	1	2	3	1	1
Austria	16	8	2.1	2.3	7	3	1	1	4	—	—
Belgium	22	13	1.6	1.4	2	5	—	—	13	—	2
Canada	12	7	2.8	2.6	4	2	2	—	—	3	1
Denmark	21	11	1.6	1.6	8	3	1	3	1	4	1
Finland	35	17	1.0	1.1	6	4	1	—	11	5	8
France 4	16	—	0.6	—	1	—	—	—	4	9	2
5	21	15	1.6	1.3	4	1	—	—	5	3	8
West Germany	14	8	2.4	2.3	7	—	2	—	3	1	1
Iceland	12	6	2.8	3.0	4	1	—	2	3	2	—
Ireland	14	8	2.4	2.3	3	5	2	1	3	2	1
Israel	25	12	1.4	1.5	6	3	2	1	10	3	—
Italy	41	25	0.8	0.7	3	3	1	—	23	10	1
Japan	24	11	1.4	1.6	7	4	6	2	2	2	1
Luxemburg	10	5	3.0	3.6	5	1	1	1	1	1	—

Netherlands	18	11	1.8	1.6	7	3	—	—	6	1	1
New Zealand	15	9	2.3	2.0	12	3	—	—	—	—	—
Norway	16	11	2.1	1.6	9	—	2	1	2	2	1
Sweden	17	10	1.9	1.8	9	—	1	1	4	1	1
UK	12	6	2.8	3.0	2	6	1	2	—	1	—
TOTAL	380	195			114	50	24	16	95	51	30
Average over all countries	19	9.8	1.85	1.92	5.7	2.5	1.2	0.8	4.8	2.6	1.5
% of total	100	51.6			30.5	12.6	6.3	4.2	25.0	13.4	7.9
					{ 43.1 }		{ 10.5 }		{ 46.4 }		

Note: The fixed terms and elections of Swiss governments render the analysis uninformative for Switzerland, which is therefore omitted from the statistics in this chapter.

Sources: Keesing's Contemporary Archives; H. Paloheimo, *Governments in Democratic Capitalist States 1950–1983: A Data Handbook* (Tampere: Finnish Political Science Association, 1984), K. von Beyme, *Political Parties in Western Democracies* (Aldershot: Gower, 1985).

disagreement and squabbling can be seen as having effects on subsequent elections (Implication 6 (i)) and on prospects for continued co-operation between previous partners (Implication 6 (ii)). Unless politicians have severely truncated time-perspectives, events associated with the fall of a government cannot be totally dissociated from the formation of its successor. We shall see in the sixth section the extent to which such factors can be said to exert a continuing influence.

First, however, given that breakdown and termination have not been studied much at all,[4] we examine the immediate circumstances surrounding each government's demise. Classifying these gives us a comparative description more than anything else, but this provides a good basis for the theoretically orientated analyses which follow.

CIRCUMSTANCES OF GOVERNMENT TERMINATION

Table 6.1 begins by reporting the average duration of governments for the period 1950–83, as well as for 1965–83. This enables us to check whether there is any tendency for national governments to last longer or to terminate more quickly in the later period. No clear-cut difference emerges, either between the overall average of 1.85 and 1.92 years or within any of the individual countries.

The main differences in duration appear between countries, not time periods. Those with single-party governments tend also to have ones which are longer-lived. Besides most of the Anglo-Saxon democracies this group includes Austria, Norway, and Sweden, which have experienced coalition from time to time. However, Germany and Luxemburg have equally long-lived governments in spite of having almost permanent coalitions. On the other side, Australia, which has entirely single-party government (counting the Liberal–Country electoral coalition as effectively one party), and Japan, dominated by the LDP, have quite short-lived governments. The tendency for countries with single-party governments to have longer-lived ones is clearly only a tendency, with many exceptions, which require further investigation (notably comparisons between different kinds of government within the same country, which we go into in the next section[5]).

The other columns of Table 6.1 present the immediate circumstances associated with government termination—which may of course not be the ultimate or underlying causes of demission. To take one obvious example, a government may resign to clear the way for anticipated elections, and this provides the immediate 'institutional' explanation of its end. For descriptive purposes we can stop here, but later we shall go on to ask why it feels the need to anticipate elections in the first place. Is it because the constituent parties cannot agree and see no prospects of forming another coalition—or on the contrary, do they feel they have succeeded so well that they want to catch the opposition parties off guard and increase their own vote?

The categories into which 'immediate' 'institutional' reasons fall in Table 6.1 are common-sense ones which require little justification or explanation. To begin with we have elections (which in most countries require the existing government's formal resignation and reconstitution as a caretaker administration). Elections may occur either because the government calls them (the case considered above) —counted under 'Anticipated' in the table—or because the constitution specifies a particular date, in which case governments have no choice, when the deadline occurs, but to offer their resignation and fight the election—counted under 'Fixed' in the table. In a sense, of course, fixed election dates provoke 'involuntary' termination, but not in the same sense that inability to agree on a coherent (or any) policy does. The Implications of Table 2.4 are worded so as to emphasize the distinction. In the analysis below, survival up to a fixed election date is regarded as a sign of relative success rather than weakness.

In general, substantially more governments end because of constitutionally prescribed dates of re-election than because they try to anticipate them. The exceptions are Belgium and the UK, where elections are anticipated in almost all cases, and Ireland (a few more cases). Apart from these countries, anticipated elections bring an end to relatively more governments in Finland and Japan than elsewhere. By contrast, some countries never have anticipated elections: Germany, Norway, and Sweden fall into this category. The table also reports the overall percentage of governments ending with elections: 30.5 per cent of all cases with fixed elections and 12.6 per cent of all cases with anticipated ones. Only in a few countries (Belgium, Finland, France, Israel, and Italy) is this general tendency not repeated. In the majority of countries elections of one sort or another are the major immediate event putting a stop to government tenure.

According to the terms of our overall definition of a government stated in Chapter 1, its life may also be ended by a change in Prime

Minister or in party composition, or by resignation for whatever reason even if followed by reconstitution with the same parties and Prime Minister. Looking first of all at resignation of the Prime Minister, we can distinguish between voluntary resignations, for whatever reason (sometimes of course because of weariness or inability to reconcile warring factions) and resignations on health grounds (which of course are also sometimes excuses for inability to manage). This category accounts for 6.30 per cent (voluntary) and 4.20 per cent (health) of all cases. Japan has a high number of voluntary resignations, due to the alternation of factions within the ruling Liberal Democratic party. Denmark has an unusually high proportion of Prime Ministers who actually died in office! Otherwise this remains a minor category.

The remaining factors distinguished within the table are more directly political than any considered up to now (except, possibly, anticipated elections). They are: intragovernmental reasons (change of party composition or mass resignation of ministers precipitating demission of the whole government); loss of a vote of confidence in Parliament; and intervention by an external authority, usually the Head of State. On many occasions one of these events can get mixed up with others, or with the circumstances examined previously (for instance, dissent within government can provoke a vote of no confidence in Parliament, leading to Prime Ministerial resignation and an election). What we have done, here and elsewhere in the table, is to distinguish the major immediate cause of the government's fall and locate it within the appropriate categories. The entries in the table are mutually exclusive, therefore, each recording the leading event bringing about termination, without seeking to imply that the other circumstances were totally absent.

Dissension *within* government is the second most important of the leading reasons for termination after elections. It accounts for 25.0 per cent of all cases. Belgium, Finland, the two French regimes, Israel, and Italy are notable here: these are countries with coalitions grouping large numbers of parties and (with the exception of the Fifth French Republic), often putting together bourgeois and socialist tendances. Internal government dissension is also important as a cause of termination in The Netherlands which to some extent shows the same characteristics. All these cases go some way to supporting the Implications of Table 2.4. For a full check we shall have to go into more detail, which we do in the next two sections.

Parliamentary termination is also a fairly important factor, accounting for 13.4 per cent of all cases of government demise. It is particularly important in the classic parliamentarian regimes of Fourth Republic France and Italy, but accounts for a fair number of cases in Canada, Finland, and Denmark (where minority governments often rely on informal legislative coalitions).

Interference from outside these arenas is less common, as most countries lack institutions which could take initiatives corresponding to those of the government or Parliament. The most common source of alternative authority is an executive President, so not surprisingly Finland and the Fifth French Republic, which have this institution, are the countries where it compares in frequency with other circumstances of demission. Because of the fact that external sources of constitutional authority exist in relatively few countries, this category accounts for only 7.9 per cent of all cases of termination.

As we remarked at the outset, the categories used in the table are the common-sense groupings into which the circumstances surrounding government termination seem to fall. No claims are made for them as ultimate or fundamental reasons for breakdown and demise. As a first general categorization they do seem to make sense, however; and in all countries except New Zealand, cases occur in most categories, indicating a broad general relevance rather than an association with idiosyncratic conditions in specific countries. The fact that elections are the most usual reasons for the termination of governments is as it should be in the parliamentary democracies we are considering.

EFFECTS OF GOVERNMENT COMPOSITION ON TERMINATION AND DURATION

Going a little deeper into the reasons for government demission—that is, searching for analytic rather than institutional or legal explanations —we look first at the composition of governments, so often cited in the mainstream literature as the basis for internal dissension and hence governmental paralysis and breakdown. We have already mentioned this idea at the outset of the chapter. Specifically, Dodd claims that minimal winning coalitions last longer than other coalitions.[6] This claim rests in part on a different definition of government termination from the one generally used, and adopted for this book. Dodd takes governments as changing only when the Prime

Minister alters or a party leaves and/or enters government. He thus
omits the criteria of elections and of resignation, our use of which
underlies the findings of Table 6.1. Obviously elections would not
emerge as a major event associated with the end of governments were
they not considered, by definition, to end governments!

Grofman has queried Dodd's findings on the grounds that cross-
national comparisons confound various other influences with those of
composition *per se*: in particular, societal cleavages and fragmentation
of the party system will independently provoke intragovernmental
conflict quite apart from the nature of the coalition.[7] He argues
convincingly that the way to avoid this is to compare the various types
of government *within* each country, a procedure which automatically
controls for extraneous national effects.

In this section we examine both cross-national averages and within-
country comparisons, using, however, the generally accepted definition of government termination (governments end with elections,
change of Prime Minister, change of party composition, or formal
resignation even if later reconstituted in the same form). It is interesting to see how the change of definition affects results; and our findings
about the effects of party composition provide a good entry to our
analysis in the next section of the influence of ideological homogeneity
and policy agreements.

Before looking at duration directly we link composition to reasons
for termination, as classified in the previous section (Table 6.2). As far
as we know, this is not a relationship which has been examined before,
and the results are instructive. Single-party majority governments
overwhelmingly (in two-thirds of the cases) terminate with elections
—in half the cases ones with a fixed date, a result which testifies to their
greater capacity for survival. About one-third of majority coalitions
also terminate with elections. Caretaker governments, which are
usually resorted to when the parties cannot agree, and have a clear,
often technical, remit, terminate with elections in 56 per cent of the
cases. This is not surprising, as often their remit is precisely to call and
supervise elections.

What is unexpected in Table 6.2 is that the contrast between
single-party administrations and coalitions also holds within the
category of minority governments. Single-party minority governments end with elections twice as frequently as minority coalitions
—44 per cent to 22 per cent. The contrast between single parties and
coalitions extends further: the former more frequently anticipate

TABLE 6.2. The relationship between type of government and mode of termination, 1950–1983

| Reason for termination | Type of government (%) | | | | | Caretaker | No. of governments |
| | Single-party majority | Surplus majority coalition | Minimal winning coalition | Minority | | | |
				Single-party	Coalition		
Fixed election	48.4	24.1	28.3	24.6	12.5	32.0	116
Anticipated election	18.6	6.9	8.0	19.7	9.4	24.0	48
PM resigns voluntarily	11.0	1.7	5.3	9.8	3.1	—	24
PM resigns through ill health	4.4	1.7	5.3	3.3	3.1	—	16
Governmental dissension	8.8	34.5	35.4	9.8	28.1	36.0	95
Parliamentary dissension	5.5	17.2	11.5	26.2	21.9	4.0	51
Constitutional intervention	3.3	13.8	6.2	6.6	21.9	4.0	30
TOTAL	100.0	100.0	100.0	100.0	100.0	100.0	
Total no. of governments	91	58	113	61	32	25	380

elections, both in the majority and the minority cases. As pointed out in Chapter 2, the act of anticipating an election could be attributable either to weakness or to strength. Failed governments might see it as the only way out of an impossible situation. But on the other hand, successful governments could well be capitalizing on a favourable turn of events or on general popularity in order to reap electoral gains. The fact that single-party governments opt for anticipated elections both in majority and minority situations argues for the second possibility, though we have no way of demonstrating this conclusively in the absence of directly relevant information. So far as it goes, however, it seems to uphold Implication 5(ii) of Table 2.4, on the greater probability of coalitions terminating on an unpremeditated basis, compared to single-party governments.

Further evidence from Table 6.2 also shows the contrast between single parties and coalitions with regard to voluntary resignation of the Prime Minister (again more likely to be premeditated and strategic in purpose), and compares the two types of government with regard to whether they terminate owing to dissensions, resignations, and other events inside government, or from external causes. Internal terminations again seem more likely than external to arise from irreconcilable policy disagreements, beyond anyone's ability to compose, and are clearly fewer within single-party governments. The consistent differences between single-party and coalition government, within both majority and minority situations, argue more powerfully in favour of anticipated elections being strategic than if they occurred with either taken separately. The only point on which single-party minority governments do resemble their coalitional counterparts is termination by Parliament (quite naturally, given their minority status).

The other striking feature of Table 6.2 is the roughly equal proportions of surplus majority coalitions and of minimal winning coalitions (just over one-third) that end through internal or external dissension (in both cases the proportion is higher than for minority coalitions). The failure of contrasts to emerge is surprising because conventional reasoning has it that coalitions are stripped to the minimal number of members precisely to *reduce* risks of internal disagreement. If, on the other hand, minimal winning coalitions come together *faute de mieux*, because parties cannot agree on policy (Table 2.3 Rule v (*b*)), the relatively high rate of internal dissension is not surprising.

Overall Table 6.2 demonstrates that government composition is

TABLE 6.3. Average duration of governments according to type and mode of termination, 1950–1983

Type of government	Reason for termination						
	Election		Resignation of PM		Political		
	Fixed	Anticipated	Voluntary	Health	Governmental dissension	Parliamentary dissension	Constitutional intervention
Single-party majority	2.89	1.61	1.66	2.02	1.76	2.06	1.93
Surplus majority coalition	2.34	0.95	1.40	1.80	1.27	1.19	1.53
Minimal winning coalition	2.47	2.17	1.73	2.52	1.47	1.39	1.54
Minority	2.07	1.32	1.56	1.82	1.07	1.47	1.25
Caretaker	0.45	0.22	—	—	0.36	0.40	0.60
All types	2.04	1.25	1.27	1.63	1.19	1.30	1.37
Total no. of governments	116	48	24	16	95	51	30

indeed related to modes of termination. We can approach the question of how it is related to government duration indirectly, by seeing first how reasons for termination relate to duration (Table 6.3). This comparison shows that where governments end with fixed elections their longevity is greater on average than where they end for other causes. This is hardly surprising and almost tautological. Apart from Prime Ministerial resignation for reasons of health, governments do not vary much in average duration across the other modes of termination: there is indeed a surprisingly limited range, from 1.19 to 1.37 years. The major variations in the table occur within columns, between the different types of government. While, on the whole, single-party majority governments last the longest, minimal winning coalitions last longer when governments terminate by anticipated elections or by resignation of the Prime Minister on health grounds; they last more or less as long where the Prime Minister resigns voluntarily; and are of distinctly lesser duration only where the government terminates on 'political' grounds. Rather than giving us new substantive information, these variations underline the point made previously: duration is not an automatic indicator of stability and success, since successful governments may well terminate themselves in order to capitalize on their advantages. Without further information (which we have not succeeded in obtaining) on actual reasons for termination, one cannot really push the discussion much further.

Table 6.4 gives figures for the average duration of each type of government within each country. Confirming overall comparisons, single-party governments are clearly the longest-lived within most countries, with some interesting exceptions involving minimal winning coalitions (Belgium, Ireland, Norway). Minority governments are generally the shortest-lived (apart from caretakers, for obvious reasons) but in Finland, Denmark, and Austria and under both French regimes they last longer on average than minimal winning coalitions. An interesting point opens up with the comparison of surplus majority and minimal winning coalitions: in six democracies the former last longer, in three (Belgium, Finland, and Italy) the latter. On office-seeking interpretations the opposite result would be expected, but of course these interpretations also equate longevity with success, which we are not doing here.

Taken as a whole, the within-country comparisons of Table 6.4 uphold the cross-national conclusions drawn from Table 6.3. The

TABLE 6.4. Average duration of governments according to type, by country, 1950–1983

Country	Average duration (years)					Total no. of governments
	Single-party majority	Surplus majority coalition	Minimal winning coalition	Minority	Caretaker	
Australia	1.88	—	—	—	0.10	19
Austria	2.78	—	1.78	1.90	—	16
Belgium	1.80	1.08	1.81	—	0.33	22
Canada	4.20	—	—	1.47	—	12
Denmark	—	—	2.04	2.19	0.25	21
Finland	—	1.25	1.58	1.85	0.31	35
France 4	—	0.68	0.25	0.54	—	16
5	1.80	1.53	0.48	0.60	0.10	21
West Germany	—	4.00	2.17	—	—	14
Iceland	—	3.30	3.13	2.20	0.30	12
Ireland	2.57	—	2.63	2.25	—	14
Israel	—	2.14	1.33	1.20	0.50	25
Italy	—	0.81	0.94	0.77	0.40	41
Japan	1.71	—	—	1.14	0.33	24
Luxemburg	—	—	3.40	—	—	10
Netherlands	—	2.40	1.86	—	0.33	18
New Zealand	2.27	—	—	—	—	15
Norway	2.49	—	2.57	1.68	—	16
Sweden	1.05	—	2.15	2.12	—	17
UK	3.23	—	—	0.85	—	12
Total no. of governments	91	58	113	93	25	380

differences between national systems suggest, however, that there are other factors at work than simply government type. This of course is quite in accord with our expectation that policy and ideologically based agreements and disagreements will affect the general functioning and stability of governments. We turn to a more direct examination of these in the next section.

EFFECTS OF AGREEMENT ON TERMINATION AND DURATION

The preceding analysis demonstrates that composition has an effect on the way governments end and on how long they stay in office. The main difference, however, opens up between single-party governments and others. As a major distinguishing mark of single-party government is its ideological homogeneity and more extensive internal policy agreements, the possibility emerges that effects of composition indirectly manifest the influence of policy. If this were true it would relate reasons for termination, and durability, to the other aspects of party behaviour in government covered by our theory. Several of the Implications of Table 2.4 cover this point, arguing that the less governments agree on policy, the more likely they are to terminate involuntarily (5 (i)—this leaves out the case of fixed elections discussed above). The general assertion is then applied to the particular case of single-party government (5 (ii)), already considered and to the ideological 'mix' of coalitions (5 (iii)). Given the difficulties already noted (Chapter 3) of discovering whether or not parties agree on specific major policies, it is easier to test these extensions of the reasoning. The point about single-party governments avoiding internal dissent is already supported by Table 6.2. Table 6.5 now relates the specifically ideological composition of each government to modes of termination.

Findings here broadly confirm our reasoning about the effects of ideological homogeneity (and, by inference, policy agreement) in producing more stable and long-lived governments. The single-party governments and Socialist-dominated coalitions are less likely to terminate through internal dissent or parliamentary defeat, and conversely more likely to survive till fixed elections occur.

What is unexpected in Table 6.5 is the implication that the nature of the ideology exerts an effect on modes of termination independently of the degree of simple homogeneity. Socialist single-party governments

TABLE 6.5. The relationship between ideological complexion of government and mode of termination, 1950–1983

Reason for termination	Ideological complexion (%)				
	Bourgeois hegemony	Bourgeois dominance	Bourgeois–socialist balance	Socialist dominance	Socialist hegemony
Fixed election	30.2	23.4	22.2	51.4	48.9
Anticipated election	13.0	14.1	13.9	2.9	10.6
PM resigns voluntarily	8.0	1.6	1.4	2.9	12.8
PM resigns through ill health	4.9	0.0	1.4	5.8	4.3
Governmental dissension	19.8	32.8	33.3	14.3	4.3
Parliamentary dissension	13.6	17.2	11.1	14.3	10.6
Constitutional intervention	10.5	10.9	16.7	7.4	6.4
TOTAL	100.0	100.0	100.0	100.0	100.0
Total no. of governments	162	64	72	35	47

Note: 'Ideological complexion of government' is a composite index based on the representation of socialist and non-socialist (i.e. bourgeois) parties in government. 'Hegemony' occurs when one tendance has 100% of Cabinet positions; 'dominance' is when one has 67% or more; 'balance' takes in the remaining situations.

—and, even more significantly, Socialist-dominated coalitions—are more likely to survive to the time of fixed elections, and less likely to perish through internal or parliamentary dissension, than bourgeois single-party governments, and significantly more so than bourgeois-dominated coalitions. The latter indeed are almost as likely to perish through internal dissension as those where there is a socialist–bourgeois balance, and more likely to terminate through votes in Parliament.

How can we explain this? And does the finding go against some of the implications of our theory? The answer to the second question is not clear, because we lack more precise information. It is possible to argue that the ideological divisions between bourgeois parties are potentially greater than those between parties of the Left—in particular, that Christian Democrats and to a lesser extent Agrarians are likely to diverge considerably from free-market Liberals (cf. the policy differences revealed in Chapter 5). Divisions between Social Democrats and Left Socialists will be of degree rather than of direction. Given such an interpretation we should then expect bourgeois governments, particularly coalitions, to be less stable than socialist ones. The trouble is that we lack good information about the exact level of policy agreement inside each government, so are not in a position to check the interpretation directly.

We cannot therefore provide a precise explanation of the bourgeois–socialist differences apparent from the table, and must return an open verdict on the standing of our hypotheses in light of the data. There is no doubt that the contrasts which emerge between bourgeois and socialist governments are extremely interesting, however, and demand further exploration.[8]

We can follow them through here by looking directly at the duration of governments of the various ideological complexions within each country. Table 6.3 provides an obvious basis for inferring that governments which continue till the date of the fixed elections last longer, and that the socialist–bourgeois differences which emerge in this regard will be equally obvious in terms of ability to survive for more extended periods. Table 6.6 gives the average duration of governments of varying ideological complexion within each country. We can make comparisons across more and less ideologically homogeneous governments in fourteen democracies (in the remaining ones only hegemonic situations occur). In eight of these fourteen, however, ideologically mixed governments last longer than ideologi-

TABLE 6.6. Average duration of governments according to ideological complexion, by country, 1950–1983

Country	Average duration (years)				
	Bourgeois hegemony	Bourgeois dominance	Bourgeois–socialist balance	Socialist dominance	Socialist hegemony
Australia	1.51	—	—	—	1.73
Austria	1.80	0.50	1.83	2.30	3.03
Belgium	1.36	1.67	1.39	—	—
Canada	2.83	—	—	—	—
Denmark	1.90	1.77	1.03	1.61	1.54
Finland	1.22	0.70	1.06	0.40	—
France 4	0.43	0.44	1.18	—	—
5	1.12	—	—	—	1.67
West Germany	2.27	—	2.90	—	2.54
Iceland	3.15	2.98	2.95	1.65	—
Ireland	2.17	2.47	2.60	—	—
Israel	0.90	—	1.71	1.13	—
Italy	0.82	0.81	1.03	—	—
Japan	1.42	—	—	—	—
Luxemburg	3.53	0.90	3.86	—	—
Netherlands	1.23	—	1.30	2.80	—
New Zealand	2.28	—	—	—	2.23
Norway	1.87	1.20	—	1.10	2.62
Sweden	3.00	1.88	—	2.33	2.00
UK	3.30	—	—	—	2.44
Total no. of governments	162	64	72	35	47

cally homogeneous ones; only in six democracies does greater homogeneity go with greater longevity.

Like much of the other evidence presented in this chapter, the exact status of this finding is unclear. Should we, for example, leave the generally long-lived hegemonic governments in the remaining six democracies altogether out of account? If we brought them in, the balance would again tilt in favour of homogeneity as producing longevity. But this could be due to extraneous national factors.[9]

Longevity cannot in any case be considered as automatically conterminous with stability and success, so these ambiguities in the findings of Table 6.6 do not affect our theoretical expectations very directly. In the next section, however, we go on to look at the effects of policy success and failure, first on modes of termination and then on duration of governments. This will give us more of a basis on which to assess the validity of duration as an indicator of performance, as well as allowing us to check Implications 5(iv) and 5(v) of Table 2.4, on the political effects of policy—and particularly of economic—success and failure.

EFFECTS OF POLICY PERFORMANCE ON MODES OF TERMINATION AND DURATION

Internal agreement and ideological homogeneity, important though they are, form only one of the channels through which policy can influence government breakdown or survival. Another aspect which needs to be investigated is performance, in the sense of party priorities being implemented or blocked in government. To the extent that they can be implemented, there will be fewer grounds for discontent, either internally at the level of the government, or among party supporters in the electorate, and therefore less strain on coalition partners or on the factions within a single-party government. Again, these points have been formulated as Implications from the policy-pursuit principle of our original theory (Table 2.1 Assumption 2), stating that failure in implementing characteristic policies, particularly economic policies, leads to internal dissension and premature dissolution (Table 2.4 Implications 5 (iv) and 5 (v)).

We can operationalize this kind of success or failure in terms of the characterizations of policy made in the last chapter. A socialist government which has not put major effort into creating and maintaining a Welfare State, or at least into growth-creating economic expansion and high employment, is obviously not succeeding well in terms of its traditional values and the expectations of its supporters. Conversely, after 1973, a bourgeois government can be regarded as having failed, in relation to its own aspirations, if it has not kept down inflation even at the cost of increasing unemployment and expenditure cuts.

Policy success or failure is therefore relative. One cannot associate any one line of policy with success or failure *per se*, but it can be judged to be unsuccessful if it does not correspond to the party's traditional stance. This is the reason why Table 6.7 takes the form it does, with governments distinguished according to their ideological complexion *before* being judged to have followed 'appropriate' or 'inappropriate' policies, since the content of such policies varies between the different types of government. Appropriate policy objectives for socialist (hegemonic or dominated) governments are high employment and extensive welfare; for bourgeois (hegemonic or dominated) governments, low inflation; and for 'balanced' governments, all three. Inappropriate policies are of course the reverse of these.

What Table 6.7 does is to relate appropriate and inappropriate performance to the mode of termination of governments—in this case distinguishing between 'regular' modes of termination, such as fixed elections and Prime Ministerial resignation and 'political' modes, indicating dissent or dissatisfaction. Anticipated elections, whose meaning is ambiguous (do they represent a reaction to success or to failure?), are left out of account.

If our expectations are correct, governments taking action appropriate to their own ideology should terminate 'regularly' more often. We are a little limited in some situations by small numbers: information about policies is confined to the later post-war period, and there are data missing and other cases omitted because of anticipated

TABLE 6.7. The relationship between policy performance and mode of termination, according to ideological complexion of government, 1965–1983

Ideological complexion	Mode of termination	Policy performance on welfare, employment, and inflation			
		Appropriate		Inappropriate	
		No.	%	No.	%
Socialist hegemony	Regular	14	100	5	62
	Political	—	—	3	38
Socialist dominance	Regular	10	59	1	20
	Political	7	41	4	80
Socialist–bourgeois balance	Regular	3	30	4	33
	Political	7	70	8	66
Bourgeois dominance	Regular	1	50	8	38
	Political	1	50	13	62
Bourgeois hegemony	Regular	17	85	10	50
	Political	3	15	10	50
All types	Regular	45	71	28	42
	Political	18	29	38	58

elections; the smaller numbers also inhibit us from going to individual country level). However, a general tendency does emerge for governments undertaking appropriate action to be seemingly less prone to fatal internal dissent. The exception, as one might expect, occurs in balanced situations, where hardly any difference occurs between governments pursuing appropriate policies and those pursuing inappropriate ones. Possibly, governments pursuing the goals of high employment, welfare, and low inflation (the policy line labelled as 'appropriate' here) are likely to generate conflict between opposed coalition partners in any case. On the whole, however, Table 6.7 does uphold our expectations, both for four out of the five types of government and on the basis of a general comparison across all types.

We can supplement the findings on modes of termination by looking at the effects of inappropriate and appropriate performance on the actual duration of governments. Again we would assume on the whole that governments satisfying their own and their supporters' policy aspirations would last longer, even though a very successful government might choose to capitalize on its success (where it can) by calling a snap election. On the other hand, elections are also anticipated when the government boxes itself into an impasse it cannot otherwise resolve. These considerations render the interpretation of straight duration, as before, rather ambiguous. For what they are worth, we give the figures in Table 6.8.

We have seen from Table 6.3 that mode of termination is related to duration. As dissent and dissatisfaction may stem from factors other than policy performance, we have controlled for this in Table 6.8 as well as for ideological type. Whether one looks at these more detailed average durations or at the overall figures for each different type of government (or indeed for all governments), it is clear that governments pursuing appropriate policies generally last longer. Sometimes the contrast is a slight one but it holds in all but three instances, in one of which the comparison is based on only one case of inappropriate action. Otherwise the idea that governments performing appropriately will survive longer is upheld—even though, as noted, some successful governments may deliberately go to the polls early. Some information on this point is—at last!—provided by Table 6.9, which we discuss next.

Given the central importance of economic policy to every government's activities (emphasized in our Implication 5(v) of Table 2.4) there is another, more 'objective' approach than comparing ideology

TABLE 6.8. Average duration of governments, according to ideological complexion, in relation to policy performance and mode of termination, 1965–1983

Ideological complexion	Mode of termination	Social and economic policy performance	
		Appropriate	Inappropriate
Socialist	Regular	2.33	1.98
hegemony	Political	1.27	1.34
	All	1.92	1.66
Socialist	Regular	2.34	2.00[a]
dominance	Political	2.00	0.60
	All	2.17	0.88
Socialist–bourgeois	Regular	1.70	1.98
balance	Political	1.37	1.16
	All	1.43	1.38
Bourgeois	Regular	1.13	1.70[a]
dominance	Political	1.10	0.70
	All	1.12	1.03
Bourgeois	Regular	2.73	2.08
hegemony	Political	1.56	1.45
	All	1.94	1.80
All types	Regular	2.16	2.03
	Political	1.42	1.18
	All	1.72	1.56

[a] Figure based on only one case.

to effects from which to estimate good or bad policy performance. That is, we can look directly at whether the government's tenure is associated with general prosperity or not (as measured on the OECD 'misery index'—a composite indicator of unemployment and inflation). Table 6.9 provides this information on the basis of dichotomizing above-average and below-average performance, and relating this to modes of termination for all governments, and for the different types already distinguished.

The table clearly shows a shift from governments ending with fixed elections to termination for 'political' reasons, as performance goes from above to below average. Interestingly, the percentage of governments ending with anticipated elections is higher—for every type of

TABLE 6.9. The relationship between economic performance of various types of government and mode of termination, 1965–1983

Reason for termination	Economic performance							
	Above average (%)				Below average (%)			
	Single-party majority governments	Majority coalition governments	Minority governments	All governments	Single-party majority governments	Majority coalition governments	Minority governments	All governments
Fixed election	42.9	42.9	47.8	44.9	25.0	22.2	24.1	23.5
Anticipated election	17.9	21.4	19.1	15.4	12.5	11.1	13.8	12.3
PM resigns voluntarily	7.1	7.1	4.8	7.7	—	2.2	3.5	2.0
PM resigns through ill health	3.6	3.6	4.8	3.9	4.2	4.4	3.5	4.1
Governmental dissension	14.3	14.3	9.5	15.4	25.0	26.8	24.1	25.5
Parliamentary dissension	7.1	7.1	9.5	6.4	20.8	22.2	24.1	22.4
Constitutional intervention	7.1	3.6	4.8	5.2	12.5	11.1	6.9	10.2
TOTAL	100.0	100.0	100.0	100.0	100.0	100.0	100.0	100.0
No. of governments	28	28	21	77	24	45	29	98

Note: 'Economic performance' is judged on the 'misery index' as employed by OECD (*Social Expenditures 1960–1990* (Paris: OECD, 1985). It is a composite index of mean rate of unemployment and inflation (annual), i.e. $\frac{U+I}{2}$ (see also H. E. Keman and T. van Dijk, 'Policy Formation as a Strategy to Overcome the Economic Crisis', in F. Castles and R. Wildermann (eds), *The Future of Party Government* (Berlin: De Gruyter, 1987), 127–62. Caretaker governments have been excluded from the statistics.

TABLE 6.10. Average duration of various types of government according to economic performance, 1965–1983

Type of government	Economic performance			
	Above average		Below average	
	Average duration (years)	No. of governments	Average duration (years)	No. of governments
Single-party majority	2.15	28	2.49	24
Majority coalition	2.16	28	1.49	45
Minority	1.63	21	1.30	29
All	1.97	77	1.76	98

Note: Economic performance is judged on the OECD's 'misery index'. Caretaker governments have been excluded from the statistics.

government—where economic performance has been above average than where it has been below average. It does seem that anticipating elections is more a strategy of successful, united governments than of disunited or failed ones.

We can supplement this finding by looking directly at the relationship between economic success and duration (bearing in mind the point just made about anticipated elections, which will lower duration also for successful governments). Table 6.10 presents the relevant figures. Above-average performance obtains a longer stay in office for all types of government save one-party majority governments, where the less successful governments hang on significantly longer. It is tempting to interpret this in terms of such governments' greater recourse to anticipated elections when they are successful. However, no difference appears in Table 6.9 between their termination in this way and that of other types of government. An alternative explanation is that single-party majority governments have a greater ability—and need, in view of their clear political responsibility—to carry on, compared to the other types. Whatever the explanation in this particular case, the link between duration and economic success holds in the other cases and overall.

The findings of this section, therefore, do generally demonstrate a relationship between good policy performance (whether measured 'subjectively' or 'objectively') and government stability and success (whether measured by mode of termination or by duration). Use of multiple indicators in this area seems advisable—one is always conscious of approaching 'stability' and 'success', the phenomena which really interest us, somewhat indirectly. On the whole, however, investigation on the basis of mode of termination bears out what we discover from the figures for duration. Good policy performance is more likely to ensure a government's survival with some kind of 'regular' termination, while bad or inappropriate performance exposes it to the risk of premature collapse, through 'political' recriminations.

EFFECTS OF POLICY PERFORMANCE ON FUTURE ELECTIONS AND GOVERNMENTS

A general expectation throughout the party literature is that successful parties will be rewarded electorally for their governmental performance and will thus have a better chance of constituting a future government. This is a common assumption of rational-choice and 'economic' theories of party democracy (otherwise parties have no motivation to be responsive in government).[10] It is perforce an even stronger assumption of theorists of the political-business cycle, who assume governments manipulate the economy to present a good face to electors and ensure their electoral success.[11]

Our own theory takes a more negative view of this process, assuming that parties are more likely to be blamed for failure than rewarded for success. To the extent that parties do not carry through characteristic policies, therefore, we expect them to lose votes (Table 2.4 Implication 6(i)), on the grounds that this causes certain dissent among activists and supporters, whereas winning over new voters is more problematic. Further, we expect that policy disagreements between coalition partners will have effects on their ability to form a future government together (Implication 6(ii)).

Our pessimism about an automatic reward for success is shared by some of the more critical writing on the political-business cycle.[12] An interesting general finding which bears on this point is that only 38.8 per cent of parties we have studied over the whole post-war period actually gained in elections (on average, 5.9 per cent in legislative seats). Conversely, 61.2 per cent experienced losses, at an average of

TABLE 6.11. Electoral fate of parties in government, 1965–1983

	All gain votes	Some gain votes, some lose votes	All lose votes
Coalition governments[a] in which this occurs (%)	8.9	68.4	22.8
Average increase/decrease in no. of parliamentary seats (%)	3.7	−0.25	−7.9

[a] The number of such governments is 79.

6.8 per cent. As many of these were parties in government at the time of the election, it does seem that incumbency is a mixed blessing. Much depends, of course, on circumstances within the government at the time, and on its relative success.

As a preliminary, we look at the electoral performance of incumbent parties and the effects this has on future governmental participation. Relevant figures for the later post-war period are reported in Tables 6.11 and 6.12. In the former we see reflections of the general tendency of government parties to lose rather than to gain votes. There are substantially more cases where all government parties lose rather than where all gain. In two-thirds of the cases, however, some gain and some lose. What happens as a result? From Table 6.12 we see that previously incumbent, electorally gaining parties have a slightly greater chance of gaining control of more ministries in the next government than of losing posts. But the differences are marginal and not at all as great as we might have expected in the abstract. The disjunction between election results and governmental rewards is heightened by the fact that 54.2 per cent of all post-war parties who made the greatest gains at an election did not get into the ensuing coalition.

Electorally unsuccessful parties, on the other hand, certainly lose government posts rather than gain them, though half retain the same number without apparent consequences from their electoral failure. Failure does therefore seem to be punished more than success is rewarded, as anticipated, but not *much* more. The main lesson of the table is to caution us against facile assumptions that electoral performance is translated very directly into government position—particularly in the case of coalitions.

We can look at this relationship more directly on the basis of Table 6.13, which gives us the vote gains and losses associated with 'appropriate' and 'inappropriate' policy actions (cf. Table 6.7 and supporting discussion) for the different ideological families of parties. The table confirms previous expectations by showing that inappropriate performance tends fairly consistently to produce electoral losses. Appropriate performance on the whole serves only to limit losses, except in the case of socialist governments, which make very marginal gains. Presumably, electoral resentments tend to build up against all governments, so that an appropriate policy response is only a basis, or first stage, in a strategy to promote electoral success, and not in itself a guarantee that it will follow.

The religious parties are entirely anomalous—possibly for two reasons. (1) Their policy position, as we have seen from Chapters 4 and 5, is half-way between that of socialists and the more mainstream bourgeois parties. Hence they may be subject to more mixed expectations, so it is unclear what an appropriate response is in their situation—certainly maintaining welfare, but otherwise is it to maintain employment or reduce inflation? (2) They are almost always in coalition, and may limit losses in inappropriate situations by distancing themselves from government partners—a tendency, however, that may work against them where appropriate action is taken, and the credit goes to the partner.

There is of course a possibly simpler explanation: the anomalous gain for religious parties in the last column is based on only three cases—the lowest entry in the table. Apart from this, all the figures

TABLE 6.12. Effect of electoral fate of parties in government upon their share of ministries in the subsequent government, 1965–1983

	No. of ministries		
	Increases	Remains the same	Decreases
% of parties having gained votes in which this occurs[a]	29.9	43.2	26.9
% of parties having lost votes in which this occurs[b]	14.3	50.8	34.9

[a] The number of such parties is 67.
[b] The number of such parties is 63.

TABLE 6.13. The relationship between policy performance and electoral fate of parties in government, according to character of dominant party in government, 1965–1983

Character of dominant party in government	Policy performance			
	Appropriate		Inappropriate	
	No. of governments	% change in votes	No. of governments	% change in votes
Socialist	17	+0.17	10	−2.50
Religious	20	−1.73	3	+1.30
Liberal	6	−0.10	7	−4.03
Conservative	14	−0.12	19	−1.92
All types	57	−0.60	39	−2.07

Note: Iceland, Israel, and Luxemburg are excluded from the statistics. Only governments in existence just before an election are included. The percentages represent the *net* gain or loss over all relevant cases. Governments include both single-party and coalition governments (identifying as dominant the PM's party).

confirm our expectations. As we trace out the consequences of government parties' policy decisions, therefore, we find, as is natural, that links become more tenuous the further we go into the future. There appears to be quite a direct relationship between the adoption of appropriate policies and the internal cohesion of governments (Tables 6.7 and 6.8). However, this becomes weaker in terms of electoral rewards and punishments (in the sense that appropriate actions do not gain an immediate reward). In any case, as Table 6.12 indicates, electoral consequences are themselves only muddily reflected in the allocation of government posts.

All this has consequences for theories of parliamentary democracy which assume automatic rewards for parties which carry through their electoral mandate. (Downs, however, explicitly noted the lesser responsibility and accountability of parties in coalitions, which form the bulk of our cases.[13]) The finding that inappropriate policy responses, already seen to be associated with greater internal dissent and disagreement (Tables 6.7 and 6.9), are generally punished with electoral losses certainly upholds our general theoretical expectations, regardless of the fact that appropriate responses do not attract greater immediate rewards.

TABLE 6.14. The relationship between mode of termination of a coalition government and similarity of composition of the subsequent government, 1950–1984

(%)

Parties involved in subsequent government	Reason for termination						
	Election		Resignation of PM		Political		
	Fixed	Anticipated	Voluntary	Health	Governmental dissension	Parliamentary dissension	Constitutional intervention
All	37.1	50.0	50.0	100.0	56.3	36.0	22.2
Some	20.0	14.3	50.0	—	18.7	24.0	33.3
None	42.9	35.7	—	—	25.0	40.0	44.4
TOTAL	100.0	100.0	100.0	100.0	100.0	100.0	100.0
No. of coalitions	35	14	4	6	48	25	9

Note: Israel is excluded from the statistics.

Source: Authors' own data, and K. von Beyme, Political Parties in Western Democracies (Aldershot: Gower, 1985).

We complete our analysis by studying the effects of experiences in one government upon participation in the next, in Table 6.14. This relates the circumstances in which a coalition government terminates to the composition of the next government. We expect (Table 2.4 Implication 6 (ii)) that parties which end up by quarrelling and bringing government to a premature close will find it harder to collaborate with each other in a successor government, and if they do it will be on the purely office-holding basis of a minimal coalition. Operationally, therefore, we expect governments which end with elections or Prime Ministerial resignation to encourage continued collaboration more than governments terminated for 'political' reasons.

Table 6.14 offers no support for this idea, however. Parties in governments terminating with elections are consistently less likely to co-operate again; and if they all do, this is more likely than in the other cases to be on the basis of a minimal winning coalition (61 per cent of parties all collaborating after a fixed election and 86 per cent after an anticipated election form minimal winning coalitions, as compared to 44 per cent and 59 per cent in the other cases). It is possible that the findings reflect the change in relative party positions brought about by elections and that our operationalization of regular circumstances of termination as opposed to 'political' here reaches its limit. But there is no support for Implication 6(ii) in these data.

CONCLUSIONS

Breakdown and termination are perhaps the most difficult aspects of government behaviour to analyse, in part because of the lack of previous research and in part because of difficulties in pinning down and putting into focus such diffuse phenomena. In practically all previous studies straight duration has been taken as an unproblematic indicator of stability and effectiveness. A more direct indicator, though not an unproblematic one, is the way in which governments end; 'effectiveness' can also be approached more directly in terms of policy performance. Putting all these together, we have found support for the relationships postulated in our original theory (Table 2.4 Implications 5(ii)–5(v)) between lack of policy agreement and premature and involuntary dissolution; and some evidence for the effects of these continuing into subsequent elections (Implication 6(i)). They do not appear to affect the constitution of the next government, however (Implication 6(ii)). Difficulties of measurement and limits on numbers of cases and the information available render it difficult to be more conclusive than this. But the main thrust of our policy-based theory is clearly supported.

The wider significance of the results, against the background of previous rational-choice theory, is that just as minimal-winning, core, and other theories have linked instability and shorter duration to non-conformity with their prescriptions for 'good' coalitions, so here we have an indication that governments formed without policy agreements will be shorter-lived, less effective, and less stable. Putting together the evidence from this chapter with that from Chapter 3, we now have strong support for the idea that policy criteria have not only a determining role in the initial formation of governments, but also a continuing influence over their functioning.

Parties Steering the State: Evaluation and Development of the Theory

If accepted, as the weight of the evidence indicates it should be, our theory carries major methodological and substantive implications. On the methodological side we have two 'firsts': a truly comprehensive account of parties in government (including but not confined to coalition and government formation), which actually fits the experience of post-war Westernized democracies! Substantively, the theory incorporates a view of parties as significant, if not *the* significant actors within parliamentary democracies. This contrasts sharply with critiques which see parties as constrained by other, more powerful economic forces to pursue policies and actions which are practically indistinguishable. Our theory provides a good way to 'bring parties back in', not least because its precisely stated and validated assertions lend it credibility in relation to critiques which are often imprecise about key concepts and consequently not susceptible either to proof or disproof.

Since substantive weight depends to a considerable extent on methodological standing, we devote the next three sections of this chapter to a comprehensive evaluation of the theory in relation to other accounts and models of party government. The evaluation has an interest in its own right, as our theory has been developed and tested with spatial models of party behaviour in mind, and it is important to see how they stand in relation to each other after the analysis.

The theoretical evaluation centres round the question of government formation, since it is on this that most models and theories up to now have concentrated. Substantively, our main interest centres round policy—how far parties implement significantly different policies and thus appear as major influences shaping State action. We deal with this in the last section, following the methodological discussions.

A SATISFACTORY EXPLANATION?

The striking methodological paradox about parties in government is the ease with which, at a practical level, we can anticipate and explain what they do, and the difficulty we experience in constructing a theory which performs equally well. To take specific examples, it is clear that the *pentapartito* in Italy will continue in some form to the end of the decade, its frequent internal crises not affecting the stability of the underlying arrangement; that the Dutch Christian Democratic Appeal will continue to dictate the composition of government co-alitions in the absence of any major intervening event; and that in the Nordic countries and Ireland predominant-party governments will alternate with coalitions of the other significant parties.

The laborious theoretical constructions which litter the field do no better than this predictively, and often much worse.[1] The solution is not, however, to abandon theory in favour of *ad hoc* judgements. Chapter 1 pointed out that practical judgements are invariably based on general assumptions, so we always operate on the basis of *some* theory, though it is usually implicit. Failure to articulate the theoretical assumptions, however, leaves open the possibility that we may make right judgements for wrong reasons, or for other reasons than those we think we are basing them on.

To advance our knowledge of parties there is really no alternative to operating with theory; only we should make it a better and more relevant theory than what has gone before. This implies that we should consider seriously why practical predictions are often better than theoretical ones, and why the latter should be so often wrong.

The answer to one question is bound up with the other. Most theorizing has gone wrong because it bases itself exclusively on a one-dimensional (often literally and spatially one-dimensional) assumption about party motivation. Over the last thirty years formal theory has moved from exclusive concentration on office-seeking to obsessive concern with ideology. As we argued above, the greater ease of formalization offered by a one-variable theory is counterbalanced by difficulties in approximating to the real world. So it is no wonder that its characterizations are often more misleading than instructive.

What, on the other hand, accounts for the success of practical judgements is not an excessive detailing of particular situations, but an appreciation of the structural and ideological continuities underlying party systems, combined with the realization that these will be modified if the pressures are strong enough. Without being excessively historicist, practical judgement does therefore take some account of changing circumstances in a way that the traditionally static, ahistorical formal theories do not.

The obvious way to improve explanation in this field, therefore, is precisely by generalizing the continuities and forces for change underlying practical judgements. Of the continuities, the major ones are ideology—which provides parties not only with a distinct motivation but also with their very identity—and structure, in the sense of the parties' long-term relationships and basic strength. Both are featured in existing formal theory. Where practical judgements differ is in recognizing that ideological influences vary in their effects, sometimes focusing everyone's attention on a single central issue or set of issues, sometimes allowing for shades of variation between individual parties, and sometimes being suppressed altogether in face of dramatic and threatening events. Not being tied to a theoretical insistence on ideology dominating in the same way all the time, practical judgement is able to make sense of the interaction of party preferences with situational factors, such as an international crisis or a rise in internal tensions between social groups.

It is precisely this interaction which we have tried to summarize in our theory through the specific assumptions and derivations set out in Chapter 2 (Tables 2.1–2.4). The remarkable fit between these theoretical expectations and actual behaviour in a variety of governmental situations in very different countries entitles us to regard them as a good approximation of the rules governing party actions. They form an explanation of such actions in the precise sense of relating diverse aspects of party and government behaviour to consistent underlying motivations, and of thus reducing the complexity of the real world to simpler basic principles which make it more understandable and predictable.

Certainly our explanation cannot and does not purport to cover every specific case of party or governmental behaviour. It is a statistical theory which accounts for a majority of the actions undertaken in particular situations, not for all of them. To do this is already a great deal, however. Whether one tries to explain Social Democratic pensions policy in Sweden during the 1950s or the change of preference of the German Free Democrats for coalition partners in West Germany in 1983, the theory presented here is illuminating. Even to account for 'exceptional' cases we need a theory covering 'normal' ones, since without it we cannot begin to distinguish what is exceptional.

Our theory explains how party democracy works by referring behaviour back to the ideologically based preferences of the parties and assigning an order to these. As these preferences are taken as enduring and stable, they clearly come before the time-bound behaviour they are supposed to explain, and so fall into a classic cause-and-effect sequence. In fact, all theories of party behaviour, including mathematical and formal ones, similarly draft ideologies and preferences to explain behaviour, and assume a causal sequence of the same kind.

An objection could be made none the less that these party preferences, with their ordering of defence of democracy followed by Left–Right conflicts followed by group-based objectives (Table 2.1 Assumption 3), are postulated arbitrarily, with no real justification of why parties should have these particular preferences and such an ordering. What gives them such unique importance and how did they come to acquire it in the first place?

An obvious answer is that theories cannot explain everything. It is enough to show that the behaviours under consideration can be related to each other and traced to simpler underlying processes: there is no inherent obligation to explain the particular shape of party preferences too. That constitutes a problem for another theory and another investigation.

In this case there is, however, no need to take refuge in methodological evasion, however justified. The best-known theory of the development of party systems traces the preferences we attribute to parties back to the group interests they mobilized in the period of mass enfranchisement at the end of the nineteenth and beginning of the twentieth centuries.[2] We could hardly base ourselves on a more extensive or generally accepted explanation than that.

This theory of party development, it is true, gives equal weight to all types of group-related preferences, with no special priority for the defence of democracy or for Left–Right cleavages over others (moral–religious, regional, urban–rural). There is, however, a case, supported by much evidence, for the predominance of the Left–Right cleavage when it comes into play.[3] And developmental theory itself traces the last great split in the party system to the alignment of Social Democrats with their bourgeois rivals from 1920–2, in support of constitutional principles, against Communists and Fascists. From there it is not a great step to asserting the priority given to defence of democracy when it is in question. Thus the ordering we postulate for party preference fits comfortably with the developmental theory of party systems, even if not wholly derived from it. Plausibility is all that is really required to justify the assumption in the context of our theory: to demand that every assumption itself be fully justified and explained is to push it unfairly into an infinite regress.

We have tried to demonstrate that, besides its remarkable fit to the empirical evidence, our theory conforms to all the general requirements that can reasonably be made of a satisfactory explanation. Two more specialized objections can still be raised, however, stemming from the basic strategies we have adopted in its construction. Essentially, what we have done is to learn from the historical experience, codifying and abstracting it into a set of understandable general principles of party behaviour. Of course in doing this we have not been uninfluenced by the way in which earlier theories have organized and explained their material—one rarely starts without some initial ideas of what is relevant and salient, derived from earlier discussion. However, we have tried to confront the historical experience freshly and without imposing preconceived ideas too rigidly upon it.

In doing so we have steered a course between excessive coverage of each specific post-war situation (in which event the theory would have ended up as mere redescription of particular cases) and the kind of over-formalistic abstraction which has deprived earlier theory of practical credibility. Such a strategy opens us to criticism from two sides: from historians, first, for over-simplification and over-generalization where the truth is in fact embedded in the detailed unfolding of events bounded by a specific time and place; and from formal theorists, secondly, for having put together various assumptions which reflect rather than explain the post-war democratic experiences.

The first objection we consider immediately; we then devote the third section of the chapter to the general standing of our theory *qua* theory and the fourth to a detailed consideration of how it can aid the general development of knowledge in this field.

The answer to the first objection is in fact quite simple: to construct a theory at all one has to simplify and generalize, rather than describe. There is no point in constructing a general explanation clogged up with minutiae of time and place. The purpose of a theory is to catch and specify general tendencies, even at the cost of not fitting *all* cases (hence one can check it only statistically, and it is no disproof to cite one or two counter-examples). The theory should, however, fit the majority of cases at least in a general way, and provide a sensible and above all an applicable starting-point for discussion of any particular situation, even one which in the end it turns out not to explain—here it can at any rate serve as the basis of a special analysis which shows which (presumably unique or idiosyncratic) factors prevent it from fitting.

A general theory of this kind serves the historian by providing him with an entry point and starting-ideas. These, we would argue, he always brings to the case anyway; with a validated theory he knows they are reasonably founded and has a context within which he can make comparisons with greater confidence. As we suggested at the outset, there is no inherent conflict between historical analysis and general theory. Each can, indeed must, be informed by the other and supplement the other's efforts. Theory is therefore a *necessary* simplification and generalization of particular motives and influences, not simply a restatement of them, though complete loss of contact with historical reality will render it too abstract and ultimately irrelevant.

AD HOC OR GENERAL THEORY?

This still leaves us facing a second line of criticism, that our assumptions are *too* historically based and *too* close to the reality they seek to explain to be taken as real theory. To qualify as a 'real' theory rather than an *ad hoc* one, assumptions need to be abstract in form and generally applicable, without regard to time and place.

Riker's *obiter dictum* in regard to his minimal-winning formulation might be generalized in this context: 'In social situations similar to n-person zero-sum games with side payments, participants create coalitions just as large as they believe will ensure winning and no larger.'[4] Here a general body of mathematical reasoning about the interactions of rational actors (n-person zero-sum game theory) was applied to governmental coalition formation on the basis that parties are unified rational actors concerned with the division of finite and limited benefits. One could adapt a similar formulation for the theories of the core or of proto-coalition formation outlined in Chapter 1: 'In political situations similar to n-person variable-sum games, participants support only those coalitions producing outcomes which favour themselves as much as possible given the constraints imposed by actual and potential allies.' Again a body of general, contentless propositions about the behaviour of rational actors is being drawn up to explain the actions of political parties, once they are identified as rational actors in the sense specified.

In contrast, our own assumptions make use of the concepts of rational choice only in the very general sense, common also to historians, that parties do not knowingly act so as to thwart their own goals, that they are reasonably consistent in adapting ends to means, and so on. There is no pretence of specifying and applying precisely defined and general game-theoretical concepts to party behaviour. Instead the theory starts and ends with political parties and is simply irrelevant to the behaviour of, for instance, firms, nuclear-defence strategists, or gamblers—all of which and many more are forms of strategic behaviour covered by game theory. In that sense our theory is clearly specific and specialized.

On the other hand, it may be asked in what precise sense, once we move from zero-sum applications and minimal winning coalitions, variable-sum formulations do represent direct applications of game theory to party behaviour. Certainly game-theoretical ideas influence the way the theory is conceived and presented, but there is no clear derivation from a specific mathematical game. The relationship of game theory to formal models of party behaviour seems in fact analogous to the general influence of 'rational choice' on our own formulation—that is, it is inspirational rather than strictly generative.

That said, there are clearly different levels of generality among formal models themselves. Of the two mentioned specifically in Chapter 1, the theory of proto-coalition formation among parties (where coalition-building proceeds in stages, as parties that are contiguous in policy space combine on the basis of a compromise policy and then do the same with other parties or proto-coalitions when they lack the strength to dominate on their own) seems more specialized to party behaviour than does the theory of the core, or that of uncovered sets (where any set of actors in a policy space will only settle on a coalition within certain limits defined by their collective preferences). Core theory could apply to any actors engaged in bargaining over potentially conflictual preferences. Only in institutional settings which provide the time and the structure for sequential bargaining is proto-coalition formation likely.

These differences, however, become less significant when we consider the additional assumptions entailed in the application of any general theory to the specific field of parties. There is a tendency among formal theorists to consider the act of application as a mere formality before the mathematics begin: one need only assume that parties are unified rational actors to permit their representation as points in a space with preference vectors; then formal reasoning can be applied on the basis, essentially, of the original contentless postulates. When, however, we actually examined the assumptions required to generate the policy space within which preferences are represented, we saw that much more was involved than that. Indeed, the assumptions which translate the abstract model into a theory of *party* behaviour look strikingly like our own (compare Table 1.1 with Table 2.1).

Certainly 'points in one- or two-dimensional space', and 'distances' between them, compared to 'crisis', 'Left–Right conflict' and 'group-related preferences', represent a more generalized and widely applicable vocabulary. To apply the theory, however, one has to postulate not only an interpretation for the dimensions but also a meaning for the distances measured on them, which quickly brings analysis to a highly specific level—in effect, often boiling down to a simplistic assertion of the unvarying dominance of Left–Right divisions. It is significant that the suggestions made in the companion volume in this series[5] for improvements to formal theory correspond closely to the various assumptions specified in our Table 2.1 (on the pivotal role of the legislative vote of confidence, for example).

There is clearly an advantage in having a theory of party behaviour directly derived from wider theory, especially if it can be expressed mathematically. While some formal models of party behaviour are capable of wider application, there is no direct derivation from game theory. Moreover the very process of applying them to party behaviour deprives them of their general abstract character and forces them to operate on postulates very similar to those of our theory. There is thus no question within the party context of one theory being more or less *ad hoc* than another. All depend equally on assumptions about substantive party preferences to attain definite conclusions. On formal as compared to substantive criteria all are equally parsimonious and economical (again compare Tables 1.1 and 2.1).

Other things being equal, mathematical models of party behaviour would clearly be preferred to verbal ones, and theories generalizable to non-party contexts to party-specific ones. Recent research has shown other things not to be equal, however. Minimal-winning theory clearly does not correspond to most party behaviour in government. Analysis of party electoral and governmental programmes (the best information we have on policy positions and distances), shows that no policy-based theory adequately explains the observed phenomena.[6] If programmatic emphases are reflected in government outputs, this seems to be through the party control of ministries in which they are interested.[7] No formal theory of party behaviour accommodates such a tendency, but ours does (see Chapter 4).

More broadly, it could be said that our policy-based theory fits where spatial ones do not, precisely because it avoids over-specification of the phenomena involved. Politicians are more likely to think in broad terms of crisis/non-crisis, confrontation of Left and Right, and group-related politics, rather than of making finely calculated moves along a graduated continuum. Theory-building thus becomes a choice between representing party thought processes in their own terms and so improving the empirical fit, or devising an elegant abstract formulation more closely linked with developments in other fields. For reasons already discussed in Chapter 1, we have chosen the former. Far from downgrading the kind of explanation involved, achieving an empirical fit this way seems to us an advance. It provides a basic context for further research, as we have indicated already in the discussion of its relationship with historical analysis. The uses of a validated theory do not stop with historical analysis, however. Because the assumptions of our verbal formulation so closely parallel those of applied spatial models, there is a possibility of developing aspects of spatial reasoning within the context it provides. We detail these in the next section.

SPATIAL EXTENSIONS AND REFINEMENTS

An obvious place to start, because so crucial to any theory of government formation, is the question of what constitutes a viable government. As we saw in Chapter 1, even spatial theories which have abandoned zero- or constant-sum assumptions in favour of policy still use minimal-winning criteria to define the end-point of government formation. While this is inconsistent with their variable-sum assumptions, it is understandable since 'viability', while clearly defined in general terms,[8] has never been operationalized very precisely. Pushing it back to the ability to gain a legislative vote of confidence (Table 2.1 Assumption 1) merely poses the same question within a more specific context: What are the characteristics which ensure that governments will win a vote of confidence? There are three alternative lines of approach.

(*a*) One can apply data-based procedures, as in the third section of Chapter 3, extrapolating from experiences over the post-war period. That is, if governments always have over 50 per cent of legislative seats but barely more on average, one can deduce that the condition of viability is minimal-winning. If the average is 60 per cent and over, one can deduce that viable governments need a surplus majority. If governments tend to be minority, with a particular party composition (perhaps the presence of a centre party), one can deduce that 40 per cent or less of seats are required if that party is present in government. If a definite 'government formula' seems to operate in certain periods, one can take governments conforming to it as viable and others not.

The problem with such a procedure is that the data-based extrapolations are then applied to test hypotheses on the same data, with a consequent risk of tautology. We mostly avoided this in Chapter 3 since we were testing a specialized hypothesis on a limited subset of data, but it is a clear danger in testing general theory.

(*b*) Theoretical examples of what viable governments might look like in the context of parties exclusively concerned with the same policy field, have been proposed by Budge and Laver.[9] Figure 7.1 illustrates the essence of the argument. Clearly the coalition BCD is most likely to emerge, since it is preferred by A to any involving E, and by E to any involving A, while the likely coalition partners prefer each other to either of the other two.

Fig. 7.1. An example of a viable government coalition with a minority of seats, in a one-dimensional policy space

Note: A, B, C, D, and E are parties, positioned on the one-dimensional policy continuum L–R. The numbers represent the percentage of seats held by each party.

One problem with the example (within its own terms) is what to do when more than one policy field is involved. An attempted solution is to identify for every relevant dimension the party in the position of C in Figure 7.1 (i.e. possessing the median legislator and hence likely to be crucial to every coalition that might form). If the same party had the median legislator on all or almost all dimensions, a government containing it might be taken as 'policy-viable'.[10] If no such party existed, all governments might be arbitrary, short-lived, and unstable (following the suggestions of core theory: see the fifth section of Chapter 1).

(c) This, however, is a pure policy-based conception of viability. Parties using possession of a preferred ministry as the major way to implement policies of interest could act quite differently: for instance, A and E could form a coalition by splitting ministries 50–50. On the realistic assumption that there could be acceptable trade-offs between ministries and programmes, even for policy-pursuing parties, this seems implausible.

An example of what might be involved is given in Figure 7.2, showing the same policy dimension as Figure 7.1 but taking into account what parties might expect in the way of ministries within the possible coalitions they might form. This transforms the prospects for government formation since parties A and E, being relatively extreme, might well hope to get full control of ministries in their preferred policy sector or sectors from a coalition with their ideological opposite, or failing that with the centre party C. The slightly off-centre parties B and D would expect fewer ministries from any coalition precisely because they are closer to the other parties and their preferences for ministries overlap with A, C, and E. (A somewhat similar suggestion is made by Leubbert, that parties with tangential policies might prefer each other to those closer; in this case C might be preferred as a coalition partner by the two extreme parties.[11])

One could indeed go further and speculate that A and E, precisely because they can hope for very little in a policy-based coalition, may well downgrade their concern with general government policy in favour of ministerial allocations—not because they are exclusively concerned with office but simply because ways of achieving policy ends other than through implementation within ministries are blocked. In this case the very nature of the figure would cease to be Euclidean: the dimensions would be weighted differently for the different parties.

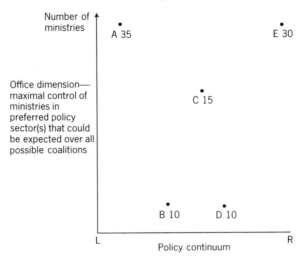

FIG. 7.2. An example of viable alternative coalitions, in a mixed two-dimensional space representing policy and distribution of ministries

Note: A, B, C, D, and E are parties; the numbers indicate the percentage of seats held by each.

Our analysis of policy-based preferences for ministries (Chapter 4) clearly demonstrates the plausibility of mixed strategies of this kind, which are hard to understand either from a formal, abstract perspective or from a historical-institutional approach. It helps us to break with the confined tradition, within spatial analyses, of concentrating exclusively on the policy programmes of parties and governments, as though general declarations were the only things which exercised the minds of party decision-makers.

A major task for mathematical and spatial analysis, therefore, is to analyse conditions for governmental viability within a mixed space, defined by party dominance of the ministries within their preferred policy sector or sectors as well as by the more familiar policy dimensions, and allowing for differential preferences for ministries among the parties. Specification of new conditions for viability would not only save variable-sum theories from the dangers of tautology and internal inconsistency. It would also start to provide a theoretical basis for tackling the trade-offs between ministries and policies discussed in the last section of Chapter 1.

A second area for formal development within the context of our overall theory relates to Assumptions 2 and 3 of Table 2.1. These specify circumstances in which almost all parties share the same policy position in face of threats or crisis, or in which left- or right-wing sympathies produce the same effect among the parties of each tendance. They also identify other situations in which parties form coalitions on the basis of policy agreement and minimal viable coalitions in the absence of these.

These substantially validated assumptions offer a taxonomic aid to formal theory, in the sense of specifying cases in which particular postulates apply and others to which they are irrelevant—for example, when parties converge on one or two common preference points. Here spatial analysis has nothing to add. Where a more everyday type of party politics holds sway, and parties spread out over disparate, group-related preferences, this type of policy-based analysis (and mixed policy–office analysis as illustrated in Figure 7.2) can be illuminating. It remains an open question in that situation whether politicians' actions are best modelled in subtly graduated spaces or whether abrupt dichotomies and discontinuities best characterize their thinking. It is clear, however, that the more traditional types of policy-based analysis could apply here, providing a basis for the application of theories like those we have discussed—of proto-coalition formation and the core, among others.

Clearly, if we can distinguish a class of government-formation situations to which formal policy models particularly apply, it should substantially improve their fit and predictive ability. This among other things is what our verbal theory is able to do, and it is one reason for saying that it provides an overall context within which formal theory applies. There has been a tendency, given the very mixed success of all policy-based theories, to argue that each theory models processes within certain countries while others are fitted better by another theory. We would argue on the basis of our analysis that the difference arises less through country differences than from the occurrence of different types of government-formation situations in varying proportions within different countries. Specifying clear institutional conditions under which different models apply is clearly a more satisfactory theoretical strategy than tying them, without a clear rationale, to different national politics.

One task for formal policy models is to determine, more precisely than we have done in Chapter 3, when no basis of policy agreement for a coalition exists, under the conditions of 'normal' politics. In such cases zero-sum, minimal-winning ideas will be more applicable than variable-sum, policy-based ones since nothing remains but to share out offices, general policy being blocked on the major questions. It is clear after our analysis that minimal-winning ideas cannot be left unchanged, however. Two major modifications are needed to make this approach useful:

(a) 'Winning' needs to be modified to 'viable', which will involve different criteria under different configurations of parties.

(b) Depending on party preferences for ministries and the extent to which they clash, the game will be more or less zero-sum.

The models would thus need to be substantially modified. But there is no doubt that minimal-winning ideas provide a better initial approach to coalition formation in this type of situation than pure policy-based ones. Again our theory provides a way of distinguishing the different situations to which different models might optimally apply.

To sum up, not only is our comprehensive formulation of party behaviour in government perfectly compatible with the application of formal, mathematical theory: it actually facilitates that application by showing where it is most appropriate and by enriching it with new ideas. It has the ability to reconcile previous approaches by demonstrating that each is more applicable under certain circumstances.

As stated at the outset of this investigation, validation of any one theory in this field represents a general advance, as the necessary similarity of many assumptions means that it can provide stable points of reference for others. This is what our theory clearly does in relation to spatial theory and historical analysis. It may indeed be its major contribution to research in the field to demarcate the areas within which formal theory can fruitfully operate, while emphasizing the need to link government formation with other party behaviours in government, such as internal disputes and termination, distribution of offices, and above all policy-making.

SUBSTANTIVE IMPLICATIONS FOR THE THEORY OF THE STATE

It is at this point, after the methodological evaluation, that we return to the substantive concerns introduced at the beginning of the chapter. While the precise way in which parties form or end governments is not of much interest to those who believe them to be unimportant anyway, the idea that they influence the most important State policies poses an obvious challenge to critiques of parliamentary democracy which see policy as determined by other interests (such as business), parties as essentially identical, and electoral choice as a sham.

One example of such a position is formed by (neo-)Marxist analyses of party government in parliamentary democracy, which consider parties at best as intermediaries of societal interests, and at worse as mere instruments of capitalist or economic interests.[12] Another line of criticism, stemming from '(neo-)corporatist' discussions of late capitalism, views parties as being replaced by interest associations, which seemingly determine policy formation.[13] From such a viewpoint it goes almost without saying that the role of political parties in government is obsolete.

Our theory does not conclusively disprove such assertions. But it casts doubt on them by asserting that parties have quite distinct (sometimes radically distinct) policies on the most significant decisions made by governments, and that they follow these up when in power. Interests like Business and Labour do affect politics, but through their ties with parties rather than bypassing them or confronting them. The legislative strength acquired by parties through elections is a significant factor in enabling them to advance their policy through government participation, so elections do provide meaningful choices and voting is a significant act.

Our analysis has thus demonstrated that not only do politics matter, but indeed party differences on ideology and policy preferences matter as well. This is in clear contrast to a number of tenets of those 'schools' (Marxist and non-Marxist) that argue for the irrelevance of parties as agents of change, and of government as an agency for influencing society.

Three currents of criticism can be discerned in this respect: first, those who think that class divisions are the overriding determinant of state actions;[14] secondly, those who hold the view of the 'strong State', i.e. the idea that the 'Stateness'[15] of society implies that political actors are becoming less relevant;[16] thirdly, those who believe that economic interests, and particularly the way these are embedded in economic life and their degree of 'associability', ultimately steer the State's course.[17] All these views have their merits, but certainly are not convincing theoretically or empirically with respect to the essential role and position of parties in government and in society in general.

The first, class-based approach, which is closest to Marxist tradition, may not necessarily be incorrect in itself, but—apart from the fact that empirically it is still weakly founded—its tenability does not exclude the possibility of parties being viable intermediators and bearers of (class) interests. Indeed we have demonstrated throughout this study not only that Left and Right are (still) meaningful concepts, but also that the related party differences do matter with respect to policy formation and policy performance. Hence, although class divisions may affect societal power distribution structurally, in an asymmetrical sense they certainly do not prove the irrelevance of parties or governments.

In contrast, the 'strong-State critique' seeks to emphasize the role of the (relatively) autonomous State, that institution which is considered to be capable of action independent of societal actors (such as classes, parties, interests, and associations). Again, to a certain extent this view of the State and its implications for parties and government appear tenable enough. Moreover, unlike the first school it has been extensively investigated,[18] and it appears that within certain policy areas, like external security, or in periods of (economic) crisis, the State apparatus as such is capable of autonomous actions. Yet this does not invalidate our approach, nor its tenets and conclusions. As we have outlined in Chapters 1 and 5, under certain circumstances (war, anti-democratic threat, economic stagnation) parties refrain from competition and via government enlarge the room for the state to manœuvre. However, in almost all instances this situation is temporary. This only signifies, in our view, that government is a viable intermediary of various, often conflicting, interests, which is able to integrate them and procure stability.

Our analysis also shows that political institutions and related actors are at the heart of the State, mediating societal pressures and conflicts. It is easy to see, therefore, that the third school, the economistic view, is hardly tenable. Of course, the economic well-being of the nation is a *raison d'état* for any political system and serves as a constraint on political action. It has been demonstrated in this study, however, that economic management by means of party governments is feasible and is effective. In Chapter 6 we have shown that both the duration of governments and their reasons for termination not only vary cross-nationally, but that this is in large part due to the behaviour of parties and is related to the policy performance of government.

What these findings show is that a comprehensive theory of party government is essential for understanding and assessing the relationship between State and society. The alternative views discussed here are therefore not wholly mistaken or superfluous, but they would do well to relate the results presented in this study to their own points of view and to the way these are to be empirically and analytically investigated.

The theory we have tested is closely related to standard versions of the party-mandate theory of democracy, in which parties transmute popular preferences through the electoral support they gain into government policy. The substantive significance of our theory is that it translates this well-established account into empirically testable and now validated propositions, which is more than most critiques have been able to do. So far as party effects on government policy and expenditures are concerned, some of this has been done before.[19] Our investigation is the first that puts policy-influence hypotheses in the context of an overall theory of party behaviour, so that the fit of one part of the theory to the data is strengthened by a high degree of fit elsewhere, and a comprehensive contextual evaluation.

One could only evade this proof by arguing that in some sense the policy areas examined in Chapter 5 are unimportant, so that party decisions upon them do not really demonstrate that parties steer the State. In this case, however, the onus is on critics to cite policy areas which could be more important than economics, welfare, and defence, and the trade-offs between them. To most people they will appear to be at the very centre of what the State does.

Moreover, it is exactly these same policy concerns that are cited by critics of the party-control hypothesis to show that it is wrong. We have been able to show that both welfare policies and economic policies vary cross-nationally and over time, and that this can be meaningfully related to the composition of party governments. On the one hand these findings contradict the deterministic views of societal variants of State theory. On the other hand they also demonstrate the inadequacy of the relatively simple State-agent theory of Klonne and Nordlinger, for instance.[20]

Our findings show that leaving out actors like parties and agencies like governments leads to grave simplifications or at least misperceptions of the State. It is not only a matter of 'bringing the State back in', but also of qualifying in what way and to what extent 'politics' can steer society autonomously, that is to say independently of societal actors. Social welfare and economic welfare in particular are the policy areas that count nowadays. Their influence over defence expenditure has important consequences for one of the core functions of any sovereign State, external security, and also shows how ideological preferences and policy choices have an impact, albeit indirect, on this indubitably central area. Most theories of the State offer only conjecture on these points; we have demonstrated the importance of party behaviour.

An interesting aspect of our investigation is its revelation that parties, besides guiding the general direction of government policy, also penetrate State administration at the level of ministries. The fact that parties take administrative posts is hardly novel of course. The demonstration that they have substantive preferences for ministries which are closely geared to their policy interests, and that they use office to advance their policies in a particular sector (see Chapter 5), shows that they do have a considerable capacity to bend the bureaucracy to their own ends.

This finding can be contested from a neo-Marxist as well as from a neo-pluralist view. Poulantzas, for instance, argues that the 'logic of bureaucracy' makes it quite invulnerable to steering and control from political agents.[21] Yet, this Weberian approach is not only too simple but also wrong, since we have demonstrated that this 'logic'—in so far as it exists—is again much more variable cross-nationally than the critique allows for.

Not only is this mechanistic view wrong, but so also is Nordlinger, who attempts to argue that much of State action is merely the result of conscious preferences of public officials, even if they are at variance with societal actors. Although Nordlinger leaves room for other actors (such as interest associations and political parties) to manœuvre, he places bureaucrats and politicians on the same level of influence.[22] Without underestimating the weight and influence of the bureaucracy, we think we have shown that both parties and governments are capable of steering society to a large extent. If our observations are correct, then it follows that the views of Poulantzas and Nordlinger are in need of revision or empirical validation. As these views represent a major criticism of parliamentary democracy (that behind the façade of representation, State power structures—bureaucracy, police, army—go their own class-based way), our demonstration of the degree of party control at a detailed level is important. Again it goes to demonstrate that, besides controlling government, parties have an important influence on the State and, through it, on society.

Much of this argument has been rehearsed and demonstrated before, in its single parts. To our knowledge this is the first time the whole theory has been put together and tested on such a wide range of evidence. Not only is the resulting structure empirically validated, it emerges well from the evaluation of its explanatory standing undertaken earlier in this chapter. It is going too far to say that the present theory of party representation decisively refutes critiques of parliamentary democracy. It does, however, challenge them to present themselves with equal clarity and to submit themselves to the same checks against post-war experiences. While not itself a full theory of the (democratic) State, our account of party behaviour carries implications for that theory which other formulations ignore at the risk of their general credibility.

Appendix A

Party Factions and Cabinet Reshuffles

This appendix reports a check carried out on Implications 4(i) and 4(ii) of Table 2.4, relating reshuffles and turnover of ministers to the Prime Minister's freedom from constraints, and therefore to the existence of single-party governments as compared to coalitions.

Although these hypotheses follow from the main and auxiliary assumptions of Tables 2.1 and 2.2, just like other aspects of our reasoning, it proved difficult to combine this limited analysis, which is all we can undertake here, with the more extended analysis undertaken in the chapters. We therefore report it in this free-standing appendix—which is not to say that positive results will not uphold the General Theory just as much (and negative findings damage it) as ones reported earlier. The analysis was in fact done contemporaneously with the last four chapters of the book.

To recap the theoretical argument briefly, parties are assumed to act in unity when there is a premium on doing so and external pressures are great—as in coalition formation and indeed during the lifetime of coalitions. Where both the premium on unity and external pressures are less, parties become more inward-looking, and policy-pursuing factions have greater scope. The Prime Minister, as a member of a faction, will use the powers given by the constitutional conventions to dismiss or transfer representatives of other factions in order to benefit his or her own faction. Policy-pursuing motives can thus prompt the movement of individuals between offices (reshuffles). Such movement will be greater where the Prime Minister is less constrained by other constitutional powers, such as an executive or semi-executive Head of State (found only in France and Finland of the countries we are dealing with, however), and above all by coalition partners. Hence the major contrast we shall be examining in the succeeding analysis is that between coalition and single-party governments.

A published report has in fact already presented results from an earlier analysis of some of our data, for the period 1946–78.[1] We shall include some findings from this along with our updated ones for 1946–84 below. The article defined 'reshuffle' as we shall use the term here: that is, as 'the simultaneous movement or replacement of two or more Cabinet Ministers'. Such a definition deliberately avoids identifying the resignation and replacement of only one individual as a reshuffle, since very probably this would not have been precipitated by 'political' motives but by ill health or personal reasons. Certainly the transfer of two or more persons might also have been initiated by these factors, but it constitutes more than a simple substitution and at least represents a decision by the Prime Minister to make more changes in the Cabinet than necessitated by a single appointment from outside.

There is another operational definition involved in the analysis. Governments as such consist of very diverse ministries, many of which have a very limited existence, and some of which are represented within Cabinets while others are not. To permit analysis over time, therefore (and also to allow for checks of the other hypotheses in the central theory), what has been examined is changes in the tenure of the central and most important ministries—those already used in the analyses of Chapter 4. In most governments these indeed

TABLE A.1. Incidence of government reshuffles in eighteen democracies, according to type of government, 1946–1984

	Coalition governments		Single-party governments		All governments	
	No. of reshuffles	No.	No. of reshuffles	No.	No. of reshuffles	No.
Australia[a]	—	—	11	22	11	22
Austria	3	18	3	4	6	22
Belgium	4	23	—	4	4	27
Canada	—	—	24	15	24	15
Denmark	7	11	4	12	11	23
Finland	2	29	2	9	4	38
France 4	2	28	—	—	2	28
5	6[b]	21	—	—	6	21
West Germany	4	14	—	—	4	14
Ireland	1	4	8	10	9	14
Israel	2	29	—	—	2	29
Italy	0	33	—	14	—	47
Japan	4	5	24	24	28	29
Luxemburg	—	13	—	—	—	13
Netherlands	1	17	—	—	1	17
New Zealand	—	—	3	16	3	16
Norway	1	4	9	15	10	19
Sweden	3	6	7	11	10	17
United Kingdom	—	—	22	15	22	15
TOTAL	36	233	120	160	156	393

[a] The permanent and governmental alliance between the Australian Liberals and the Country party makes them a single party for the purposes of the analysis.
[b] At times the government majority in France 5 has seemed more like a single party, but it has never actually cohered in the end.

represent the whole set of Cabinet Ministries, and in any case any important reshuffle would involve changes affecting them. So although the need to select only certain ministries in some countries is a limitation on the analysis, it should not seriously affect results.

In Table A.1 we present data for each country taken individually, distinguishing in each case between coalition and single-party governments. Some countries, such as the United Kingdom and most Commonwealth democracies, have only single-party governments, of course, while the classic multi-party systems have only coalitions. A preliminary glance at these two extremes shows that the Commonwealth as a group has many reshuffles while in multi-party systems these are very limited. In the intermediate cases where both coalitions and single-party governments appear, the number of reshuffles is greater in the single-party governments, with the exception of Denmark and Belgium (Italy never has reshuffles in any case). The high number of single-party but decisively minority governments in Denmark perhaps affects behaviour there: parties, particularly the (relatively) predominant Social Democratic Party, seem to act in the same way regardless of what their present status as a government is. In Belgium single-party government is exceptional and confined to the first half of the 1950s. The average duration of Italian governments is low; this, as we shall see, is an important influence on reshuffles, since for obvious reasons they are unlikely to occur in new governments. New Zealand is also exceptional, in that strictly single-party government is associated with very few reshuffles. A special factor may be found in the small recruitment pool and great technical difficulty of finding replacements from outside government if a minister resigns rather than accepts relocation. More could be made of the contrast between the Fourth and Fifth Republics in France if we took the government majority in the latter case as essentially a single (highly factionalized) party. But the balance of considerations seems to point to governments as being essentially coalitions, though more stable and durable than those going before. Reshuffles are obviously limited under the Fifth Republic by another factor—the institutional position of the President as a separate and more powerful actor than the Prime Minister. Government reshuffles thus take the form of a change of Prime Minister along with the other ministers. Several outright reshuffles of this kind, which appear in our comparative definition as the termination of a government, have in fact taken place (involving, for instance, Pompidou in 1968, Chirac in 1976). The same holds true for Finland, where the President may often intervene to terminate a government as a preliminary to encouraging another more to his liking.

Japan is an interesting case where the frequency of reshuffles is very great. This seems clearly related to factional efforts to establish dominance in government. Japan comes closest, perhaps, to Italy in the way in which factions have become institutionalized and overtly recognized within the predominant party. In Italy, however, owing to the weaker position of the Christian Democrats compared with the Japanese Liberal Democrats, internal factional conflict cannot be confined to the party itself. Thus it provokes the downfall of governments and often the Prime Minister, rather than an internal change.

Looking at the table as a whole, the contrasts seem to uphold the general line of argument advanced above, particularly in regard to the constraints on Prime Ministerial power imposed by coalition arrangements. Evidence on institutional constraints (relationships with other ministries) is limited to the French Fifth Republic and Finland, where different factors obviously operate. The influence of constraints imposed by other factions is limited to the observation that possession of the Premiership in a single-party government, whatever the power of other factions, seems enough to enable the Prime Minister to initiate reshuffles (on this, Japan and Ireland can be contrasted with Italy and Israel). The obvious exception here is New Zealand where, whatever the reasons, the Prime Minister does not reshuffle his Cabinet.

One possible confounding factor is the effect which the duration of governments has on reshuffles. For the most part, a government has to get beyond the initial stage of organization before rearrangements can be thought of. Thus the length of time governments exist will affect the potentiality for reshuffles. This is doubly confounding because coalition governments and minority governments are generally shorter-lived than single-party majority governments. Is the apparent contrast between these types, attributed here to greater and lesser constraints on the Prime Minister, in fact due to a simple time factor?

A crucial comparison here is between coalition and single-party governments within each country, where differences in duration are not so marked. The contrast does persist in six of the nine possible comparisons of this kind, so the hypothesized finding is still found even under the control for national factors.

We can control in another way, more directly, for the effects of duration as against those of single-party versus coalition government, by incorporating both factors explicitly as variables in a multiple regression equation. Table A.2 presents several such equations, numbers 1 and 2 being based on countries as the basic case, using number of governments as an indicator of their greater or lesser duration (the more governments, the less long they last on average), and comparing the effects of this with those of the number of single-party governments on number of reshuffles.

Equation 1 is already reported for a different time period (1946–78) and with India and Sri Lanka included as well as the countries shown in Table A.1.[2] It produces a resounding confirmation for our hypotheses, as the effect of number of single-party governments is still strong even under the control for numbers of governments—that is, for duration (which, as expected also, has a smallish negative effect on the number of reshuffles). The results (equation 2) for the countries and data given in Table A.1 are less resounding,

TABLE A.2. The relationship between single-party government, government duration, and number of reshuffles, according to various multiple-regression equations

Equation		Constant	Single-party government		Duration	
			b_1	r	b_2	r
1	23 democracies (1946–78)	4.118	0.673	0.688	−0.117	−0.207
2	19 democracies (1946–84)	8.423	0.305	0.350	−0.152	−0.185
3	74 governments (1978–84)	0.475	0.522	0.532	0.030	0.401

Note: Number of reshuffles = Constant + b_1 Single government + b_2 Duration. Duration is measured by number of governments over the relevant period in each country (in Equations 1 and 2) and by number of months each government lasted (in Equation 3).

but support these observed before, with a moderately strong effect for number of single-party governments and a small negative one for number of governments.

Using countries as cases when we want to examine government-based phenomena is a slightly indirect way of proceeding. We can also look at the relationship between single-party control and reshuffles using governments as cases, the duration of each directly measured in months, and single-party government versus coalitions as a dichotomized variable scored 0 for coalitions and 1 for single-party government. Unfortunately our project ran out of money and time before we could go very far with the recoding involved, so we have data with governments as cases only from 1978 to 1984. These six years suffice to give another test to our hypothesis, however, the results of which are again in the expected directions (except that duration appears as exerting insignificant rather than negative effects).

The advantage of looking at the relationship in several different ways is to establish that it holds under a range of different circumstances, which it clearly does. How can we interpret the findings? It is certainly true that, in itself, the ability of Prime Ministers to demote or move ministers around to suit their own purposes might equally be interpreted as office-seeking (or office-preserving) rather than policy-pursuing behaviour. This is one of several cases where office-seeking and policy-pursuing assumptions give rise to similar predictions. The latter are better supported in the other tests made previously, so taken in context the result of the analysis made here is to validate further the reasoning of the General Theory set out in Chapter 2.

Appendix B

Data: Sources and Preparation

The data used for analysis throughout the book are all aggregated and organized by country. The period studied covers at most the post-war era (1945 to 1984), but quite often lack of data or cross-national limitations on availability restricted it to 1950 onwards or even 1965 onwards (particularly in regard to economic data).

The data—apart from those related to policy—are organized on different levels of aggregation:

1. On the level of the political system (in addition, some specific variables were added to the files or derived from system-level information)
2. On the level of governments as a whole
3. On the level of separate ministries
4. For sectors of ministries
5. For modes of termination

The following democracies are the ones for which at least some data were available: Australia (1), Austria (2), Belgium (3), Canada (4), Denmark (5), Finland (6), France (Fourth Republic) (7), France (Fifth Republic) (8), the Federal Republic of Germany (9), Ireland (10), Italy (11), Japan (12), The Netherlands (13), New Zealand (14), Norway (15), Sweden (16), Switzerland (17), the United Kingdom (18), Iceland★ (30), India (40), Israel★ (50), Luxemburg★ (60), Sri Lanka (70). Asterisked countries are those omitted at some points through lack of policy-relevant information. Because of difficulties of comparability India and Sri Lanka are only referred to in the course of particular analyses.

The following variables have been used to describe the various *parliamentary systems* of the countries under review:

Number of parliamentary seats (total)
Code-number of parties in Parliament according to Mackie and Rose
Number of parliamentary seats held by each party (only those, naturally, which have ever entered Parliament)
Percentage of votes for each party
Role of party in government (2 = participating; 1 = supporting; 0 = other)
Number of portfolios held by each party
Percentage of portfolios held by each party
Party code of party of Prime Minister

Most of these variables are straightforwardly taken from Mackie and Rose[1] and updated by means of either the *European Journal of Political Research* or Keesing's Contemporary Archives.[2] The party-in-government variable as well as the portfolio variables are primarily based on Keesing's Contemporary Archives, but at the same time checked with the work of von Beyme and Paloheimo.[3]

In operationalizing the parliamentary variables one major problem arose: whether to score the actual ministers, or ministries. We opted for the latter option, that is to say we counted the number of portfolios (i.e. competences) held by each party. For in our analysis we seek to discover the impact of parties within governments, in terms of both the office-seeking capacity of a party and its capacity to transform its ideology into public policy formation and performance. Hence the minister is not the carrier of the supposed influence; it is the competence of the ministry in a policy area that is important to the party to which the office-holder is affiliated.

Both von Beyme and Paloheimo inform us on the role of parties in government, and in general the differences between them are not great. Their definition of a government, however, is different from ours: we return to this later. If there was a difference of opinion we resorted to Keesing's Contemporary Archives, unless it concerned the Federal Republic of Germany or Austria, or Finland where we considered von Beyme and Paloheimo respectively country-specialists. There were differences between Keesing's Contemporary Archives and Paloheimo with regard to the number of portfolios held by each party. The reason for this is twofold: on the one hand, Paloheimo counts persons rather than competences; on the other, it is genuinely difficult in some cases (in particular, Parliaments on the 'Westminster model') to know what is a governmental organization and what is not. Hence 'there are problems in determining the exact number. Again, when in doubt, we resorted to Keesing's Contemporary Archives.

The variables listed below have been used to depict the format and working of the various *party systems*:[4]

Anti-democratic feelings (1 = yes; 0 = no)
Left–Right feelings (1 = yes; 0 = no)
Absolute majority of government (1 = yes; 0 = no)
Anti-system party (1 = yes; 0 = no)
Normal party of Government (1 = yes; 0 = no)
Tendance of party (1 = Bourgeois; 2 = Socialist)
Party Family (1 = Conservative; 2 = Liberal; 3 = Christian Democratic; 4 = Social Democratic; 5 = Special Interest)

Although most of these variables appear to be quite static, we have nevertheless assumed them to be dynamic. Therefore the most problematic issue with respect to them has been less the distinction as a dummy and more if and when change occurred. Invariably the cut-off points used will show some arbitrariness. However, we are convinced that the decisions made would be agreed to by most specialists.

Another problem has been to determine whether a party belongs to the Conservative or the Christian Democratic party family. The same applies to the distinction between Liberal and Conservative. In this we have followed the categorization of parties made by Keman[5] and applied it to this sample.

The third cluster of variables consists of those representing *specific features of governments*. Before discussing the separate elements of each variable we shall elaborate (again) the definition of 'government' as it has been used throughout this study: it encompasses any administration that is formed after an election and continues in the absence of

(a) change of Prime Minister;
(b) change in the party composition of the Cabinet; or
(c) resignation in an inter-election period followed by re-formation of the government with the same Prime Minister and party composition.

This definition is obviously more strict than most others, particularly those used in much of the literature on coalitions. This is particularly true in regard to formal resignation. Yet it makes sense to include this as a cut-off point, since a resignation generally changes the political situation in some significant aspects. The effect of our decision has been to increase the total number of governments, hence the total number of cases. However, the differences with both von Beyme and Paloheimo, although they exist, are not enormously great, and are explicable by our inclusion of caretaker governments and the operation of the resignation rule.

Another respect in which we differ from some of the other specialist treatments concerns the date of the initial constitution of a government. Whereas there is great unanimity as to dates of termination there is less in regard to formation. The main reason lies in the different ways in which governments are brought into being in some countries and in their constitutional processes: in a number of the continental European countries a considerable lapse of time occurs between the ending of a government and the installation of a new government by the Head of State. Most conspicuous in this respect are Belgium, Denmark, and The Netherlands (the maximum lapse of time being almost nine months, in which there is no new government and the old one is not allowed to introduce new bills or to make politically controversial decisions). To a lesser extent these lapses of time can be found in Finland, Italy, Norway, and Sweden. Von Beyme only gives the beginning not the ending of a government, whereas Paloheimo follows the same practices as we have. Any difference has been checked by means of Keesing's Contemporary Archives.

In addition to these government variables (dates of initiation and termination) we have created the following:

Government number (1 . . . n) (numerically coded)
Identity of Prime Minister (alphanumerically coded)
Duration of government (in years, up to the nearest half-month)
Percentage of ministries held by party
Type of government (1–5)

'Ideological complexion of government' is an indicator which introduces a more qualitative aspect to government formation. It attempts to account for the relative strength of parties in government with reference to the Left–Right dimension, through a five-point scale in which the proportional shares of the Left, Centre and Right are transformed into scores (1 to 5) representing the degree of dominance of either party:

1 = right-wing dominance (share of Cabinet seats of these parties greater than 66.6 per cent)
2 = Right–Centre complexion (share of Cabinet seats of Right and Centre parties between 33.3 and 66.6 per cent each)
3 = balanced situation (share of Centre greater than 50 per cent; or if Left and Right form a government together not dominated by one or the other)
4 = Left–Centre complexion (share of Cabinet seats of Left and Centre parties between 33.3 and 66.6 per cent each)
5 = left-wing dominance (share of Cabinet seats of these parties greater than 66.6 per cent)

These scores are collected and calculated for the period 1950–83 on an annual basis and then compiled for each government.[6]

The following are the five types of government in our classification:

1 = One-party government: one party takes all government seats.
2 = Minimal winning coalitions: all participating parties are necessary to form the government.
3 = Surplus coalition: this comprises those coalition governments which exceed the minimal-winning criterion.
4 = Minority government: the party or parties in government do not possess a majority in Parliament.
5 = Caretaker government: the government formed is not intended to undertake any kind of serious policy-making, but is only temporarily minding the shop.

As mentioned in Chapter 4, Cabinet Ministries are lightly standardized into common types—which in fact vary only in minor ways across countries. Coding is as follows: 01 = Prime Minister, 02 = Deputy Prime Minister, 03 = Foreign Affairs, 04 = Defence, 05 = Interior, 06 = Justice, 07 = Finance, 08 = Economy, 09 = Labour, 10 = Social Affairs, 11 = Education, 12 = Health, 13 = Housing, 14 = Infrastructure, 15 = Agriculture, 16 = Industry/Trade/Commerce, 17 = Religion, 18 = Other. These data have not yet been collected cross-nationally in any other study known to us. On the one hand, this implies that there are no differences with other data sources. On the other, it has meant that there were some problems concerning comparability and reliability.

In many countries different labels are used for the same competence (for instance, the Treasury in the UK is similar to Finance in most continental countries; in other cases Justice is differently organized, not only in a ministry, but also in a separate non-governmental institution). These problems have been solved by consulting country studies or, if available and understandable, government and/or parliamentary year-books.

In most countries some of the competences listed above are combined in one ministry; in others they are separated. For example, in some countries Defence is organized in different ministries (Navy, Air Force, and Army in The Netherlands, for instance, up to 1959); in Scandinavia Agriculture is subdivided into Forestry, Fisheries, and Agriculture itself. Conversely, Labour and Social Affairs (often labelled 'Employment') may be headed by one minister, as may the Economy, Trade, and Industry. In each case of doubt we consulted Keesing's Contemporary Archives. If more than one of the coded competences was mentioned we scored them both. Where there was a subdivision, we either attributed it to the party holding all relevant ministries or scored the party holding the main competence—in the Scandinavian cases, Agriculture; in the Dutch case, Navy, Air Force, and Army together as Defence (since after 1959 Navy and Air Force became sub-ministries within Defence).

To increase comparability and reliability we have developed the concept of sectors of ministries. We contend that the main areas of policy concern are generally not covered by just one ministry, but by various ministries. For our analysis of the relation between policy formation, policy performance, and party control of certain offices, we have designated as 'relevant ministries' the following:

Economic Policy sector: Finance, Labour, Economy
Social Welfare sector: Social Affairs, Education, Health,
External Security sector: Prime Minister, Foreign Affairs, Defence

Not all ministries existed in a country for the whole period of the study, so there were variations in the absolute number of relevant ministries. We therefore employed proportional representation of parties within a sector rather than absolute values. The dominance of a sector was decided by looking at the party (family) with the greatest representation. If two parties had equal numbers of specific ministries the Prime Minister's party—if represented—was considered to be the dominant one.

A separate file has been generated to deal with *modes of termination of governments*. Apart from von Beyme's work,[7] we have not come across such data in the existing literature. Following von Beyme,[8] we developed a classification for modes of termination:

1.1 Fixed elections. These include any election stipulated by law or constitution—for the Anglo-Saxon countries, in the fifth year of the electoral calendar.

1.2 Anticipated elections. These include all elections not required as under 1.1, and those, in Anglo-Saxon countries, occurring before four years have gone by.

2.1 Voluntary resignation of the Prime Minister.

2.2 Resignation of the Prime Minister due to health reasons. Both these last two reasons can be considered as non-political ones, but mode 2.1 may well be a cover-up for factional dispute within a party or government (as for instance in Japan). Yet, as we cannot distinguish 'real' from 'fake' reasons, we have accepted them on face value.

3.1 Dissension within government. This covers those instances when either a coalition breaks up without external pressure or there are publicized quarrels and/or movement of personnel. Often these incidents are not discussed in the literature since in many cases they have no visible consequence for a government defined in a more relaxed way than we have defined it.

3.2 Lack of parliamentary support. This reason of termination, of course, lies at the heart of any parliamentary democracy. We have counted here every instance when either parties withdrew support from government, or there occurred a (successful) vote of no confidence (or similar parliamentary action).

3.3 Intervention by the Head of State. Apart from semi-presidential regimes (such as Finland and France), however, the role of the Head of State is much less essential for government termination than with respect to government formation.

We collected these data from Keesing's Contemporary Archives. In addition we compared our data with those of von Beyme. There was little disagreement except for the fact that we have identified more governments and thus have found more reasons of termination. Another difference has been that electoral reasons are not subdivided by von Beyme as by us. Finally, more than one reason is often mentioned by von Beyme: in these cases we have followed Keesing's Contemporary Archives. In a number of cases (about 10 per cent) we were not able to locate a reason of termination.

Finally we have developed a number of variables relating to *policy formation* (or outputs) and *policy performance* (or outcomes). These include indexes of economic policy, social welfare, and one measure of the trade-off between military expenditure and welfare. In addition we used indexes representing the extent to which socio-economic welfare has been achieved.

Policy formation indexes. Measurement of economic policy output is based on the interpretation of certain policy measures which supposedly form, in combination, a nation's macro-economic policy strategy. To this end we have examined the degree to which a country allowed a Budget deficit and a high increase in money supply; and the size of the public economy (total outlays on all government services). Unlike social welfare output, we have defined the index qualitatively in the following manner:

1 = High levels of spending, regardless of the Budget deficit and the velocity of money circulation.

2 = Moderately high levels of public spending, with a relatively low Budget deficit.

3 = Modest levels of public spending, with avoidance of Budget deficits and of an increase in the money supply.

4 = Low levels of public spending, hardly any Budget deficits, and no increase of money supply.

The index is based on rank-ordering scores on each dimension, for each country, on a yearly basis (1963–84). The data source is OECD (various volumes).[9]

External security is simply based on total expenditure on defence expressed as a percentage of GDP (source: SIPRI, various volumes). The 'trade-off' measure is a constructed variable. It is the combination of the annual growth-rates of social welfare and military expenditures. If they both increase or decrease simultaneously we have labelled this a positive and negative pay-off respectively. If one increases and the other decreases we called this a positive trade-off (if social welfare grows) or a negative trade-off (if defence grows). Thus there are four distinctive outcomes:[10]

1 = Positive trade-off
2 = Positive pay-off
3 = Negative pay-off
4 = Negative trade-off

Policy performance index. This is identical to the 'misery index' as used by OECD: (rate of inflation + rate of unemployment) divided by 2. This measure shows the relative success of a country in coping with socio-economic circumstances. The index is based on annual OECD data.

All policy-related variables are based on yearly figures and are transformed into rank-ordered values. This procedure has been undertaken in order to increase comparability, sometimes at the expense of precision. However, we feel that, since the data are collected and calculated on an annual basis, this certainly improves cross-national comparisons and analysis over time.

In conclusion, we should note that this appendix represents only a summary description of the data we have employed. With the aid of a grant from the British Economic and Social Science Research Council (R000231598) work will be going on to refine and complete our data collection, and to publish all variables in full in a handbook, in association with other collections of data on parties in government. In addition we intend to lodge the fully computerized data set or sets at the major European Social Science Archives. Thus all the information we have drawn up should be available for public use and secondary analysis from the end of 1990 onwards. Obviously it may undergo some changes of detail in the mean time, but this appendix should remain valid as a broad description of the leading features of our collection. We should like to end with a tribute to the work of our predecessors in the field, whose works have been cited frequently in the notes to this appendix, and hope our data may prove as useful to future investigators as theirs has proved to be to us.

Notes

Introduction

1. India and Sri Lanka, which are also countries where parliamentary democracy has survived, with certain vicissitudes, over the whole postwar period, could also be included. We omit them from the main analyses because their cultural and social backgrounds are too diverse to render comparisons meaningful. We do point out, in parenthesis, where our hypotheses would apply to them; and we note findings for these countries, where relevant, in footnotes.

2. H. E. Keman, 'Securing the Safety of the Nation State', in F. Castles (ed.), *The Impact of Parties* (London: Sage, 1982); Keman, 'Politics, Policies and Consequences: A Cross-National Analysis', *European Journal of Political Research*, 12 (1984), 101–8; id., 'Strategies of Economic Policy-Formation: Dutchmen, Dutch Diseases and Dutch Crossings', paper presented at the ECPR Joint Sessions, Göteborg, 1986; I. Budge, I. Crewe, and D. J. Farlie (eds.), *Party Identification and Beyond* (London and New York: Wiley, 1976); Budge and Farlie, *Voting and Party Competition* (London and New York: Wiley, 1977); Budge and Farlie, *Explaining and Predicting Elections* (London: Allen & Unwin, 1983); I. Budge, D. Robertson, and D. J. Hearl (eds.), *Ideology, Strategy and Party Movement* (Cambridge: Cambridge UP, 1987).

3. M. J. Laver and N. Schofield, *Multiparty Government: The Politics of Coalition in Europe* (Oxford: Oxford UP, 1990).

4. Cf. Budge and Farlie, *Explaining and Predicting Elections*.

5. I. Budge and M. J. Laver, 'Office-Seeking and Policy-Pursuit in Coalition Theory', *Legislative Studies Quarterly*, 11 (1986), 485–506.

6. D. B. Robertson, *A Theory of Party Competition* (London and New York: Wiley, 1976); Budge and Farlie, *Voting and Party Competition*, ch. 11.

7. Ibid., pp. 157–62; C. Rallings, 'The Influence of Election Programmes', in Budge, Robertson, and Hearl (eds.), *Ideology*.

8. Castles (ed.), *The Impact of Parties*; Keman, 'Strategies'; id. and T. van Dijk, 'Policy Formation as a Strategy to Overcome the Economic Crisis', in F. Castles and R. Wildenmann (eds.), *The Future of Party Government* (Berlin: De Gruyter, 1987), 127–62.

Chapter 1

1. Cf. I. Budge, 'The Political Impact of Information Technology', *Teoria politica* (forthcoming), for ways in which this may be changing.
2. For a specific discussion, see I. Budge, 'Parties and Democratic Government: A Framework for Comparative Explanation', *Western European Politics*, 7 (1984), 95–118.
3. For a 'Newtonian' formulation of election theory, see I. Budge and D. J. Farlie, 'Newtonian Mechanics and Predictive Election Theory', *Brit. J. Pol. Science*, 7 (1977), 413–17; for an 'events' analysis of governments which reflects such a formulation, see E. Browne, J. Fendreis, and D. Gleiber, 'An "Events" Approach to the Problem of Cabinet Stability', *Comparative Political Studies*, 17 (1984), 167–97.
4. A. Downs, *An Economic Theory of Democracy* (New York: Harper, 1957).
5. W. Riker, *The Theory of Political Coalitions* (New Haven: Yale UP, 1962), 32–3.
6. M. Leiserson, 'Factions and Coalitions in One-Party Japan', *American Political Science Review*, 68 (1968), 770–87; W. A. Gamson, 'A Theory of Coalition Formation', *American Sociological Review*, 26 (1961), 373–82.
7. See e.g. L. S. Shapley and M. Shubik, 'A Method for Evaluating the Distribution of Power in a Committee System', *American Political Science Review*, 48 (1954), 787–92; J. Coleman, 'Control of Collectivities and the Power of a Collectivity to Act', in B. Lieberman (ed.), *Social Choice* (New York: Gordon Breach Science Publishers, 1971).
8. I. Budge and M. J. Laver, 'Office-Seeking and Policy-Pursuit in Coalition Theory', *Legislative Studies Quarterly*, 11 (1986), 485–506; M. J. Laver and N. Schofield, *Multiparty Government: The Politics of Coalition in Europe* (Oxford: Oxford UP, 1990); see also Table 2.1.
9. M. Winer, 'Cabinet Coalition Formation: A Game-Theoretic Analysis', in S. Brams, G. Schwodiauer, and A. Schotter (eds.), *Applied Game Theory* (Wurzburg: Physica Verlag, 1979); B. Grofman, 'A Dynamic Model of Protocoalition Behavior', *Behavioral Science*, 27 (1982), 77–90.
10. I. Budge and D. J. Farlie, *Voting and Party Competition* (London and New York: Wiley, 1977), 157–62.
11. Downs, *An Economic Theory of Democracy*, pp. 103–9.
12. V. H. Herman and J. Pope, 'Minority Governments in Western Democracies', *Brit. J. Pol. Science*, 3 (1973), 191–212.
13. M. J. Taylor and M. J. Laver, 'Government Coalitions in Western Europe'. *European Journal of Political Research*, 1 (1973), 205–48; I. Budge and V. H. Herman, 'Coalitions and Government Formation', *Brit. J. Pol. Science*, 8 (1978), 459–77.
14. L. C. Dodd, *Coalitions in Parliamentary Government* (Princeton, NJ: Princeton UP, 1976).
15. B. Grofman, 'The Comparative Analysis of Coalition Formation and

Duration: Distinguishing Between Country and Within Country Effects', paper presented at the International Conference on Coalition Theory and Public Choice, Fiesole, Italy, 25–29 May 1987.

16. N. Schofield, (ed.), *Social Choice and Democracy* (Heidelberg: Springer-Verlag, 1985), chs. 2 and 3.

17. E. Browne and M. Franklin, 'Coalition Payoffs in European Parliamentary Democracies', *American Political Science Review*, 67 (1973), 453–64.

18. See esp. Gamson, 'A Theory of Coalition Formation'.

19. M. Olson, *The Logic of Collective Action* (Cambridge, Mass.: Harvard UP, 1965); N. Schofield and M. J. Laver, 'Bargaining Theory and Portfolio Payoffs in European Coalition Governments', *Brit. J. Pol. Science*, 15 (1985), 143–64.

20. Gamson, 'A Theory of Coalition Formation'; M. Leiserson, *Coalitions in Politics* (Ann Arbor, Mich.: University Microfilms, 1966).

21. R. A. Axelrod, *Conflict of Interest* (Chicago: Markham, 1970).

22. Leiserson, *Coalitions in Politics*; A. De Swaan, *Coalition Theories and Cabinet Formation* (Amsterdam: Elsevier, 1973).

23. Ibid., p. 88.

24. Axelrod, *Conflict of Interest*; A. Lijphart, *Democracies* (New Haven, Conn.: Yale UP, 1984), 52, table 4.1.

25. S. M. Lipset and S. Rokkan, *Party Systems and Voter Alignments* (New York: The Free Press Collier-Macmillan, 1967), 7–69.

26. Grofman, 'A Dynamic Model'.

27. M. J. Laver and I. Budge (eds.), *Party Policy and Coalition Government in Western Europe* (forthcoming).

28. N. Schofield, 'Existence of a "Structurally Stable" Equilibrium for a Non-Collegial Voting Rule', *Public Choice*, 51 (1986), 267–84.

29. R. D. McKelvey, 'Dominance and Institution-Free Properties of Social Choice', *Am. J. Pol. Science*, 9 (1986), 300–2.

30. Ibid.; see also new work on voting-cycles among limited sets of centrally located dominant parties: Laver and Schofield, *Multiparty Government*.

31. G. M. Luebbert, *A Theory of Government Formation in Multiparty Democracies* (Stanford, Calif.: Stanford UP, 1986).

32. Laver and Schofield, *Multiparty Government*.

33. Laver and Budge (eds.), *Party Policy*.

34. R. I. Hofferbert and H.-D. Klingemann, 'The Policy Impact of Party Programmes and Government Declarations in Federal Germany', paper presented to the ECPR Manifesto Research Group Meeting, Hotel Mediterraneo, Palermo, 10–13 Dec. 1987.

35. Ibid.; see also Ch. 5.

36. Cf. E. Browne and K. Feste, 'Qualitative Dimensions of Coalition Payoffs', *American Behavioral Scientist*, 18 (1975), 530–56; Budge, 'Parties and Democratic Government'.

37. Downs, *An Economic Theory of Democracy*.

38. Budge and Laver, 'Office-Seeking and Policy-Pursuit'.
39. Hofferbert and Klingemann, 'The Policy Impact'.

Chapter 2

1. I. Budge and M. J. Laver, 'Office-Seeking and Policy-Pursuit in Coalition Theory', *Legislative Studies Quarterly*, 11 (1986), 485–506.
2. I. Budge, D. Robertson, and D. J. Hearl (eds.), *Ideology, Strategy and Party Movement* (Cambridge: Cambridge UP, 1987), ch. 18.
3. D. Hibbs, 'Political Parties and Macro-Economic Policy', *American Political Science Review*, 71 (1977), 1476–87.
4. S. M. Lipset and S. Rokkan, *Party Systems and Voter Alignments* (New York: The Free Press Collier-Macmillan, 1967).
5. R. Inglehart, *The Silent Revolution: Changing Values and Political Styles among Western Publics* (Princeton, NJ: Princeton UP, 1977).
6. Ibid.; D. B. Robertson, *Class and the British Electorate* (Oxford: Blackwell, 1984).
7. N. Schofield and M. J. Laver, 'Bargaining Theory and Portfolio Payoffs in European Coalition Governments', *Brit. J. Pol. Science*, 15 (1985), 143–64; B. Grofman, 'The Comparative Analysis of Coalition Formation and Duration: Distinguishing Between Country and Within Country Effects', paper presented at the International Conference on Coalition Theory and Public Choice, Fiesole, Italy, 25–29 May 1987.
8. M. J. Laver and N. Schofield, *Multiparty Government: The Politics of Coalition in Europe* (Oxford: Oxford UP, 1990).
9. A possibility now also being examined in terms of spatial theory: B. Grofman, N. Noviello, and P. Strafflin, 'A New Model of Coalition Formation in which One Party Is Asked to Form a Government', paper presented at the International Conference on Coalition Theory and Public Choice, Fiesole, Italy, 25–29 May 1987.
10. Though, for a suggestion that the relative power of parties may affect the result, see Schofield and Laver, 'Bargaining Theory'.
11. E. Browne and M. Franklin, 'Coalition Payoffs in European Parliamentary Democracies', *American Political Science Review*, 67 (1973), 453–64; confirmed for the whole post-war period by Schofield and Laver, 'Bargaining Theory'.
12. E. Browne and K. Feste, 'Qualitative Dimensions of Coalition Payoffs', *American Behavioral Scientist*, 18 (1975), 530–56.
13. I. Budge, 'Party Factions and Government Reshuffles', *European Journal of Political Research*, 13 (1985), 327–34.
14. M. Leiserson, 'Factions and Coalitions in One-Party Japan', *American Political Science Review*, 68 (1968), 770–87; R. A. Axelrod, *Conflict of Interest* (Chicago: Markham, 1970); A. De Swaan, *Coalition Theories and Cabinet Formation* (Amsterdam: Elsevier, 1973).

15. Laver and Schofield, *Multiparty Government*.
16. A. Downs, *An Economic Theory of Democracy* (New York: Harper, 1957).

Chapter 3

 1. K. von Beyme, *Political Parties in Western Democracies* (Aldershot: Gower, 1985).
 2. I. Budge and V. H. Herman, 'Coalitions and Government Formation', *Brit. J. Pol. Science*, 8 (1978), 459–77; Switzerland has now been added and India and Sri Lanka excluded from the analysis.
 3. G. Sartori, *Parties and Party Systems* (Cambridge: Cambridge UP, 1976), 121–5.
 4. We shall allude to findings for India and Sri Lanka later in this chapter, so we should note that they had no experience of serious anti-democratic threats (up to the end of 1984) and no anti-system party, and that the Left–Right division was always cross-cut by others. Congress is the 'normal' party of government in India.
 5. L. Hurwitz, 'An Index of Democratic Political Stability', *Comparative Political Studies*, 4 (1971), 41–68; D. Sanders and V. Herman, 'The Survival and Stability of Governments in Western Democracies', *Acta Politica*, 3 (1977), 346–77.
 6. A. De Swaan, *Coalition Theories and Cabinet Formation* (Amsterdam: Elsevier, 1973).
 7. See *The Economist* (1946), p. 2.
 8. N. Schofield and M. J. Laver, 'Bargaining Theory and Portfolio Payoffs in European Coalition Governments', *Brit. J. Pol. Science*, 15 (1985), 143–64.
 9. I. Budge and M. J. Laver, 'Office-Seeking and Policy-Pursuit in Coalition Theory', *Legislative Studies Quarterly*, 11 (1986), 485–506.
10. Budge and Herman, 'Coalitions and Government Formation'.

Chapter 4

 1. R. I. Hofferbert and H.-D. Klingemann, 'The Policy Impact of Party Programmes and Government Declarations in Federal Germany', paper presented to the ECPR Manifesto Research Group Meeting, Hotel Mediterraneo, Palermo, 10–13 Dec. 1987.
 2. For a recent confirmation of the existence of two types of liberalism, see I. Budge, D. Robertson, and D. J. Hearl (eds.), *Ideology, Strategy and Party Movement* (Cambridge: Cambridge UP, 1987), ch. 18.
 3. For the historical origins, see esp. S. M. Lipset and S. Rokkan, *Party Systems and Voter Alignments* (New York: The Free Press Collier-Macmillan, 1967), 9–67.

4. I. Budge and D. J. Farlie, *Explaining and Predicting Elections* (London: Allen & Unwin, 1983).
5. E. Browne and K. Feste, 'Qualitative Dimensions of Coalition Payoffs', *American Behavioral Scientist*, 18 (1975), 530–56.
6. Cf. the similar results of Browne and Feste, ibid.
7. E. Browne and M. Franklin, 'Coalition Payoffs in European Parliamentary Democracies', *American Political Science Review*, 67 (1973), 453–64; confirmed more recently by N. Schofield and M. J. Laver, 'Bargaining Theory and Portfolio Payoffs in European Coalition Governments', *Brit. J. Pol. Science*, 15 (1985), 143–64.
8. Ibid.
9. The use of flow diagrams should make possible in the future a computerization of the whole theory and tests against comparative data—which would, however, have to be extended and refined to permit sensitive testing. The relative crudity of the data available has limited this first analysis to non-machine evaluation, but the total specification of relationships through the flow diagrams and the holistic testing of these through tables like 4.3 render computerization possible in principle.
10. M. J. Laver and N. Schofield, *Multiparty Government: The Politics of Coalition in Europe* (Oxford: Oxford UP, 1990).
11. H. Paloheimo, *Governments in Democratic Capitalist States 1950–1983: A Data Handbook* (Tampere: Finnish Political Science Association, 1984).

Chapter 5

1. G. Sartori, *Parties and Party Systems* (Cambridge: Cambridge UP, 1976); for a similar tactic, see S. Lessman, *Budgetary Politics and Elections* (Berlin: De Gruyter, 1987).
2. H. E. Keman and T. van Dijk, 'Policy Formation as a Strategy to Overcome the Economic Crisis', in F. Castles and R. Wildenmann (eds.), *The Future of Party Government* (Berlin: De Gruyter, 1987), 127–62.
3. F. Castles (ed.), *The Impact of Parties* (London: Sage, 1982).

Chapter 6

1. e.g. L. C. Dodd, *Coalitions in Parliamentary Government* (Princeton, NJ: Princeton UP, 1976), 18.
2. For a critique of Dodd, see B. Grofman, 'The Comparative Analysis of Coalition Formation and Duration: Distinguishing Between Country and Within Country Effects', paper presented at the International Conference on Coalition Theory and Public Choice, Fiesole, Italy, 25–9 May 1987.
3. Cf. M. J. Laver and N. Schofield, *Multiparty Government: The Politics of Coalition in Europe* (Oxford: Oxford UP, 1990).

4. The exceptions are G. Bingham Powell, *Contemporary Democracies* (Cambridge, Mass.: Harvard UP, 1984); K. von Beyme, 'I partiti socialisti al potere', *Laboratorio politico*, 5 (1983), 79–94; id., *Political Parties in Western Democracies* (Aldershot: Gower, 1985).
5. Cf. Grofman, 'The Comparative Analysis of Coalition Formation and Duration'.
6. Dodd, *Coalitions in Parliamentary Government*, ch. 1.
7. Grofman, 'The Comparative Analysis of Coalition Formation and Duration'.
8. Cf. H. E. Keman, *The Development toward Surplus Welfare* (Amsterdam: CT Press, 1988).
9. Grofman, 'The Comparative Analysis of Coalition Formation and Duration'.
10. A. Downs, *An Economic Theory of Democracy* (New York: Harper, 1957).
11. E. Tufte, *The Political Control of the Economy* (Princeton, NJ: Princeton UP, 1978).
12. P. Whiteley, *Political Control of the Macroeconomy* (London: Sage, 1986); M. G. Schmidt, 'Allerweltsparteien in Westeuropa', *Leviathan*, 13 (1985), 329–54.
13. Downs, *An Economic Theory of Democracy*, pp. 120–40.

Chapter 7

1. Cf. G. Pridham (ed.), *Coalitional Behaviour in Theory and Practice* (Cambridge: Cambridge UP, 1986).
2. S. M. Lipset' and S. Rokkan, *Party Systems and Voter Alignments* (New York: The Free Press Collier-Macmillan, 1967); Rokkan, *Citizens, Elections, Parties* (Oslo: Universitets Forlaget, 1970).
3. I. Budge, D. Robertson, and D. J. Hearl (eds.), *Ideology, Strategy and Party Movement* (Cambridge: Cambridge UP, 1987), ch. 18; M. J. Laver and N. Schofield, *Multiparty Government: The Politics· of Coalition in Europe* (Oxford: Oxford UP, 1990).
4. W. Riker, *The Theory of Political Coalitions* (New Haven: Yale UP, 1962), 32, 33.
5. Laver and Schofield, *Multiparty Government*.
6. M. J. Laver and I. Budge (eds.), *Party Policy and Coalition Government in Western Europe* (forthcoming).
7. R. I. Hofferbert, H.-D. Klingemann, and F. Pétry (eds.), *Party Policy and Government Expenditure* (forthcoming).
8. I. Budge and M. J. Laver, 'Office-Seeking and Policy-Pursuit in Coalition Theory', *Legislative Studies Quarterly*, 11 (1986), 485–506.
9. Ibid.
10. K. Strom and J. Leipart, 'Coalition Politics in Norway', in Laver and Budge (eds.), *Party Policy*, ch. 4.

11. G. M. Leubbert, *A Theory of Government Formation in Multiparty Democracies* (Stanford, Calif.: Stanford UP, 1986).
12. e.g. K. Offe, *Contradictions of the Welfare State* (London: Hutchinson, 1984), 179 ff.; G. Therborn, *Why Some Peoples Are More Unemployed than Others* (London: New Left Books, 1986).
13. A. Cawson (ed.), *Organized Interests and the State* (London: Sage, 1985); W. Grant, *The Political Economy of Corporatism* (London: Macmillan, 1986).
14. e.g. R. Miliband, *The State in Capitalist Society* (London: Quartet, 1973); N. Poulantzas, *State, Power, Socialism* (London: New Left Books, 1978); Therborn, *Why Some Peoples Are More Unemployed than Others*.
15. See J. P. Nettl, 'The State as a Conceptual Variable', *World Politics*, 20 (1968), 559–92.
16. See also P. B. Evans, D. Rueschemeyer, and T. Skocpol (eds.), *Bringing the State Back In* (Cambridge: Cambridge UP, 1985).
17. e.g. C. E. Lindblom, *Politics and Markets* (New York: Basic Books, 1977).
18. See e.g. S. D. Krasner, *Defending the National Interest* (Princeton, NJ: Princeton UP, 1981); M. Weir and T. Skocpol, 'State Structures and Social Keynesian Responses to the Great Depression in Sweden and the United States', *International J. of Comparative Sociology*, 24/1–2 (1983), 4–29.
19. F. Castles (ed.), *The Impact of Parties* (London: Sage, 1982); D. Hibbs, 'Political Parties and Macro-Economic Policy', *American Political Science Review*, 71 (1977), 1476–87.
20. E. A. Nordlinger, *On the Anatomy of the Democratic State* (Cambridge, Mass.: Harvard UP, 1981).
21. Poulantzas, *State, Power, Socialism*.
22. Nordlinger, *On the Anatomy of the Democratic State*, pp. 43 ff.

Appendix A

1. I. Budge, 'Party Factions and Government Reshuffles', *European Journal of Political Research*, 13 (1985).
2. Ibid.

Appendix B

1. T. Mackie and R. Rose, *The International Almanac of Electoral History* (2nd edn.; London: Macmillan, 1982).
2. Bristol: Longman, 1945– .
3. K. von Beyme, *Political Parties in Western Democracies* (Aldershot: Gower, 1985), appendix pp. 377–406; H. Paloheimo, *Governments in*

Democratic Capitalist States 1950–1983: A Data Handbook (Tampere: Finnish Political Science Association, 1984).

4. Most of these variables reflect the literature on parties and party systems (see G. Sartori, *Parties and Party Systems* (Cambridge: Cambridge UP, 1976)) as well as certain dimensions of what might be called common-sense observation in most Western parliamentary democracies. In addition to Sartori, these data are derived from the following works. With respect to party families: von Beyme, *Political Parties*; Paloheimo, *Governments in Democratic Capitalist States*; J. Raschke (ed.), *Die politischen Parteien in Westeuropa* (Reinbek-Bei-Hamburg: RoRoRo Verlag, 1978). With respect to tendance: I. Budge and D. J. Farlie, *Explaining and Predicting Elections* (London: Allen & Unwin, 1983). With respect to anti-democratic and Left–Right feelings, and tendance of party: I. Budge, 'Parties and Democratic Government: A Framework for Comparative Explanation', *Western European Politics*, 7 (1984), 95–118. Finally, various country studies were used where necessary.

5. H. E. Keman, *The Development toward Surplus Welfare* (Amsterdam: CT Press, 1988).

6. For this, see also M. G. Schmidt, 'The Welfare State and the Economy in Periods of Economic Crisis: A Comparative Analysis of 23 O.E.C.D. Nations', *European Journal of Political Research*, 11 (1983), 1–26; Keman, *The Development toward Surplus Welfare*.

7. Von Beyme, *Political Parties*, appendix.

8. Ibid., pp. 329 ff.

9. For an extensive discussion of this variable, see H. E. Keman and T. van Dijk, 'Policy Formation as a Strategy to Overcome the Economic Crisis', in F. Castles and R. Wildermann (eds.), *The Future of Party Government* (Berlin: De Gruyter, 1987), 127–62.

10. For a full discussion of this method of calculation, see H. E. Keman, 'Welfare and Warfare: Critical Opinions and Conscious Choice in Public Policy', in F. Castles, F. Lehner, and M. G. Schmidt (eds.), *Managing Mixed Economies* (Berlin: De Gruyter, 1988).

Bibliography

AXELROD, R. A., *Conflict of Interest* (Chicago: Markham, 1970).

BOGDANOR, V. (ed.), *Coalition Government in Western Europe* (London: Heinemann, 1983).

BROWNE, E., and DREIJMANIS, J. (eds.), *Government Coalitions in Western Democracies* (London: Longman, 1982).

—— and FESTE, K., 'Qualitative Dimensions of Coalition Payoffs', *American Behavioral Scientist*, 18 (1975), 530–56.

—— and FRANKLIN, M., 'Coalition Payoffs in European Parliamentary Democracies', *American Political Science Review*, 67 (1973), 453–64.

—— FENDREIS, J., and GLEIBER, D., 'An "Events" Approach to the Problem of Cabinet Stability', *Comparative Political Studies*, 17 (1984), 167–97.

—— —— —— 'The Process of Cabinet Dissolution: An Exponential Model of Duration and Stability in Western Democracies', *Am. J. Pol. Science*, 30 (1986), 625–50.

BUDGE, I., 'Parties and Democratic Government: A Framework for Comparative Explanation', *Western European Politics*, 7 (1984), 95–118.

—— 'Party Factions and Government Reshuffles', *European Journal of Political Research*, 13 (1985), 327–34.

—— 'The Political Impact of Information Technology', *Teoria politica* (forthcoming).

—— and FARLIE, D. J., *Voting and Party Competition* (London and New York: Wiley, 1977).

—— —— 'Newtonian Mechanics and Predictive Election Theory', *Brit. J. Pol. Science*, 7 (1977), 413–17.

—— —— *Explaining and Predicting Elections* (London: Allen & Unwin, 1983).

—— and HERMAN, V. H., 'Coalitions and Government Formation', *Brit. J. Pol. Science*, 8 (1978), 459–77.

—— and LAVER, M. J., 'Office-Seeking and Policy-Pursuit in Coalition Theory', *Legislative Studies Quarterly*, 11 (1986), 485–506.

—— CREWE, I., and FARLIE, D. J. (eds.), *Party Identification and Beyond* (London and New York: Wiley, 1976).

—— ROBERTSON, D., and HEARL, D. J. (eds.), *Ideology, Strategy and Party Movement* (Cambridge: Cambridge UP, 1987).

CASTLES, F. (ed.), *The Impact of Parties* (London: Sage, 1982).

CASTLES, F. and WILDENMANN, R. (eds.), *The Future of Party Government* (Berlin: De Gruyter, 1987).

—— LEHNER, F., and SCHMIDT, M. G. (eds.), *Managing Mixed Economies* (Berlin: De Gruyter, 1988).

CAWSON, A. (ed.), *Organized Interests and the State* (London: Sage, 1985).

COLEMAN, J., 'Control of Collectivities and the Power of a Collectivity to Act', in B. Lieberman (ed.), *Social Choice* (New York: Gordon Breach Science Publishers, 1971).

DE SWAAN, A., *Coalition Theories and Cabinet Formation* (Amsterdam: Elsevier, 1973).

DODD, L. C., *Coalitions in Parliamentary Government* (Princeton, NJ: Princeton UP, 1976).

DOWNS, A. *An Economic Theory of Democracy* (New York: Harper, 1957).

EVANS, P. B., RUESCHEMEYER, D., and SKOCPOL, T. (eds.), *Bringing the State Back In* (Cambridge: Cambridge UP, 1985).

GAMSON, W. A., 'A Theory of Coalition Formation', *American Sociological Review*, 26 (1961), 373–82.

GRANT, W., *The Political Economy of Corporatism* (London: Macmillan, 1986).

GROFMAN, B., 'A Dynamic Model of Protocoalition Behavior', *Behavioral Science*, 27 (1982), 77–90.

—— 'The Comparative Analysis of Coalition Formation and Duration: Distinguishing Between Country and Within Country Effects', paper presented at the International Conference on Coalition Theory and Public Choice, Fiesole, Italy, 25–9 May 1987.

—— NOVIELLO, N., and STRAFFLIN, P., 'A New Model of Coalition Formation in which One Party Is Asked to Form a Government', paper presented at the International Conference on Coalition Theory and Public Choice, Fiesole, Italy, 25–9 May 1987.

HERMAN, V. H., and POPE, J., 'Minority Governments in Western Democracies', *Brit. J. Pol. Science*, 3 (1973), 191–212.

HIBBS, D., 'Political Parties and Macro-Economic Policy', *American Political Science Review*, 71 (1977), 1476–87.

HOFFERBERT, R. I., and KLINGEMANN, H.-D., 'The Policy Impact of Party Programmes and Government Declarations in Federal Germany', paper presented to the ECPR Manifesto Research Group Meeting, Hotel Mediterraneo, Palermo, 10–13 December 1987.

—— —— and PÉTRY, F. (eds.), *Party Policy and Government Expenditures* (forthcoming).

HURWITZ, L., 'An Index of Democratic Political Stability', *Comparative Political Studies*, 4 (1971), 41–68.

INGLEHART, R., *The Silent Revolution: Changing Values and Political Styles among Western Publics* (Princeton, NJ: Princeton UP, 1977).

Keesing's Contemporary Archives (Bristol: Longman, 1945–).

KEMAN, H. E., 'Securing the Safety of the Nation State', in Castles (ed.), *The Impact of Parties*.

—— 'Politics, Policies and Consequences: A Cross-National Analysis', *European Journal of Political Research*, 12 (1984), 101–8.

—— 'Strategies of Economic Policy-Formation: Dutchmen, Dutch Diseases and Dutch Crossings', paper presented at the ECPR Joint Sessions, Göteborg, 1986.

—— *The Development toward Surplus Welfare* (Amsterdam: CT Press, 1988).

—— 'Welfare and Warfare: Critical Options and Conscious Choice in Public Policy', in Castles, Lehner, and Schmidt (eds.), *Managing Mixed Economies*.

—— and VAN DIJK, T., 'Policy Formation as a Strategy to Overcome the Economic Crisis', in Castles and Wildenmann (eds.), *The Future of Party Government*, pp. 127–62.

—— PALOHEIMO, H., and WHITELEY, P. F. (eds.), *Coping with the Crisis: Alternative Responses to Economic Recession in Advanced Industrial Society* (London: Sage, 1987).

KRASNER, S. D., *Defending the National Interest* (Princeton, NJ: Princeton UP, 1981).

LAVER, M. J., and BUDGE, I. (eds.), *Party Policy and Coalition Government in Western Europe* (forthcoming).

—— and SCHOFIELD, N., *Multiparty Government: The Politics of Coalition in Europe* (Oxford: Oxford UP, 1990).

LEISERSON, M., *Coalitions in Politics* (Ann Arbor, Mich.: University Microfilms, 1966).

—— 'Factions and Coalitions in One-Party Japan', *American Political Science Review*, 68 (1968), 770–87.

LESSMAN, S., *Budgetary Politics and Elections* (Berlin: De Gruyter, 1987).

LIJPHART, A., *Democracies* (New Haven, Conn.: Yale UP, 1984).

LINDBLOM, C. E., *Politics and Markets* (New York: Basic Books, 1977).

LIPSET, S. M., and ROKKAN, S., *Party Systems and Voter Alignments* (New York: The Free Press (Collier-Macmillan), 1967).

LUEBBERT, G. M., *A Theory of Government Formation in Multiparty Democracies* (Stanford, Calif.: Stanford UP, 1986).

MCKELVEY, R. D., 'Dominance and Institution-Free Properties of Social Choice', *Am. J. Pol. Science*, 9 (1986), 283–311.

MACKIE, T., and ROSE, R., *The International Almanac of Electoral History* (2nd edn.; London: Macmillan, 1982); continued in *European Journal of Political Research* (1983–8).

MANN, C., and HILL, M., *The Policy Process in Modern Capitalist States* (Brighton: Wheatsheaf, 1984).

MILIBAND, R., *The State in Capitalist Society* (London: Quartet, 1973).

NETTL, J. P., 'The State as a Conceptual Variable', *World Politics*, 20 (1968), 559–92.

NORDLINGER, E. A., *On the Anatomy of the Democratic State* (Cambridge, Mass.: Harvard UP, 1981).

OFFE, K., *Contradictions of the Welfare State* (London: Hutchinson, 1984).

OLSON, M., *The Logic of Collective Action* (Cambridge, Mass: Harvard UP, 1965).

Organization for Economic Co-Operation and Development (OECD), *National Accounts of OECD Countries*, vol. ii (Paris: OECD, 1979, 1983, 1985).

—— *Social Expenditures 1960–1990* (Paris: OECD, 1985).

PAGE, E. C., *Political Authority and Bureaucratic Power* (Brighton: Wheatsheaf, 1985).

PALOHEIMO, H., *Governments in Democratic Capitalist States 1950–1983: A Data Handbook* (Tampere: Finnish Political Science Association, 1984).

POULANTZAS, N., *State, Power, Socialism* (London: New Left Books, 1978).

POWELL, G. B., *Contemporary Democracies* (Cambridge, Mass.: Harvard UP, 1984).

PRIDHAM, G. (ed.), *Coalitional Behaviour in Theory and Practice* (Cambridge: Cambridge UP, 1986).

RALLINGS, C., 'The Influence of Election Programmes', in Budge, Robertson, and Hearl (eds.), *Ideology, Strategy and Party Movement*, ch. 1.

RASCHKE, J. (ed.), *Die politischen Parteien in Westeuropa* (Reinbek-Bei-Hamburg: RoRoRo Verlag, 1978).

RIKER, W., *The Theory of Political Coalitions* (New Haven: Yale UP, 1962).

ROBERTSON, D. B., *A Theory of Party Competition* (London and New York: Wiley, 1976).

—— *Class and the British Electorate* (Oxford: Blackwell, 1984).

ROKKAN, S., *Citizens, Elections, Parties* (Oslo: Universitetsforlaget, 1970).

SANDERS, D., and HERMAN, V., 'The Survival and Stability of Governments in Western Democracies', *Acta Politica*, 3 (1977), 346–77.

SARTORI, G., *Parties and Party Systems* (Cambridge, Cambridge UP, 1976).

SCHMIDT, M. G., 'The Welfare State and the Economy in Periods of Economic Crisis: A Comparative Analysis of 23 O.E.C.D. Nations', *European Journal of Political Research*, 11 (1983), 1–26.

—— 'Allerweltsparteien in Westeuropa', *Leviathan*, 13 (1985), 329–54.

SCHOFIELD, N. (ed.), *Social Choice and Democracy* (Heidelberg: Springer-Verlag, 1985).

—— 'Existence of a "Structurally Stable" Equilibrium for a Non-Collegial Voting Rule', *Public Choice*, 51 (1986), 267–84.

—— and LAVER, M. J., 'Bargaining Theory and Portfolio Payoffs in European Coalition Governments', *Brit. J. Pol. Science*, 15 (1985), 143–64.

STROM, K., and LEIPART, J., 'Coalition Politics in Norway', in Laver and Budge (eds.), *Party Policy*, ch. 4.

TAYLOR, M. J., and LAVER, M. J., 'Government Coalitions in Western Europe', *European Journal of Political Research*, 1 (1973), 205–48.

THERBORN, G., *Why Some Peoples Are More Unemployed than Others* (London: New Left Books, 1986).

TUFTE, E., *The Political Control of the Economy* (Princeton, NJ: Princeton UP, 1978).

VON BEYME, K., 'I partiti socialisti al potere', *Laboratorio politico*, 5 (1983), 79–94.

—— *Political Parties in Western Democracies* (Aldershot: Gower, 1985).

WEIR, M., and SKOCPOL, T., 'State Structures and Social Keynesian Responses to the Great Depression in Sweden and the United States', *International J. of Comparative Sociology*, 24/1–2 (1983), 4–29.

WHITELEY, P., *Political Control of the Macroeconomy* (London: Sage, 1986).

Index

Index